S. Boniface and the Conversion of Germany

By Mrs. Hope

PREFACE

The following pages contain the life of one of the most notable of Englishmen, As a legislator, he was as great as Alfred; his heart was as brave as that of Cosur-de-Lioni. As a Saint, he was an Apostle and a Martyr. Besides which there clusters round S. Boniface a whole group of saintly English men and women, whose history gives us a delightful insight into the inner life of the Christians of the time. The object, however, of the book is not to present to the reader an interesting biography, or a life of a Saint. Its origin lay in a deep conviction on the part of both author and editor, that the great proof of the Divine origin of the Church, is its history, I believe that the more the grand story of the Catholic Church is known, the more it will be certain that the Christian revelation lies historically in the Church in communion with Rome that that has ever been the centre of its life, and that all bodies out of it, are visibly sects in a state of dissolution and of death. In order, however, to show this, the history must be known in its totality. What is needed is the truth, the whole truth, and nothing but the truth.

It may seem to be a truism that the object of history is truth, yet to some it may appear a paradox. History is often written as if its end were- edification. It must be remembered, however, that in the long run truth is always edifying, though isolated facts may often be scandalous and startling. The annals of the Church sire those of the battle of God s revelation with sin and error. To slur over scandals is to omit the enemy in the story of a fight. On the whole the career of the Church has been one of most marvelous victory, and if it requires to be told courageously as a whole in Gander to make this clear. History is God acting through facts, and each fact is to be considered a sacred being, because it throws light on a portion of His deal with mankind.

For this reason an attempt has been made to arrive at accuracy, even in matters apparently indifferent. Of course to say this is to invite criticism, and in a book which covers so much ground in so small a compass mistake are inevitable. However, we trust that the great features of the time are accurately rendered. It is important that Catholics should be familiar with the results of modern research. That Charlemagne was a Frenchman that Francia in the eighth century meant France that any individual then called himself an Anglo-Saxon, are myths which it is high time to explode; because, harmless as they appear, they give a false view of the whole period.

Precisely the same reverence for truth has led to the insertion of the miraculous parts of the narrative. If I am asked why I have not exercised the same minute criticism in this respect as in other portions of the book, I answer that my reason is, that after all deductions to be made for the indiscriminating faith of the period, the greater part of the stories are true. I have preferred to leave here and there tales which are startling and rest on insufficient evidence, to running the risk of omitting what after all has probably a basis of fact. It is not that criticism is unlawful. The Breviary itself has been frequently altered when light has been obtained by research and few of the stories in this book have the authority of the Breviary. What is unlawful is to assume a priori that at that period no miracles were done. This is not only wrong, but unhistorical. It is quite undoubted that S. Gregory warns S. Augustine not to become proud on account of the miracles wrought by him and that Elfric asserts that signs and wonders took place in his time. It is simply impossible to eliminate the miracles from the histories of the period. In this very age of S. Boniface there occurs a notable instance of a mistake in fact, made by an eminent writer in attempting to expel the super natural. In his new and excellent history of France Guizot asserts that the abbey of Fritzlar was burned by the Saxons, in opposition to the story of S. Boniface s promise, told in these pages. The one thing, however, which is certain is that the abbey was spared, whether supernaturally or not. This is asserted both by Eginhard and by the Annals of Lauresheim, though they differ in the supernatural cause which they assign. In order to avoid the supernatural, M. Guizot has been obliged to sacrifice the natural. In fact, I am not afraid to maintain that modern research has on the whole been favorable to the acts of saints and martyrs. For instance, Rossi s profound study both of martyrologies and of the catacombs has marvelously corrected, while it establishes, the lovely legend of St. Cecilia. In like manner Friedrich, on such a point a most unsuspicious authority, has shown the truth of the story of the martyrdom of that mysterious Theban legion, which seemed with such unaccountable ubiquity to flit from the banks of the Ehine and the Moselle to St. Maurice in Switzerland. The learned Professor has traced step by step the quarters of the legion and the march of Maximian, and shows the minute truth of the bloody story of frantic heathen cruelty and courageous Christian faith; while antiquarian researches in Cologne and Treves have laid bare the very bodies of the slain and the instruments of their martyrdom. Such coincidences between historical facts and the acts of the martyrs carry conviction with them in spite of mistakes in detail. Even the legend of S. Ursula has gained by the help of science since the time when Baronius in his martyrology complained, that the loss of the real story of the Virgin Martyrs had given rise to fictions, "to the great detriment of truth." The reputation of the legend has unfortunately suffered by its connexion with the fictitious visions of Elizabeth of Schonau. It must not however be forgotten, that Dr. Dollinger has but little to boast of in his exposure of these revelations. Baronius had long ago disposed of Pope Cyriacus, and Eusebius Amort of the visions. Mr. Baring-Gould s attempt to turn S. Ursula into a goddess of German heathen mythology, a view which he has borrowed from Simrpck, has already been destroyed by Friedrich, who considers that "the martyrdom of the Virgins of Cologne in the Roman period is an established fact"; By a scientific examination of the inscription pre served in S. Ursula s Church it is proved, that in the very first years of the sixth century the fame of the martyrdom of a number of virgins, was sufficiently wide-spread to bring an eastern pilgrim to their shrine. It is quite true that the whole of the details of the present legend are so utterly baseless, that even the name of Ursula has but little foundation. In a sermon preached in the beginning of the ninth century the complaint is already made, that the story of the virgins was fading from the memory of man. Even at that time, however, tradition spoke of Britain as the native country of the multitude of martyrs, among whom it is said were several married women, at the head of who was the virgin Pinnosa. After having thus cleared the story from a large in crustation of fiction, the pilgrim to the shrine of S. Ursula s Church at Cologne, may still be sure that he is venerating the relics of British women martyred for the Christian faith. As the battle of Chalons was fought the year after the date assigned to the establishment of the kingdom of Kent by Hengist, history falls in with the view, that the martyrs were a party of British emigrants flying from the Saxon invaders, and massacred by the Huns in hatred of the Christian faith. In times like the present, when the Church of God is a state of suffering, it is a consolation to look back upon her past history. She is not in greater danger now than at the time when S. Gregory, as he writes to the Emperor Maurice, saw from the walls of Rome, at the time of Agilulph s invasion, "Roman citizens dragged like dogs with ropes round their necks to be sold for slaves to the Franks;" There was not a single part of the Christian world to which Gregory could look with complacency. His long residence in Constantinople had taught him how little dependence could be placed on the pedantic inter-meddlers with dogma, who filled the imperial throne. The few remnants of the empire left to them in Italy, could only be an incumbrance, not a help. In the East Christianity was undermined by Monophysitism. The Lombards and the Spanish Goths were Arians. North Africa was filled with wild sects of Donatist origin. The Frankish kingdom, it is true, was Catholic; yet it is enough to say that in S. Gregory s time Fredegonde reigned in Neustria, and Brunehaut in Austrasia. Ireland was the most promising part of Christendom, yet not even Ireland was quite satisfactory. Admirable as were the Irish as leaders of forlorn hopes in the attacks on Teutonic heathendom, they organized little, and founded comparatively few bishoprics. S. Columba s letter to Boniface IV betrays a certain rudeness of tone, which must have brought home to the Holy See the fact, that the Celtic spirit was not sufficiently flexible to be a perfect instrument in the conversion of the continent. The rest of Europe was savage and heathen. Root and branch, the old Christian Church of Britain had perished. It was at such a time that Gregory cast his eyes upon Pagan England. The beautiful story of the Yorkshire boys is no doubt true, but will hardly account for the sort of passionate yearning for England, which lasted so many years, and haunted Gregory amidst the anxieties of his high office. There was a supernatural sagacity in thus resolving to win England, which, if converted, would become a fortress for Christianity amidst the shifting revolutions of the continent, and which was inhabited by a race, whose young energy contrasted with the feebleness of the decaying civilization and half civilized barbarism, with which he had to do.

S. Gregory s success in the conversion of England illustrates the principle of compensation, which is a law in the dealings of Christ with His Church. Simultaneously with the separation of a large portion of the Teutonic race through the influx of Protestantism, the success of S. Francis of Xavier and the spread of Christianity in the newly-discovered world across the Atlantic, compensated a thousand-fold for the losses sustained in Europe. There are now many millions more Catholics in the world than could be counted at the time when Luther died. The same principle was in operation in the conversion of England and of Germany. The East was lost to Christianity by the success of the Mahometan arms at the very moment when the conversion of England was effected. Syria, Palestine, Persia, and Egypt, were torn from Christianity in about twenty years, between A.D. 630 and A.D. 651. At that very moment was the crisis of the Christian cause in England. Up to that time it had made little progress beyond Kent, its original seat, for A.D. 633 was "the accursed year" in which Edwin was slain, Paulinus was expelled from York, and a Pagan reaction took place in the North. In these twenty years East Anglia and Wessex were converted, and Northumbria was finally won to the Cross of Christ. By the time that the seal was set to the Christianizing of England by the conversion of Sussex and the Isle of Wight, the North of Africa and a great part of Spain had ceased to be Christian. Hardly had all England received the faith when it began its marvelous work in Germany. The foresight of S. Gregory was justified by the event; the consequences of S. Augustine s mission went far beyond the spiritual conquest of the English. They spread all over the Teutonic race. The loss of the East which had failed in its mission and allowed the State to interfere with its faith, was more than compensated by the gain of the nation, to whom the future of Europe and the world was entrusted.

What sufferings may await the Church we cannot tell, but we may be quite certain that the persecutions which she may have to undergo can only be her gain.

As the question has been asked, it may be well to say something as to the amount of my work as editor of this book. I have exercised such supervision as was compatible with my occupations and limited knowledge of the subject. A few pages here and there, not much more than a dozen altogether are mine. The book is boni fide due to the industry, ability, and zeal for God s glory of the author.

J. B. DALGAIRNS

CHAPTER I.FIRST ENGLISH MISSIONS

In the crowd of monks and scholars who, for many centuries flocked from all parts of Europe to Ireland, there mingled many of the recent converts from England, and especially from Northumbria, who retired thither either in pursuit of learning, or in order to lead a stricter life. Some of these devoted themselves in monasteries to the practice of virtue, while others chose rather to apply themselves to study, and wandered from one master s cell to another. The Irish received them all with generous hospitality, and supplied them with food, books, and teachers, free of all cost. Among these Northumbrian pilgrims were S. Chad, afterwards Bishop of Lichfield, three young nobles, S. Egbert, Ethelhun, and his brother Ethelwin, afterwards Bishop of Sidnachester or Stone in Lindsey, and also S. Oswy s illegitimate son, Aldfrid, who succeeded Egfrid on the throne of Northumbria.

Egbert and Ethelhun who were closely united by friendship, took up their abode in the convent of Rathmelsigi, now called Melfont. In the year 664, soon after their arrival, the dreadful pestilence, which made such ravages in both England and Ireland, broke out. Many of the monks of Rathmelsigi died, and Egbert and Ethelhun fell desperately ill. Egbert, believing himself to be at the point of death, left his cell, and sitting down in the open air, began to review his past life as in the sight of God. Struck with compunction for the sins of his childhood and youth, he shed floods of tears, and prayed to God fervently that he might not die till he had made amends for them; and he solemnly vowed, if God would spare his life, to recite the whole Psalter daily, in addition to the usual canonical office, to fast for one whole day and night in every week, and never to return to England, which was the greatest self-denial that the home-loving Angle could offer. Then going back to his cell, and finding Ethelhun asleep, he lay down to compose himself to rest.

Meanwhile it had been revealed to Ethelhun in his sleep what Egbert had prayed for, and that his vow had been accepted. Wherefore, waking soon after and looking at him, he said, "Alas! Brother Egbert, what hast thou done? I was in hopes that we should have entered together into life everlasting. But know that what thou prayed for, is granted"; The next night Ethelhun died, but Egbert survived sixty-four years, till he was ninety years old. He led a life of great humility, meekness, continence, simplicity, and justice and did much good to those among whom he lived by his example, his industry in teaching, his authority in reproving, and his charity in distributing the alms bestowed on him by the rich. Not only did he keep his above-mentioned vow, but he also added to it by eating only a little bread with a small measure of stale skim milk once a day in Lent, and for forty days before Christmas, and after Whitsuntide.

After he had lived thus in exile for above twenty years, he conceived, A.D. 686, a great desire to go and preach the word of God to some of the German nations, from whom his people were sprung, who had never heard the Gospel, and were still practicing Pagan rites. He thought of sailing round Britain, and going to the Frisians, Danes, Saxons, and Bructerii, to try whether he could deliver any of them from Satan, and win them to Christ and if he should fail in this, he would go to Rome, to visit the tombs of the apostles and martyrs. He accordingly chose several companions, remarkable for courage, learning, and virtue, and made all necessary preparations for the voyage.

But one morning when every thing was nearly ready, one of his companions, who had been a monk in Melrose Abbey under Boisil, came to him and told him, that his old master had appeared to him the night before, and had said to him, "I am come to bring Egbert a message from our Lord and Savior, which must be delivered to him by you. Tell him, therefore, that he cannot perform the journey that he has undertaken; for it is the will of God that he should rather go to instruct the monastery of Columba"; On hearing this, Egbert desired the brother not to mention to any one what he had seen and heard, lest it should prove a delusion and though he believed it was a real vision, he did not desist from his preparations for the voyage.

A few days after the brother came once more to him, and told him that Boisil had again appeared to him that night after matins and said to him, "Why did you tell Egbert in so light and cold a manner what I bade you? Go now and tell him, that whether he will or no, he shall go to Columba s monastery; because their ploughs do not go straight, and he is to bring them into the right way"; Egbert now felt sure that the vision was from God but still he bade the brother tell no one, and resolved to try to make the voyage. Every thing was put on board ship, and they were only waiting for a fair wind, when one night a violent storm arose, and the ship being driven ashore, great part of the cargo was lost. But all that belonged to Egbert was saved. Then he said to his companions, "This tempest has happened on my account" and he gave up the undertaking, and stayed at home.

God had indeed prepared another great work for him to do. For in the year 716 he went to Iona, and being honorably received by the monks, he persuaded them to give up their peculiar customs, and to conform to the Catholic practice, both as to Easter and the tonsure. He remained thirteen years with them; and by a singular favor, he died after celebrating Mass in their presence on the true Easter day, A.D. 729.

But though Egbert had been personally hindered in his missionary enterprise, he did not abandon it. S. Wigbert, one of his companions, who was famous for his learning and contempt of the world, and had led for many years a very holy life as a hermit in Ireland, was induced to take it up, and went to Friesland.

The Frisians then possessed the country north of the Waal, all the islands now called Seeland, and the coast as far as the mouth of the Ems, and probably to the Eyder, since Heligoland certainly belonged to them. They were a very barbarous people, "living like fish in the water, and holding intercourse with other nations only by sea." Their land was quite barren and uncultivated, and so inhospitable that scarcely a human habitation was to be seen. Drusus Germanicus is said to have visited the country in search of the Pillars of Hercules but the poverty of the Frisians, their courage, their passionate love of freedom, and their peculiar skill in navigating the rivers and arms of the sea with their "kiule" or little ships, had hitherto protected them from foreign conquest and preserved their independence.

About A.D. 678, S. Amand, Bishop of Maastricht, S. Eligius, Bishop of Noyon, and other Frank missionaries, tried to draw them into the Christian fold. But they looked with such jealousy and aversion on the very name of the Franks that the attempt totally failed. The following year, however, the stormy ocean waves brought them the heavenly message of peace and love in a less suspicious form. For S. Wilfrid was driven on their coast, as already related, and being hospitably received by Aldgisl, preached with success to his subjects. As all the first English missionaries belonged to S. Wilfrid s diocese, it was probably this accident which led to Wigbert s selection of Friesland as his field of labor. Moreover, the Frisians were closely allied by blood to the English, and at that time both spoke the same language. But Wigbert found on his arrival that Aldgisl was dead, and the throne was filled by Ratbod, a bigoted Pagan. Still he was not discouraged and during two years he preached the faith to Ratbod and his people. At the end of that .time, perceiving that he reaped no fruit from his great labors, he returned to Ireland and resumed his life of solitude, "taking care, since he could not be profitable to strangers by teaching them the faith, to be the more useful to his own people by his example."

Notwithstanding the failure of Wigbert s mission, Egbert was not deterred from his pious design. He resolved to make another attempt, and selected Willibrord for the task.

Willibrord was born of noble parents in Northumbria, A.D. 657. His father Wilgils, after leading with his wife and all his household a very devout life in the world, became a monk and as his spiritual fervor increased, he retired to a small island at the mouth of the Humber, where he built an oratory in honor of S. Andrew, intending to live there in solitude. But the fame of his sanctity spread on all sides, and crowds flocked to him for advice and consolation till at length S. Oswy and his nobles gave him some land on the adjoining coast, on which he built a monastery, which he ruled till his death.

Before Willibrord s birth his mother had a dream, in which she saw the new moon increasing till it reached its full and understanding this to signify that her child was destined to dissipate the errors of darkness by the light of truth, she and his father gave him, while still an infant, to S. Wilfrid, then Abbot of Ripon. Here he received the tonsure at an early age, and as he grew up he excelled his young companions in activity, humility, and application to study his gravity far exceeding his childish years, so that it was said of him as of the little Samuel, that "he advanced, and grew on, and pleased both the Lord and men."

When Willibrord was twenty years of age, he was attracted to Ireland by the love of travel, and the reputation for learning and sanctity of many holy men who were to be found there, and especially of Egbert and Wigbert, to the former of whom the title of Saint was given even in his lifetime. Accordingly with the consent of Wilfrid and his brethren, he went to Ireland, and placed himself under Egbert and Wigbert. His intercourse with them kindled the spirit of missionary enterprise within his breast, and ripened his virtues so as to fit him for the great work which lay before him. At length, A.D. 690, when he was thirty-three years of age, he devoted himself, at Egbert suggestion, to the conversion of the Germans and with eleven companions of like spirit to himself, several of whom became martyrs, he set sail for Friesland.

The little missionary band landed at the mouth of the Rhine, whence they went to Utrecht, where Ratbod then resided. But soon finding that there was no hope of success in that quarter, they turned their steps towards Pepin Heristal, who, as Mayor of the Palace then governed France. Pepin, being very anxious to spread Christianity, was rejoiced to have such zealous and learned teachers for his people and set them to work at various places within his own frontiers, which were still Pagan. But Willibrord had learned at Ripon and in Ireland, that something more was necessary to secure success. He therefore went to Rome to obtain the Pope s permission and authority for his work and as soon as he had accomplished this object, he returned to his companions.

The missionaries labored successfully among the frontier tribes, and as they advanced, they found it desirable to have a bishop. They therefore chose Swidbert, one of their number who had formerly been Abbot of Dacre, in Cumberland, and sent him to S. Wilfrid to be consecrated by him A.D. 692. After his return Swidbert went to preach to the Bructerii, who were so much better disposed to the faith than the Frisians that he made many converts among them. But soon after the Bructerii being almost extirpated by an inroad of the Saxons, Swidbert retired to Pepin court with such of the survivors as he could collect. At the pressing entreaty of his wife, Plectrude, Pepin gave the fugitives an island in the Rhine, now called Kaiserswerth, six miles from Düsseldorf, where Swidbert lived till his death, A.D. 717.

Two others of S. Willibrord s companions, also natives of Northumbria, resolved to go and preach to the Saxons in Germany. Both had the same name and they were distinguished, on account of the color of their hair, as Black Ewald and White Ewald. Both were very holy, but Black Ewald was the most learned in the Scriptures. On their arrival in Saxony they wont to the house of a certain steward, and asked him to take them to his ealdorman, for whom they had a message which was much to his advantage. The steward received them into his own house, and entertained them hospitably for some days, promising to send them on to the ealdorman. But when the Saxons discovered by their constant praying, singing of psalms, and celebration of Mass, that they were Christians, they became alarmed lest their ealdorman should be converted by them to the new religion and falling suddenly on them, they killed them on the 3rd of October, A.D. 692. White Ewald they slew with the sword, but Black Ewald they put to the torture, and then tore limb from limb after which they threw the bodies of both into the Ehine. When the ealdorman heard what had happened, he was very angry that the strangers had not been allowed to come to him and he burnt the village, and put all the inhabitants to death. As for the bodies of the martyrs, they were carried up the stream about forty miles to the place where their companions were, a pillar of light rising every night up to heaven over the spot where they lay; till at length being discovered, they were buried by Pepin s command with due honor in the church at Cologne.

Meanwhile Pepin had sent Willibrord again to Rome to Pope Sergius, requesting that he might be consecrated Archbishop of the Frisians. The Pope complied with the request, and consecrated him on the feast of S. Cecilia, A.D. 694, in her Church, giving him the name of Clement, and conferring the pall on him. So great was Willibrord s anxiety to return to his work, that this second visit to Rome did not extend beyond fourteen days; and hurrying back to his see, lie resumed his labors with indefatigable energy.

Pepin was very successful in his war with Ratbod and as he advanced, Willibrord followed in his footsteps, sowing the seed of peace en the track of blood-stained victories. Pepin having now conquered Hither Friesland, made over the country between the Rhine and the Meuse to Willibrord, and gave him the city of Utrecht for his episcopal see; for he had learned from experience that the best way to secure his conquests was to Christianize them.

The boundaries of the Frank dominions, however, did not limit Willibrord s zeal, which, overstepping all national barriers carried him into the unconquered parts of Friesland, and even to Ratbod s court. But though he met with a courteous reception, his missionary efforts proved fruitless. For Christianity was linked in the minds of the Frisians with Frank dominion; and their love of independence led them to reject the proposals of the stranger, while they treated him with the hospitality which their national laws commanded.

Finding his progress barred in Friesland, Willibrord turned his steps to Denmark. But here he was equally unfortunate. For the King of Denmark was more ferocious than any wild beast and harder than any stone and was sunk in sensuality as well as in the darkness of Paganism. The only fruit that Willibrord could obtain from his journey was thirty children whom he brought away with him, intending to educate them and send them back to their own country, either as missionaries, or as good Christians whose example would prepare the way for the entrance of the Gospel. But as he was returning by sea, ho took the precaution to instruct them and prepare them for baptism, lest any disaster should befall them on the way.

On the homeward voyage they were driven by contrary winds to an island at the mouth of the Elbe, called Fositesland from the god Fosite, to whom it was dedicated, and Heligoland from the reverence with which it was regarded. So great was the awe which this Pagan sanctuary inspired, that no one dared to molest the wild animals which made it their abode, or to draw water from a spring within its confines except in solemn silence. Willibrord being detained in the island took the opportunity to baptize three of the children, and had some of the wild animals killed for food. The natives expected to see the sacrilegious strangers struck with sudden madness; but as nothing befell them, they seized them and carried them to Ratbod. Death alone could atone for so horrible a sacrilege, and Ratbod, transported with fury, cast lots three times on three successive days, to ascertain who were the guiltiest. The lot fell on one alone, who, offering himself a sacrifice to the true God, joyfully suffered martyrdom. Ratbod poured out threats and reproaches on Willibrord for his offence against the island god. But Willibrord answered fearlessly, "There is but one true God, Who created the heaven, the earth, tho sea, and all that in them is we who serve Him, will go into eternal life. And I, the servant of this true God, conjure thee this day to turn from tho folly of the old delusion, with which thy fathers were entrapped, and to become wise and believe in the One Almighty God." Ratbod could not but admire tho saint courage, and allowed him to return homo unharmed. Pepin rejoiced at his escape, and exhorted him to confine himself for the future to preaching within his territory.

Within this sphere Willibrord found many Pagans to be converted, and many idols to be overthrown. He traveled over the whole district, visiting the places where he had formerly preached, confirming the faith of the weak, building churches and convents, and establishing priests and teachers wherever it was possible. One day he went to the Isle of Walcheren, in which was a famous sanctuary dedicated to Woden, where the people were wont to assemble in crowds at certain seasons. Going up to the image of Woden, he dashed it down in spite of the resistance of its guardian, whose weapon fell harmless on his head. The inhabitants were converted, and held his memory in such reverence, that they afterwards chose him for their patron saint, and were accustomed to wear his relics when they went to battle.

Thus Willibrord worked on for fifty years. Like all great missionary apostles, he had the gift of miracles and of prophecy, and many instances of their exercise are on record. One of the most striking of his prophetic sayings is connected with Pepin-le-Bref. For when Pepin was brought to him by his father Charles Martel, to be baptized, he said to Charles in the presence of the court and his own disciples, "Know that this infant will be higher and more glorious than all the dukes of the Franks who have preceded him," words which were literally fulfilled, when Pepin became the first king of the Carlovingian dynasty.

Willibrord s companions preached in various places in Friesland or its vicinity. S. Adalbert, who belonged to the royal race of Northumbria, and was a pupil of S. Egbert, chose the north of Holland for his field of labor. His teaching was well received by the Pagans, and he was long revered at Egmond, where he died S. Werentrid preached to the Batavu, who, inhabited the island formed by the Rhine and the Waal. And S. Wiro and S. Plechelm were the apostles of Gueldres.

S. Wiro is said by Alcuin, who was born only a few years after his death, to have been one of the saints of the diocese of York. A writer of about the 10th century, however, claims him as a native of that "Isle of the holy Fathers, whose saints equal the stars of heaven in number." But whether he was born in England or in Ireland, there is no doubt that he imbibed his missionary spirit in Ireland, where he was a disciple of S. Egbert, and whence he and his friend, S. Plechelm, accompanied S. Willibrord to Friesland. After some time he was chosen bishop of his district and went with Plechelm and Otger, his deacon, to Rome, to obtain authority from the Pope but with the secret hope of being1 allowed to decline the dignity. The Holy Father, however, far from falling into his wishes, confirmed his election, and with his own hands consecrated both him and Plechelm bishops.

On their return to Gaul, Pepin Heristal gave them a very lonely spot at the confluence of the rivers Meuse and Ilura, since called Ruremond, where they could best follow their devotions in solitude. Here Wiro built a church, which he dedicated to S. Mary, Ever Virgin and Mother of God, and a monastery in honor of S. Peter and from this centre Christianity soon spread over Gueldres. Pepin was in the habit of going annually in Lent to the abbey, where, laying aside his purple robes of state, he would make a retreat, as would now be said, ending with a general confession to S. Wiro, and after his death, to S. Plechelm.

But the most celebrated of S. Willibrord s coadjutors, excepting only S. Boniface, was S. Wulfram. He was the son of a Frank noble, who held a high military rank at the court of Clovis II and possessed an estate at Maurillac, now Milly, in the Gatinais. He became a monk in the Abbey of Fontanelle, A.D. 684, when he made over his paternal estate to the abbey. He was elected Bishop of Sens, A.D. 690, but after some years he resigned his see in obedience to a Divine inspiration, and returning to his monastery, obtained from it some monks, with whom he embarked on the Seine for Friesland.

Once more the Gospel was preached to Ratbod, but still in vain. Many of his subjects, and even his son, were baptized but as his son died within a few days, while he still wore his baptismal robe, Ratbod's aversion from Christianity only became the stronger.

S. Wulfram turned his attention especially to preventing the human sacrifices which were constantly offered to propitiate the gods. One day, as he was preaching to a great crowd of people, it came to pass that a youth called Ovo, on whom the lot had fallen, was led out to be hanged as an offering to the sea god, on whose favor the Frisians believed themselves to be especially dependent. Wulfram begged the king to give him the youth, in order that he might offer him to the true God. But Ratbod said, that their sacred laws, which could not be broken, forbade the release of any on whom the lot had fallen. Still Wulfram pressed his petition, and Ratbod seemed disposed to yield; but the fanatical mob objected, and cried out, "If Christ deliver him from the bonds of death, then he shall belong to Him and to thee." The holy bishop accepted the condition, and began to pray earnestly and confidently. The youth was strung up; he hung for two hours in the sight of an immense crowd of Pagans and Christians; and when at last he was cut down, he fell on the ground unhurt. He was given to S. Wulfram, who sent him to be educated in the Abbey of Fontanelle, where he became a monk and a priest.

On another occasion two young boys, seven and five years of age, were torn from their mother s arms, and carried off to be drowned. They were placed at low tide on a tongue of land, which would be covered when the tide flowed in. Ratbod and an immense crowd stood on the beach, watching the rising flood. Already the tide had covered the head of the younger, and his elder brother held him up over the water but the advancing waves were quickly submerging both of them. On hearing what was going on Wulfram had rushed to the shore, and besought the king to spare the children. But Ratbod only answered, "If Christ, your God, can rescue them from this peril, they shall be His servants." "Be it so," replied Wulfram with saintly confidence. Then raising his hands in prayer, he walked over the waves as on dry ground, seized a boy in each hand, brought them safe to shore, and restored them to their weeping mother. He instructed and baptized them, giving to one his own name, which henceforth was very common in Friesland.

Such miracles added to the power of Wulfram's words, and great numbers were converted. Even Ratbod was softened, and consented to be baptized. But as he was about to step into the font, he paused, and asked, whether the princes, his forefathers, were in that heavenly abode, which Wulfram promised him if he would be baptized, or in that dark place of punishment with which he threatened him. And when Wulfram could not assure him of their salvation, he drew back from the baptismal font, saying, "I cannot give up the society of my forefathers and the entire Frisian nation, for that of a few poor people in that heavenly kingdom nor can I lightly approve of this new doctrine, for I would rather persevere in that belief which the Frisians have so long held."

Some time after, A.D. 719, being taken dangerously ill and feeling that his life was drawing to a close, he sent for Willibrord to come to him, promising that if he should find that his teaching agreed with that of Wulfram, he would become a Christian. But Willibrord answered his messenger, "If your duke despises the preaching of our holy brother and bishop, Wulfram, what good can my words do him? Last night I saw him in a vision bound with a fiery chain." He set out with the messenger but on their way they were met by the news, that the unhappy Ratbod was dead without baptism.

Wulfram worked indefatigably in Friesland for several years, returning from time to time to Fontanelle to recruit his strength. At length, soon after Ratbod s death, the infirmities of age compelled him to give up the missionary life, and retire to the monastery for the rest of his days. After a long confinement to his bed, during which it was noticed that all the sick who approached him, were cured, he expired on the 19th of April, A.D. 720.

Willibrord survived him twenty years, dying about A.D. 744, when he had held his bishopric fifty years. He had the satisfaction of leaving the work which he had begun in the hands of S. Boniface, who carried it forward with a marvelous degree of success, to which his most sanguine hopes could scarcely have aspired.

CHAPTER II.S. BONIFACE

About the year 680, Winfred, better known as S. Boniface, the Apostle of Germany was born at Crediton, in Devonshire. The names of his parents are unknown; but his father was of noble birth, and is sometimes said to have been a king and it is possible that he "may have been one of the under-kings, who were so numerous in Wessex, and who, at the time of Winfred s birth had divided the kingdom among them selves. He had other children besides Winfred but tradition has handed down the name of only his daughter, Winna, who married S. Richard, and was the mother of S. Willibald, S. Winibald, and S. Walburga. Nor were these the only saints who threw luster on this family; for S. Lioba, S. Willibrord." S. Burchard and S. Willehad are said to have been connected with it.

Winfred was surrounded from his birth by the pomp and luxury that befitted the household of a Saxon prince. His mother nursed him with peculiar tenderness and his father preferring him to all his other children, centered his affections in him and spared no pains on his early education. Winfred quickly responded to this training. Ere long the germs of a noble disposition became visible, and the fond father joyfully watched the development of a character, on which he might well build up the most ambitious hopes.

But when the child came to be four or five years old, he took an unlooked for turn. Monks and priests were frequent visitors at his father s house, for at this time the spiritual wants of the English people were chiefly supplied by monks from the monasteries, which were scattered over the country. These itinerant missioners were honored guests in every English household; but by none were they more joyfully greeted than by the little Winfred. He loved to listen to what they said about heaven, to question them on the subjects which occupied his pure and simple mind, and to ask them what he was to do to become like them. Thus supernatural desires sprang up in his heart, and while the father was cherishing plans of worldly ambition, the child s only thought was to enter a cloister and spend his life in poverty, self-denial, and prayer awaiting that eternal kingdom which alone could satisfy his desires.

At length Winfred told his father his wishes and asked his leave to be a monk. Astonished and distressed at this unexpected proposal, the father did all in his power to divert the child from his purpose, promising to make him his heir, and seeking to touch his loving heart by gentle words, or to intimidate him by threats. But all in vain; for the more the father opposed the boy s supernatural vocation, the more ardently did the latter strive to acquire treasures in heaven.

At length He who had inspired the wish, and given the weak, gentle child strength and courage to per severe in it, removed the obstacles to its attainment. Winfred s father fell dangerously ill and as he lay at the brink of the grave, the nothingness of earthly greatness was revealed to him, and he learned to appreciate his son s aspirations after heavenly joys. Assembling all his family round his bed he consulted them, according to the custom of the time, as to Winfred s future destination and it was decided to gratify his wish, and give him to a cloister.

Though all the Germans enjoyed personal freedom, yet every free man was required to attach himself to a chief, whom he was to follow to battle when called on to do so. Consequently, the laws of England and France at that time, gave parents power to make over a child to the king or a noble, or to a bishop or monastery, either to be educated till it should be four teen years old, or for life and all through the middle ages this custom continued, and formed the strongest tie between the feudal lord and his "man." As to children made over for life to an abbey, their parents could not afterwards recall the offering made to God and give them in marriage; but the children when they grew up, were not compelled to adopt the monastic life. On reaching a suitable age they had the option of confirming their parents offering, though they were not allowed to take vows as deacons or nuns till they had attained the age of twenty five. But in any case, they were bound as long as they lived, to give their services to the abbey to which they belonged.

As soon as the family council had come to a decision, Winfred s father took the usual steps to make him over to Exminster, a Benedictine abbey near Exeter. The boy was sent thither with an attendant, who also was given to the abbey, and who was the bearer of a message to the abbot, Wulfhard. The abbot assembled the monks and consulted them, as the Benedictine rule required, about receiving Winfred. Then the boy pleaded his own cause with such simplicity and earnestness, that the gift was accepted; and Winfred joyfully devoted himself to the life to which God had so early called him.

Winfred was only six years old when he went to Exminster, A.D. 686. No particulars of his life in this abbey have been handed down. His biographer only mentions, that he showed remarkable natural talents and desire for knowledge, while at the same time the religious training which he enjoyed, elevated his youthful aspirations to the noblest objects of pursuit, and cherished within him the seeds of the highest virtue. But during this period two events occurred, which must have stirred even the stillness of his cloister. One was Ceadwalla s abdication of the West Saxon crown, and pilgrimage to Rome, A.D. 688; and the other was the departure of the first band of English missionaries under S. Willibrord, A.D. 690. It may well be supposed that these examples of heroic virtue in his own neighborhood and family, must have excited the fervor of the young Winfred, and given a color to his future life.

Exminster stood on the border of the West Saxon territory, which Cenwealh had only recently conquered. Its library was a poor one, and Winfred, in his ardent pursuit of knowledge, quickly exhausted its scanty stock of books. This was a great mortification to him, and long and earnestly he prayed to know God's will, till at last he asked the abbot and his brethren to allow him to go elsewhere. They generously consented, and by their advice he removed to the Abbey of Nutscelle, in Hampshire.

The passion for learning which S. Theodore and S. Hadrian had inspired in England was now at its height. The influence of S. Aldhelm, as Abbot of Malmesbury and Bishop of Sherborne, had been felt over all the southern counties; and the school of Nutscelle under Abbot Winbert, was rich both in books and in teachers. In this atmosphere of piety and learning Winfred made rapid progress. Before long the attention of his superiors was attracted by his exemplary observance of the rule, his application to prayer and study, not only by day but by night, and especially by his remarkable power of seizing the deep mysteries of Scripture, and explaining them to those less gifted than himself. In course of time he was placed at the head of the school, when his former teachers were glad to sit at his feet and be his pupils.

In this position Winfred was not only a teacher, but also an example in word, conduct, faith, chastity, and charity, to all around him. Daily he applied himself to manual labor, as the rule required, and far from being puffed up by his own mental attainments, he treated the inferior talents of others with respect, and preferred them to himself. All who knew him, looked up to him with mingled fear and love, fearing him as a father on account of his Apostolic exhortations, and loving him as a brother for his humility, affability, and charity. His fame soon spread to all the convents in the south of England. Crowds of monks flocked to him to examine the Scriptures, and drink with him from the inspired fount of Divine knowledge. The saintly abbesses of

Barking, Thanet, and Wimburn, too, craved his instructions for themselves and their nuns and though they were naturally less fitted for abstruse study, yet he would impart to them such a spirit of understanding and fervor, as he went hastily through a few pages of Scripture with them that they would hereafter be able to meditate profitably on the hidden mysteries of Divine love. In this intercourse with monks and nuns, he laid the foundations of many a warm and enduring friendship, which afterwards proved of great service to him.

He also preached to the people with marvelous eloquence, skillfully interweaving his expositions of our Lord s parables with such practical instructions as would be most profitable to his hearers. His exhortations and reproofs, boldly addressed alike to rich and poor, noble and serf, were distinguished by their spirit of discretion, so that, neither flattering the great nor pressing hardly on the poor, he made himself all things to all men in order to gain all.

While thus laboring for others, he did not neglect his own soul. Works of charity and prayer were his constant occupation; while by fasting, penance, and mortification of his lower nature, he attained to that perfect mastery of self, which not only sheds peace and calm over the soul, but gives irresistible power over others. He was also remarked for that peculiar union of strength and gentleness, which is characteristic of the indwelling of the Holy Spirit; and hence the fire of his zeal was ever tempered by the sweetness of love, so that love breathed through his sternest rebukes, and the strength of his words was increased by their gentleness.

Thus, in the calm seclusion of the cloister Winfred led a holy and hidden life till he reached the age of thirty, which was then the usual period for ordination to the priesthood. His humility, however, made him shrink from this dignity, and it was not till about two years later, A.D. 712, that he was induced by the pressing entreaties of Abbot Winbert and his brother monks to accept it. No words can tell with what depth of contrition he was wont to prepare for the celebration of the Holy Sacrifice. He said Mass daily, but from motives of reverence he never said it more than once a day, though others would often offer three Masses, or even more, in the same day. After he had attained to this closer and deeper familiarity with our Lord in this supreme act of His love, he daily became more and more weaned from earth, and strengthened for the great work which awaited him.

Soon after Winfred s ordination to the priesthood, a great change came over his life. S. Ina, King of Wessex, having summoned the clergy and laity of his kingdom to a council, Winfred repaired thither in attendance on his abbot. The place and date of this council are not known, but it was not the one in which S. Ina promulgated his celebrated code of laws. Its occasion was some seditious movement among his people; and as every thing was then regulated on religious principles, the bishops even sitting with the ealdorman in the hundred court to judge civil causes, the bishops and abbots joined the king and nobles in consultation about this civil emergency.

When the council had come to a decision, S. Ina asked the clergy who was the person best qualified to head the deputation, which they were about to send to S. Berchtwald, Archbishop of Canterbury, to obtain his sanction to their proposed measures. Then Abbot Winbert, Wintra, Abbot of Tisbury in Wiltshire, Beorwart, Abbot of Glastonbury, and all the rest of the clergy, strongly recommended Winfred for this important mission. He accordingly set out for Canter bury, where he explained the matter to S. Berchtwald with such clearness and judgment, that within a few days he returned to the council with a satisfactory answer from the archbishop. From this time Winfred had so high a reputation for the management of both civil and ecclesiastical affairs that he was summoned to assist at several other synods. Much important business was entrusted to him, and worldly honors and wealth were at his command.

But meanwhile a far nobler ambition was stirring his heart. It has already been told, how the Germans in their wanderings always retained a claim on the lands from which they had started, and how in many Cases they returned after the lapse of years or even centuries, to the loved home of their fathers. Thus the English, in the seventh and eighth centuries, turned towards "Old Saxony" much as the English co-mist and the American citizen now speak of England as "home" and the "old country." But Christianity had supernaturalized this pure, natural affection and England was now beginning to be agitated by that noble enthusiasm, which ere long led thousands of men and women away from their English homes and their fondly cherished ties and comforts, in order to carry the Gospel of peace and hope to their poor Pagan kindred in their old German home.

This missionary spirit had taken deep hold of Winfred; and while he was moving among kings and nobles, and was breathing the sweet incense of human applause, he was constantly revolving in his secret thoughts how, for the love of Jesus, he might quit kindred and friends and his native land, and turn his steps to some distant shore. At length he laid bare his wishes and his conscience to Abbot Winbert. At first the good abbot opposed his wish, and tried to turn him from it. But finding this impossible, he came to the conclusion that this missionary desire was inspired by God and then he and all his monks took such a deep interest in Winfred s plan that they not only joy fully gave their consent, but offered him all the temporal aid in their power. Accordingly Winfred, accompanied by two of his brethren and followed by the tears and prayers of the rest, set out on his first missionary enterprise early in the spring of the year 716. The travelers first went by land to London, and there embarking for Friesland, they landed after a short voyage at Dorstat, or Wyk-to-Duerstede.

On their arrival in Friesland they found S. Willibrord's successful work, as described in a former chapter, totally ruined. Pepin Heristal having died A.D. 714, the office of Mayor of the Palace devolved on his grandson Theodoald, who being only six years old, and the Merovingian king, Dagobert III, being an imbecile boy of fifteen, the kingdom was governed by Pepin s widow, Plectrude. That discordant Frank Empire which Pepin's strong hand could scarcely hold together, naturally fell away from the feeble grasp of two children and a woman. In the north the Neustrians set up Raginfred as a rival mayor of the palace, while the south was divided between the Burgundians, Eudes, Count of Aquitaine, and the Saracens, who, having conquered Spain after the battle of Xeres, A.D. 711, claimed the territory adjoining the Pyrenees, which had for merely belonged to the Visigoths. The Austrasians, being defeated by the Neustrians, broke open the prison in which Plectrude had immured Pepin s illegitimate son, Charles Martel, and proclaimed him Duke of Austrasia. Though only twenty years of age, Charles at once proved his genius. He gained two great victories over Raginfred and the Neustrians A.D. 717 and 719; he made peace with the Count of Aquitaine and Theodoald being now dead, he secured the undisputed possession of the nominal king and the mayoralty.

But it took several years to establish Charles's supremacy, and, meanwhile, the frontier German tribes profited by these dissensions to assert their independence and retrieve their losses during Pepin s mayoralty. Among them was Ratbod, who had seized Utrecht and recovered his lost territory in Hither Friesland after which he had burnt the Christian churches, expelled Willibrord and his clergy, and begun a cruel persecution of the Frisian converts.

Such was the unhappy state of Friesland when Winfred arrived there. Notwithstanding, he did not abandon all hopes of success. After making some fruitless efforts at Dorstat, he went on to Utrecht, where he awaited Batbod, who happened to be absent. On Ratbod s return he made repeated attempts to soften his heart and rouse his better feelings. But the moment was not propitious for such an attempt, as the unhappy prince was flushed with the pride of victory and maddened by the drunken orgies and Pagan rites common on such occasions. Still hospitality was respected, and Winfred remained unmolested. Finding nought else to do, he seized the opportunity to gain some knowledge of the country and the national customs, hoping at some future time to turn it to good account. Thus he spent the summer and autumn, and on the approach of winter he returned to Nutscelle.

About the end of the next year, A.D. 717, or the beginning of the following one, Abbot Winbert died, when the monks besought Winfred to take his place. Winfred gently expostulated with them, representing to them how he had devoted himself to the missionary work. Then, to add the weight of authority to his own poor words, he laid his case before Daniel, Bishop of Winchester, in whose diocese the abbey was situated. By dint of gentleness and humility he gradually won over the bishop and the monks to what seemed to be the will of God; and another monk of great repute, called Stephen, was elected abbot.

Then Daniel, who was an able and zealous prelate, encouraged and assisted Winfred in his pious under taking. As the latter had learned from his late failure, that the Apostolic blessing would be the best guarantee for his future success, Daniel gave him a sealed letter addressed to the Pope, and an open one recommending him to the kings, bishops, abbots, and clergy whom he should come across. At a later period, also, he aided him by his gifts and wise advice.

During this last summer which Winfred spent at Nutscelle, he had a vision, in which an angel foretold to him how rich a harvest of souls he would reap, and promised him the martyr s crown. The particulars of this vision are not recorded, but it is referred to by more than one contemporary. Strengthened by this Divine favor, Winfred joyfully bade a final adieu to his home and his brethren towards the close of the autumn, A.D. 718, and set out on his Apostolic work.

CHAPTER III.FIRST VISIT TO ROME

Embarking as before in London, Winfred landed at Cwentavich, now Staples, in Picardy. Here lie waited for some time, till he had the opportunity of joining a party of pilgrim monks, who were animated by a spirit of devotion and fervor akin to his own.

The winter was setting in when they started on their long and perilous journey, the usual difficulties of which, from thick forests, impassable swamps, and the want of roads and bridges, were at this time greatly increased by civil wars, and the disordered state of the countries through which they passed. But they kept up their courage by visiting the celebrated shrines that lay on their route, and recruited their failing strength within the hospitable abbeys, which were now to be found in every part of France. How long they spent on the road is not recorded but at length, having passed safely through all the dangers that threatened them, they arrived at the gates of Rome.

In that age of faith the pilgrim s first thought on entering Rome, was not the glories of the Eternal City, nor the memorials of the martyrs, nor even the blessing of Christ s Vicar, but the intolerable burden of his own sins. Accordingly Winfred and his companions went at once to S. Peter's, where, at the tomb of Heaven's Gate Keeper, they made full confession of the sins of their past lives, received the Apostolic absolution, and were admitted to joyful Communion with their Lord and the saints whose blood hallowed the soil on which they knelt. It was only after these pious duties had been fulfilled, that Winfred humbly sought an audience of S. Gregory II, who then filled the Apostolic throne.

Winfred arrived in Rome at a critical period. For three centuries the Roman Church had been by turns neglected, insulted, and oppressed by the Emperors of the East; but now the last link that had bound her to them, was on the eve of being severed. The year before, A.D. 717, Leo the Iconoclast mounted the Imperial throne, and a few years later he was breaking images, desecrating churches and altars, persecuting Catholics, and threatening even to hurl down the statues of the Apostolic Princes in Rome. The Italians rose in arms, and were restrained only by the Pope from choosing a rival emperor, and marching with him to Constantinople. At the very moment, however, when Rome, in fact, though not in theory, shook her self free from the Eastern Empire, the pressure of the Lombard kingdom began grievously to be felt.

All around the position and prospects of Christianity were most gloomy. The Mahometans were trampling down Church after Church in the East. Africa was lost. So also was Spain, except only the mountain fastness to which the Christians had retired. The storm was now gathering on the French frontier while infidel corsairs scoured the Mediterranean, and spread terror along the coasts of Italy.

As to the German nations to whom the Church had once looked with fond hope as her future stay and glory, it seemed as if they were indeed incapable of retaining the faith. Scarcely were they converted, than one after another they fell into heresy, or relapsed into idolatry. Bavaria and Allemania were over run by heretics. Thuringia was once more Pagan. Even the realm of Clovis, her first-born, after four centuries of Christian life, and ten generations of Catholic kings, was fast sinking back into barbarism. Heresy, gross licentiousness, and simony were rampant. Bishoprics and benefices were given to laymen and blood-stained clergy as the reward of military service. In many places idolatry was reviving, and the faith seemed to be on the point of dying out. At the same time the Pagan tribes, alive to the great fact of Christianity, were banded together in defense of their national religion and independence. The furious and invincible Saxons were the centre and chief strength of this Pagan confederacy, of which the Frisians in the northwest, and the Hessians and Thuringians in the south, were the frontier bulwarks while behind in the north were Danes and Scandinavians, and in the east, Slaves, Avars, Sarmatians, Tatars, and countless other nations, stretching out into unknown and infinite barbaric space.

When S. Gregory II took possession of the Apostolic Chair, A.D. 713, two great objects demanded his care. One was the conversion of Germany; the other was the development and consolidation of the Church s interior resources, so as to secure the preservation of the faith amid the chaos of society. But he knew not where to find instruments fitted to carry out these objects. It may, therefore, be conceived with what joy he hailed the arrival of the humble and docile Winfred, beneath whose simple- and calm exterior there lay hid all the deep enthusiasm and heroic devotion of the German, united to the plain common sense, the indomitable energy, and the dogged perseverance, which distinguished the English tribes.

Winfred at his first audience of the Holy Father told him his country and his life from childhood, what was the desire that for years had filled his heart, and what the motive of his long journey. On hearing the simple and ingenuous tale the Holy Father smiled, and looking kindly on the young stranger, asked if he had not brought any letters from his bishop. Whereupon Winfred, taking off his cloak in which he had deposited the precious documents for greater safety, drew them both forth and presented them to the Pope. On receiving them, Gregory dismissed him, promising to send for him when he should have had time to consider his request. Bishop Daniel s private letter to the Pope has been lost, but there can be no doubt about its tone; for S. Gregory at once selected Winfred for the great work that he had in hand, and gave him his confidence. Daily through the winter Winfred was admitted to private audiences of the Pope, who carefully questioned him as to the faith, instructed him on various points, and gave him special directions as to the work in which he was about to employ him.

Meanwhile, he fed and deepened his devotion by making the round of the countless touching memorials of apostles and martyrs, who had lived and died for the love of Jesus alone. And besides all these, there were points of special interest to the Englishman the slave-market, the convent of S. Andrew on the Celian Hill, the tomb of young Ceadwalla, and many another tomb where lay pilgrims of his own race, who had been irresistibly drawn to the throne and centre of Christ's kingdom on earth. The Borgo did not probably become the Saxon quarter till a few years later but no doubt he met at Rome Centered, Offa, and others of his countrymen, who had given up crowns, wealth, home and kindred for the hope of the heavenly kingdom. In converse with such, and amid such memorials, Winfred s aspirations were purified and strengthened.

Thus Winfred spent the winter, and when fine spring weather set in he prepared to depart. S. Gregory gave him a letter dated the 15th of May, A.D. 719, which may be regarded as the fundamental charter of the German Catholic Church. In it the Pope commanded him "in the name of the Indivisible Trinity, and by the immovable authority of S. Peter, Prince of the Apostles, whose office of teacher and whose Chair he filled, to haste and kindle among the nations bound in the errors of Paganism, that saving fire which our Lord came to cast on earth, so that God might grant him to lead them into the kingdom of God by the preaching of the name of our Lord God Jesus Christ, and to infuse the reasonable doctrines of Holy Scripture into their ignorant minds by the Spirit of strength, love, and sobriety." He also authorized him to administer the Sacraments according to the form and tradition of the Apostolic See, in which he had been instructed and he bade him be careful to inform him whenever he should be in any difficulty Winfred on his part bound himself by a vow to the service of the Apostolic See, and promised to apprise the Holy Father of whatever joy or sorrow befell him, so that in joy they might praise God together, and in sorrow he might be strengthened by the paternal counsels of His Holiness.

Winfred quitted Home in the company of the pilgrims with whom he had traveled thither. He stopped to rest for a time at Pavia, where he was hospitably entertained by Liutprand, King of the Lombards. Then passing through the plains of Lombardy, he ascended the Alps, from which he could cast a glance over the field of his lifelong labors.

CHAPTER IV.BAVARIA

For many centuries the Roman frontier was the line of demarcation between civilization and barbarism, Christianity and Paganism. But from the conversion of Clovis, the Frank Empire took the place of Rome and the Frank frontier became, as the Roman wall had been, the boundary between those two great powers, the spiritual and physical forces, which were then struggling for the mastery of the world. However low might be the state of Christianity and civilization within that boundary, yet there lay the last hope of the Church and of civilized humanity. The history of this period cannot, therefore, be rightly understood unless the broad fact be borne in mind, that the interests of the Frank empire and of Christianity were so closely interwoven, that the advance and prosperity of either was identified with that of the other.

At the time when Winfred stood on the summit of the Alps, the Frank empire was struggling for existence, and the prospects of the Church were very gloomy. The field of his future labors, on which he looked down, may be broadly divided into Bavaria, which had once been a Roman province, and in which Christianity still lingered, and that Old Germany which was totally Pagan, and was subdivided into Thuringia on the south, Saxony on the northeast, and

Friesland on the northwest.

Bavaria, which then included nearly one third of Germany, extended from the Alps to the old Roman frontier, along the mountain forests of Bohemia and the modern towns of Baireuth, Numberg, and Anspach, and from Styria to the river Itl, which separated it from Allemania. Christianity had early taken root there and in the Diocletian persecution its bishops, S. Maximilian, S. Dionysius, S. Victorinus, and S. Quirinus, the tribune S. Florian, the penitent S. Afra and her three associates, and many others, had suffered martyrdom. Here S. Severin, the Apostle of Noricum, S. Virgil, Bishop of Trent, and S. Valentine, Bishop of Rhcetia, had labored while this was the high-road for barbarian hordes to Italy. And here, when the flood of invasion subsided, Marcomanni, Rugu, Heruli, Goths, and other tribes, who were either Pagan or Arian, had settled.

In the middle of the sixth century Duke Garibald I formed Bavaria into an independent state. He and all his descendants were Catholics, and very zealous for the conversion of their subjects and his daughter, Theodolinda, who married successively Antharis and Ao-ilolf, Kings of the Lombards, cooperated with S. Gregory the Great in converting that nation from Arianism.

About the year 615, S. Eustasius, Abbot of Luxeuil, and S. Ao-ilus came, in obedience to S. Columban's last injunctions, to preach in Bavaria. Duke Garibald II received them well, and they founded several churches on the Danube. But they did not remain long, and their work was not enduring, for when S. Emmeran, Bishop of Poitiers, went in the middle of the same century to preach in Bavaria, he found the people either Pagans or sunk in a gross mixture of Christianity with Paganism, their priests even using the same chalice for the Holy Sacrifice of the Mass and for libations to Pagan gods. Duke Theodo I, struck by S. Emmeran s humility and zeal, strove to detain him at his court, and gave him Ratisbon for his episcopal see. He preached with great success for three years; but a shameful crime being then laid to his charge, he was put to death. His innocence was proclaimed after his death, and his body was translated with great solemnity to the chapel of S. George, which was converted into a splendid abbey dedicated to him, to which the see of Ratisbon was attached.

But in spite of the zeal of these dukes Christianity made no progress in Bavaria. Fresh seeds of Paganism and Arianism were constantly brought in through the restless shifting of the barbarian tribes. The Christian clergy did not all preach the Catholic doctrine, nor administer the Sacraments in a valid form there was neither discipline nor unity; and thus even zealous and devoted priests toiled merely as feeble individuals and not as members of the one powerful Catholic body.

Towards the close of the seventh century the throne was occupied by Theodo II, a prince of extraordinary piety, whose most fervent desire was to see all his subjects united in the Catholic faith before his death. With this view he invited to his court S. Rupert, a Merovingian and Bishop of Worms, the fame of whose sanctity had reached him. S. Rupert on his arrival, A.D. 696, instructed and baptized Theodo and many of his subjects of all classes, .whose baptism he found had been invalid. Then, having obtained leave from Theodo to place his episcopal see wherever he would, and to build churches and monasteries, he embarked on the Danube and sailed down it to the frontier of Lower Pannonia, sowing the word of life as he went along. On his return he stopped at Laureacum, or Lorch, where he made many converts and performed many miraculous cures. Resuming his journey he arrived at Walarium, where the river Vischaha runs out of the lake, and here he built a church which he dedicated to S. Peter. Afterwards hearing that there were at a place called Juvavia, now Salzburg, the ruins of fine buildings overgrown by the forest, he asked Theodo s leave to clear the spot and fix his see in it. Theodo, accordingly, gave him two square leagues of land, on which he built a church and monastery dedicated to S. Peter, in which he established the daily chanting of the Divine office. He also built many other churches and monasteries.

After some time S. Rupert went back to Worms to seek more laborers for his vineyard and he brought thence with him to Bavaria twelve disciples and his niece S. Erndruda. She, too, was a Merovingian, and had been abbess of a convent in France but the discipline becoming relaxed, and quarrels arising in her abbey, she was glad to follow S. Rupert to Bavaria. He built for her on a hill near Salzburg, a monastery dedicated to S. Mary the Mother of God, where she collected a numerous community; among whom she shone like the moon surrounded with stars, setting them a bright example of devotion and all other virtues.

About the year 700 Theodo divided Bavaria into four provinces, of which he gave one to each of his three sons, reserving the fourth for himself. He now longed to see a bishop like S. Rupert in each of these provinces, with a centre of unity on which the whole might rest; and he therefore went to Rome, A.D. 716, to ask counsel and aid of S. Peter s successor.

S. Gregory received Theodo most critically, gave him a capitular, or concordat, as the foundation of the Bavarian Church, and sent with him to Bavaria three legates, who would help him to organize it fully under the Apostolic authority. This capitular throws much light on the state of Bavaria at this time. The first article directed the duke to summon a council of all the principal persons in the dukedom, both clergy and laity, in order to examine into the faith, morals, and orders of the clergy, and remove from their offices all who should be found wanting in any of these points. Then followed the usual regulations about the erection of a metropolitan chair and three or more bishops sees and the placing of a priest in each church; the prohibition of idolatry, polygamy, and marriage within the forbidden degrees of kindred and finally, the prohibition to fast on Sunday, and exhortations to marry, to do penance as the only means of obtaining pardon for sin, to look for the resurrection of the body and the final judgment, and to reject the idea that Satan and his angels would eventually be restored to their original state. The last heads prove that Gnostic and Manichaean heresies had taken root in Bavaria.

Theodo encountered great difficulties in carrying out these measures. Pious and educated clergy could not be at once found. The restrictions on marriage naturally excited opposition, and still more so when Grimoald, one of his sons, married his brother's widow, Piltrude, in defiance of the Pope's authority. Before these difficulties could be overcome S. Rupert died on Easter Day, April 8th, A.D. 718 and the good duke followed him before the close of the year.

But just at this moment, when the struggle for unity and discipline seemed hopeless, another saint was led to Bavaria to keep alive Catholic tradition. This was S. Corbinian, a native of Chatres, near Paris. At a very early age he had built himself a cell close to the church of S. Germain, outside of Chatres, where, with a few companions, he followed the monastic life. His sanctity and miraculous gifts soon drew to his cell crowds of men and women of all ranks and ages, and among others, Pepin Heristal, all of whom asked his prayers and loaded him with gifts. Often would he complain with sighs and tears, that they robbed him of the solitude and poverty which he loved, and forced him to quit his prayers in order to receive their visits, answer their questions, and distribute their alms among the poor.

After leading this life for fourteen years, he set out with his little community for Rome, about A.D. 709. There, prostrate at the Holy Father s feet, he opened out his heart to him, told him how he had lost the solitude and poverty which he longed for, and entreated him to give him and his companions some obscure corner, where, under the patronage of the Holy Apostles, they might hide themselves and follow the Benedictine rule. But Pope Constantino, far from entering into his wishes, made him a bishop, gave him a pall, and sent him away with the Apostolic authority to preach wherever he chose.

For seven years S. Corbinian traveled with his companions through various parts of France, preaching with extraordinary success. At the end of that time, A.D. 717, he set out again for Rome, hoping to be more successful with S. Gregory II than he had been with his predecessor, and obtain leave to retire to some solitude. On his way he passed through Bavaria, where both Theodo and Grimoald tried to persuade him to remain. But no tempting offers could allure him from the object of his journey. Whereupon Grimoald gave secret orders to the villagers in the Alpine passes, to seize and detain him on his return from Rome.

It was during this journey through the Tyrol that occurred the circumstance already referred to, which showed his supernatural power over the brute creation. It happened one night that the men in charge of the packhorses fell asleep, and when they awoke in the morning, they saw a bear seated on the carcase of one of the horses, which he had killed and was eating. When Ansericus, the bishop s old and faithful attendant, told him of the accident, he heard it unmoved, and only answered, "Take this whip, and punish the bear well for the injury it has done us." And as Ansericus was afraid to obey, he added, "Go, and don t be afraid. Do as I have told you, and then put the pack and the bridle on the bear, and drive it on with the other horses," Ansericus obeyed; he whipped the bear, and laid the pack on its back and the beast bore its load, like a tame horse, to the gates of Rome, where the saint dismissed it and it went its way.

S. Corbinian s second journey to Home prospered no better than the former one. For the Pope and his council unanimously decided, that far from becoming a recluse, he must return to his missionary labors.

Retracing his steps, he crossed Lombardy, and arrived at Magiee, or Mays, near Meran in the Tyrol, where, in obedience to Grimoald s secret orders, he was seized and detained till that prince s pleasure should be known. During this delay he went one day to pray in the neighboring church of S. Valentine, and on his way thither he noticed that the country was fertile and well-wooded, and that there was a solitary and pathless spot between two rivulets, called Camina, which he fixed on as a desirable site for a monastery.

In due time the village messengers returned from Grimoald with orders to bring Corbinian to him. Corbinian reluctantly obeyed but on his arrival at the court he refused to hold any communication with Grimoald, who had lately formed the incestuous connexion with Piltrude. For forty days the guilty pair continued impenitent but at last they confessed their sin, promised amendment, and were reconciled to the Church.

Corbinian now consented to fix his see at Freisingen, where he built a cathedral and a monastery to the honor of S. Mary, the Mother of God, and S. Benedict. He also built at Camina, near Magiee, a monastery which he dedicated to S. Valentine and S. Zeno. But though Grimoald had broken off his connexion with Piltrude, she retained her influence over him and caused much annoyance to S. Corbinian, till at last she sent some men to kill him. Then, finding that he could do no good, he retired to the monastery that he had built in the peaceful solitude at Magiee, there to await happier times.

CHAPTER V.THURINGIA

When Winfred arrived in Bavaria, A.D. 719, S. Rupert and Duke Theodo had been dead about a year. The dukedom was divided between Theodo s two surviving sons, Theodebert and Grimoald; and S. Corbinian was settled at Freisingen with the latter. Gladly would they have detained him to aid their work but it was to the Pagans that the Pope had sent him, and it was to them that his own heart also turned. Twenty years later he did much in Bavaria but now, he contented himself with dropping passing rebukes and exhortations as he traveled through the provinces on his way to Allemania.

In Allemania, also, there was a Church, bishops at Constance, Spire, and Augsburg, priests scattered about here and there, and a large Christian population, either Gallo-Romans, or Germans who had been gathered into the fold by S. Gall and his sons, in whose abbey S. Columban's rule was still observed. Winfred, therefore, made no long stay in Allemania, but passed on to Thuringia.

The name of the Thuringians first appears in the fifth century, when their dominion extended over the whole of central Germany. Their origin is very uncertain, but some writers suppose that they were descendants of the Hermanduri. Only scattered fragments of their history are known; but it is distinguished by the remarkable fact, that though the nation was most bigoted in its hatred of Christianity, no less than three canonized female saints are to be found in the royal family.

It has been already related how, in the early part of the sixth century, Hermanfried, one of three brothers who jointly governed the territory, got rid of his brothers with the help of the Franks and afterwards quarrelling with them, was conquered by them and the Saxons, who divided Thuringia between them. It was after this overthrow that Hermanfried's niece, S. Radegunda, was led captive to France, where she threw the halo of sanctity over the throne of her conqueror.

The acquisition of this territory was an extraordinary gain to the Franks. For great numbers of them, afterwards distinguished as East Franks, transplanted themselves to the district since called Franconia, which became a second cradle of their race in the heart of Old Germany. From this forest home the national vigor was constantly recruited, and thus they were preserved from that decay and feebleness, into which the Goths, Vandals, and other barbarian nations, so rapidly fell after they had given up their connexion with Old Germany.

After the overthrow of the Thuringian tribe, the country relapsed into its former state of Paganism and barbaric anarchy. But after the lapse of a century, A.D. 630, Dagobert, the better to resist the incursions of the Wends, gave the government of the Franco Thuringian territory, with the title of duke, to Eadulph, a Thuringian noble, in whose family it remained for four generations. Under Eadulph and his son, Hethan I, both of whom were Pagans, the Thuringians were so violently opposed to Christianity that the few Christians who were in the land, did not dare to make open profession of their faith. So fierce was their bigotry, that when Hethan I, who had married the beautiful S. Bilhilde, one of these hidden Christians, was summoned to follow the Frank king to the field, he could not venture to leave his young wife in his heathen home, but took her to her uncle Sigebert, Bishop of Mayence. Hethan being killed, she built a convent at Minister, in which she spent the rest of her life, and after her death she was venerated as a saint.

Meanwhile Gotzbert, son of Hethan by a former marriage, had succeeded to the dukedom. He was a Pagan, like his predecessors; but in his reign the Gospel was brought to him and his subjects by a band of Irish monks, whose love of souls had drawn them from their home.

At the head of this band was S. Kilian, an Irishman of noble birth, who had early entered a monastery, in which he rose to be abbot. In this position he was so much beloved and revered, that he began to fear lest his own soul should suffer from this flattering intercourse with men and he often revolved in his mind how he should escape from it, and give himself entirely to communion with God.

It happened one day that in the Gospel there occurred the text, "Whosoever will come after Me, let him deny himself, and take up his cross, and follow Me," and as the words sounded in his outward ears, the voice of Our Lord seemed to repeat them in the depths of his heart, as if addressing them specially to him. Deeply moved, he proposed to eleven of his disciples to quit their country and their kindred, and go forth to win souls for Christ. These fervent young Irish monks quickly responded to their abbot s call and before long the party started for Pagan lands.

In the year 686 they arrived at Wurzburg, the capital of Thuringia, where they were charmed with the beauty of the country and the simplicity and nobleness of the German character. Then Kilian said to his companions, "Brethren, you see how fair and rich is this laud, and how handsome and attractive are its people. If it please you, let us go to Rome and visit the threshold of the Apostolic Princes, as we agreed on when we were in our own country. Let us O present ourselves before Pope John, and if it be God's will that we should get permission from the Apostolic See, let us return here and preach faithfully the name of our Lord Jesus Christ, according to the advice that the Holy Father shall give us." The whole party agreed to this proposal, and they set out without delay for Rome.

On their arrival in Rome they found that Pope John was dead, but "they were lovingly and honorably welcomed" by his successor, Conon. When he heard whence they came, what was the motive of their journey, and to what country they wished to devote themselves, he received their profession of the Catholic faith, and then gave them authority, in the name of God and S. Peter, to teach and preach the Gospel of Christ.

In the course of their journey back to Thuringia the little band separated, only Koloman a priest, and Totman a deacon, remaining with Kilian, and the others going elsewhere.

As soon as Kilian reached Wurzburg he began to preach. The people came at first from mere curiosity to listen to his novel doctrine; they marveled at his flow of eloquence and his supernatural gifts and thus the truth gradually made its way with them. At length the duke sent for him. Gotzbert was a man of powerful intellect, and when the fundamental dogmas of the Christian faith were expounded to him, he was deeply interested. He would often go secretly to Kilian to discuss these subjects with him, till at last he arrived at the conviction, that if Kilian s words were true, he must forsake the religion of his forefathers. Then came the struggle of conscience between the newly found truth and the lifelong error; but by God's grace the truth triumphed, and on the following Easter Day Gotzbert and many of his subjects were baptized.

And now an unforeseen trial met him. As a Pagan ho had married Geilana, his brother s widow, but Kilian told him that this was an unlawful union. On hearing this Gotzbert started and sighing deeply, for he loved the woman tenderly, he answered, "Father, this is more difficult than anything you have yet taught me. For the love of the Almighty God I have left all that was dear and pleasant to me. For the same love I now give up my most beloved wife, if it be not lawful for me to have her, for there is nothing more precious or more lovable than the love of God. I am about to march against the enemies of my country, and cannot now make arrangements to put her away but as soon as I return I will do so."

But while Gotzbert thus nobly gave up his heart's dearest treasure to God, the unhappy Geilana was infuriated, and resolved to kill the Christian teachers during Gotzbert s absence.

Kilian and his companions, foreseeing their doom, redoubled their fasts and devotions, praying night and day, and rejoicing in expectation of the crown of martyrdom. It happened one night that they lay down to take a little rest, when, as Kilian was half asleep, there appeared to him a man of most beautiful countenance in shining garments, who said to him, " Beloved Kilian, arise. I will not have thee toil much longer; one com bat alone awaits thee, and thou shalt be a conqueror with me forever." Then Kilian knew that their hour was come and waking his companions, he said, "Brethren, let us watch for our Lord will soon be here, and will knock at the door. Beware lest He find us sleeping." They therefore began to pray; and about midnight, as they were singing God's praises, two assassins entered with drawn swords in their hands. On seeing them Kilian joyfully exclaimed, "My sons, behold, the long wished for day is come! Fight the good fight with me without fear and trembling, for our Lord has said, Fear not them who kill the body, but cannot kill the soul." As he said these words the ruffians fell on them and cut off the heads of all three. They buried them in haste on the spot on which they fell, and placed their crucifix, their box of books, and their vestments, in their grave. And the better to conceal the foul deed, Geilana turned the building into a stable.

When Gotzbert returned he asked what had become of the holy men and Geilana answered, that they had gone away secretly, no one knew whither. But before long one of the assassins committed suicide and the other became mad, and went about crying, in a loud voice, "Kilian, thou parsecutest me horribly. I am burning as in a fire." Geilana, too, was possessed by a devil, and in her ravings she would call on the martyrs as if they were torturing her, and would be so violent that several men could scarcely hold her. Then people were sure that the holy men had been murdered, but the circumstances of their death were long unknown.

There was, however, one witness of the martyrdom. A noble matron, called Burgonda, whom Kilian had converted, had built herself a cell adjoining his oratory, in order that she might take part in his prayers. As she was watching and praying, she saw through a chink in the wall the murderers come in and do the wicked deed and after they departed she went into the oratory and dipped a handkerchief in the martyrs blood. She was in the habit of going secretly to pray on the spot; but fearing lest Geilana or the Pagans might remove the holy relics, she told no one what she had witnessed till, being on her death-bed, she confided her secret to a few Christian friends, who handed it on till a happier day shone on this dark Pagan land.

After S. Kilian's death Gotzbert remained firm in his profession of Christianity. But it is conjectured that he and his son and successor, Hethan II, tried to force the new religion on their subjects, with whom they were henceforth constantly embroiled. Gotzbert was murdered by his servants, A.D. 706 and about ten years after, when Pepin Heristal s death had deprived the Christian party of the support which he had afforded them, the Pagan Thuringians rebelled and killed Hethan II and all his family, except his daughter S. Irinina. She, the third female royal saint of Thuringia, continued in possession of a church in Wurzburg, which her father had built in honor of our Blessed Lady and here she was found by S. Boniface five and twenty years later, at the head of a small religious community.

Two memorials of Hethan s piety still exist, in the form of two deeds of gift to S. Willibrord. The earliest, dated May 1st, A.D. 704, made over to him certain lands and houses, with all they contained, at Arnstadt on the river Welge, at Muhlberg, four leagues southwest of Gotha, and at Munchen, between Arnstadt and Weimar. The other deed, dated April 19th, A.D. 716, gave him all the property at Hamelburg on the Saal, which Hethan had inherited. More will be heard of these gifts.

When Winfred arrived in Thuringia three years after the date of this last deed, the country was divided among numerous independent chiefs and tribes; the Saxons held the greater part of it; and the bitterest hatred of Christianity existed. Still, the Christian religion was not quite extinct, and priests were to be found here and there but heresy and immorality prevailed to a frightful extent, and even a mixture of Christianity and Paganism was not uncommon, the priests and their flocks often going direct from the celebration of Mass to take part in Pagan sacrifices and the most abominable rites.

Here Winfred found full scope for his zeal. He went about diligently among all classes, striving to infuse missionary ardor into the few pious priests whom he met, stirring up the Christians to live according to the pure precepts of their religion, and exhorting those sunk in vice and sacrilege to repent and amend their ways. He succeeded, too, in persuading some of the Pagans to destroy the images and heathen symbols, which he found in groves and at springs, where the people used to assemble to worship their demon gods.

But he did not meet with the success that he anticipated. For the country being in a very unsettled state, the people were too much agitated by civil feuds to give heed to his exhortations, while the bitter enmity against Christianity, which had been increased by the late revolt against their dukes and the Franks, restricted his intercourse with the Pagans.

Under these circumstances, being uncertain where to establish himself, he passed into Austrasia with the monks with whom he had been traveling. Here he heard that Ratbod was dead. This was a Providential opening; and accordingly he immediately embarked on the Rhine, and scattering the seed of the Gospel as he passed along, he followed the course of the river to Utrecht.

CHAPTER VI.FRIESLAND

Ratbod's death led to a total revolution in Friesland. Charles Martel, having in this same year established his authority in Neustria, was now able to turn his arms to the frontiers. He quickly recovered Hither Friesland and made the rest of the nation tributary. Thus the whole country was laid open to Christian influence. S. Willibrord returned to Utrecht, and assembled his scattered clergy in synod. They decided no longer to confine themselves to the Frank province, but to preach in all parts of Friesland. Winfred now offered his services to S. Willibrord, who gladly accepted them.

In looking at Winfred s career, one is struck with the remarkable combination of great unity and firmness of purpose, with equally great flexibility of operation, which characterized him. This was a proof of his supernatural vocation. For both the firmness and the flexibility alike show the total absence of self-will, and perfect obedience to God's Providence and the Holy Spirit s guidance. The great object of his desires was the conversion of his kindred in Old Saxony, who were "of one blood and bone" with himself. This was the central point of all his operations. Direct approach to this centre being for the present impossible, he made it his secondary object to Christianize the tribes on the frontiers of Saxony, striving thus to hem in the Pagans on the north, south, and west by Christian neighbors; and as hunters close in round their game, and a general draws his lines round a beleaguered town, so he hoped to advance his circle of Christian influences ever nearer and nearer round the Pagan host, till at last he should touch the very heart of the nation and transfix it with the fiery darts of God s truth and love. This idea gave unity to all his operations, and it ought to be borne in mind, in order to understand why he preferred Friesland, Hesse, and Thuringia to Bavaria and Allemania, and how, in going so frequently from one of these provinces to another, his movements were not of a desultory character, but always tended to the same central point. Thus was Old Germany conquered to Christianity; and though Winfred did not see the final triumph of his plans, yet their perfect success proves the supernatural wisdom which inspired them.

The following letter, addressed to him, at this time, by Bugga, an English nun, shows how he rejoiced to enter on this work in Friesland. It is further interesting, as being the* first of that series of beautiful letters, which passed between him and the monks and nuns in England, to whom he was united by so warm a friendship.

"To the venerable servant of God, adorned with many spiritual gifts and graces, Boniface or Winfred, the worthy priest of God, from Bugga, a despicable servant, the greeting of perpetual charity."

"Be assured that I never cease to thank Almighty God for the manifold mercies, which, as I learn from your letter, He hath granted you in leading you through unknown lands. First, He inclined the Bishop of the glorious See to favor the desire of your heart afterwards He overthrew before you Ratbod, the enemy of the Catholic Church and, moreover, He has revealed to you in a dream, that you will reap a harvest for God, and gather sheaves of holy souls into the barns of the King of Heaven. Wherefore, I declare all the more, that no temporal vicissitude will change my affection for you; but my love for you will burn the more brightly, because I am certain that through the help of your prayers I shall attain to the haven of rest. I, therefore, humbly remind you to deign to offer your intercessions to God for my littleness that by His grace and your protection I may be kept safe. I have not been able to procure the Acts of the Martyrs which you asked me to send you. I will do so as soon as I can. And you, dearest friend, pray send, to console my littleness, what you promised in your sweet letter, namely, the collection of extracts from the Holy Scriptures. I also entreat you to offer the sacrifice of the Holy Mass for the soul of my relative, whom I loved above all others. I send you by the bearer fifty pieces of gold and an altar-cloth. I have not been able to procure any thing better. But though the gift is a small one, it is offered by me with the greater love. Farewell in this world in holy and unfeigned charity."

During three years Winfred traveled about Friesland, turning to good account the knowledge of the country and the people, which he had picked up during his former visit. He preached boldly as he went along, and while his glowing eloquence drew crowds to listen to the new doctrine, his clear reasoning and gentle persuasiveness proved irresistible. The Christians who had fallen away during the late persecution, returned to the faith thousands of Pagans were converted the idol temples were overthrown and replaced by Christian churches; and the light of truth began to shine through the whole land. Several of the converts devoted themselves to the religious life under his guidance. He taught them to chant the daily office, to labor, and to study, in obedience to S. Benedict s rule; and while he thus prepared them to help him at some future day, the fervor of the whole party was kept up amid the distractions of active work and travel, by the observance of monastic discipline. The rest of the clergy, too, were encouraged by his example, and a spirit of zeal and courage spread through the whole body. But however indefatigably the laborers toiled, they still found themselves too few for the rich harvest of souls that seemed to be only waiting to be reaped.

While Winfred followed thus perfectly the guiding of God's providence, he seems to have looked on Friesland as no more than a temporary field of labor. This is proved by a letter written at this time to a young man called Nidhard, possibly one of his Thuringian converts, whom he seems to have left in Austrasia to pursue his studies. This letter beautifully expresses that ardent love for Holy Scripture which distinguished these monk scholars, and with which he wished to inspire his young friend, as being the means whereby to acquire "that Divine wisdom, which is more resplendent than gold, more beautiful than silver, more glowing than the carbuncle, more pure than crystal, more precious than the topaz and to which all precious things are not worthy to be compared." "For what, Christian brother," he continues, "is more worthy of pursuit by the young? Or what more valuable to be possessed by the old, than the knowledge of the Holy Scriptures, which, guiding the ship of our souls without shipwreck through perils and storms, will land us on the beautiful shores of Paradise, amid the unending joys of the angels? Wherefore, if Almighty God will, whenever on my way I return to those parts, as I purpose to do, I promise to be a faithful friend to thee in all things, and a devoted help, so far as my powers go, in the study of the Divine Scriptures. Then, as if carried away by his subject, he breaks off into verse, and closes his letter with twenty-eight lines on the joys and glory of Heaven.

S. Willibrord was now sixty-five years old; he had toiled hard for thirty years in Gaul and Friesland, and was broken by age and infirmities. At the suggestion of his clergy he proposed to Winfred, who was universally loved and revered, to become his coadjutor now, and his successor on his death. But Winfred shrank from the dignity and its responsibility, which, moreover, would withdraw him from the missionary work which was so dear to him. He urged his own unworthiness, and also that he was not yet fifty, which was then the usual age for episcopal consecration. But Willibrord, deeming the interest of his flock a sufficient reason for anticipating the usual age, still pressed the office on him, and even reproved him for declining it. Thus there arose an amicable contest between the two saints. At length Winfred, driven to extremity, said to Willibrord, Pope Gregory authorized me to preach to the Germans and in virtue of this Apostolic mission, I came to this western Pagan region and placed myself under thy jurisdiction. Up to this day I have obeyed both thee and him, to whose service I am bound by vow. But now, I dare not set aside the commands of the Apostolic See, and accept the episcopal office without the Pope s command. I beseech thee, therefore, venerable prelate permit me, who am bound by the chain of my voluntary vow, to return to those parts from whence I came. This plea was unanswerable. Willibrord, therefore, bowing to the authority of Rome, gave Winfred his blessing and permission to depart.

Winfred accordingly set out for Thuringia, A.D. 722, accompanied by the Frisian converts, who, in German fashion, had given themselves to his service. On his way he came to the Abbey of Palatiolum or Pfalzel, about three miles from Treves, the abbess of which was the Merovingian princess, Adela, daughter of Dagobert II, and sister of Irmina, Abbess of Horres in Treves. She was a widow and a grandmother; and Gregory, the son of her son Albrico, a boy between fourteen and fifteen years of age, was staying with her when Winfred and his companions arrived.

According to conventual custom, the young Gregory read aloud in the refectory during the repast. He read with so much feeling and impressiveness, that Winfred noticed it, and said to him, "Thou readest well, my son. But dost thou understand what thou hast read?" The boy thought that he did, and with childish simplicity, said so frankly. "Then tell me," my son replied Winfred, "thy thoughts about what thou hast read." The boy referred to his book, and was about to read the passage again. But Winfred stopped him, saying, "No, my son, I want thee to tell me in thine own words the meaning of what thou hast read." This the boy could not do; whereupon Winfred said, "Wouldest thou like me then to explain it to thee?" Gregory assenting, Winfred made him read the passage over again very slowly and then, in the presence of the abbess and all the community, he began to preach on its meaning with such glowing and attractive eloquence, that the youth was quite carried away and captivated, and thinking not of his parents or his native land, he came to the resolution never to quit this unknown stranger. As soon as Winfred ceased speaking, he went to his grandmother and told her that he wished to go with this man and become his scholar, in order to learn the meaning of Holy Writ. Adela loved the boy too tenderly to fall in with his views; the perils of traveling in wild, Pagan lands terrified her; she represented to her dear grandchild that he did not know the man nor even where he might be going; and she did her best to turn him from his purpose. But all in vain. Gregory could not be frightened, or reasoned with he begged, and prayed, and wept; and at last he said, that if she would not give him a horse, he would follow the man on foot. Then Adela s natural affection gave way to the spiritual love that had taken possession of her grandson. She gave him a horse and a servant and as the fishers at the sea of Galilee left their father, their nets, and their all, at the loving call of that Divine voice, so the boy drawn on by the fragrant odor of the same Divine word, which is more sweet than honey to the palate, turned his back on the royal state in which he had been nurtured, followed the stranger through toil, poverty, and peril to unknown lands, and never left him till the martyr s death parted them.

On Winfred s arrival in Thuringia he found the country in an indescribable state of misery. As there was no central government round which the people could rally, the Saxons were constantly making predatory incursions, ravaging with fire and sword, and driving the inhabitants into the towns or strong natural fastnesses, where they lived in hourly dread for their lives, till the foe retreated from sheer satiety of spoil, or till neighboring tribes could muster in sufficient force to drive them out. Then civil war would add to the desolation, the rival factions destroy ing whatever the Saxon had spared. And by all parties alike the Christians were so pitilessly persecuted, that their sole alternative was to relapse into Paganism, or to hide themselves in secluded solitudes. Thus whole tracts of land were left without cultivation, and the scattered inhabitants were in want of the necessaries of life.

Winfred and his companions shared the common privations. They had to support themselves by manual labor and their lives were in constant peril. But in spite of the hardships that they endured, they sought out the scattered Christian flock in the wilds in which they lay hid, consoling those who held firm to the faith, and restoring many lapsed wanderers to the fold.

In the midst of this gloom a ray of light soon appeared. Charles Martel crossed the Rhine, drove the Saxons out of the territory which had formerly been tributary to the Franks, and reduced the Thuringian factions to subjection. The presence of his troops added, it is true, to the misery of the province, but it was a sure harbinger of returning peace and order. Winfred followed in the track of the Frank army. He seems to have been unknown to Charles, being only a humble priest and Charles was at this time no friend to the Church, which was constantly reproaching and threatening him for giving bishoprics and abbeys to his military retainers. Still Charles s presence was an involuntary aid to Winfred. Three years before the latter had met with but faint response in Thuringia, but now he made thousands of converts, idol temples were overthrown, and Christian oratories rose on their ruins.

Winfred took advantage of these prosperous circumstances to gain a firm standing-point in Old Germany, by laying the first stone of those monasteries, which became the chief instrument by which the Germans were converted and civilized.

The object of Duke Hethans gift of the lands at Hamelburg on the Saal, near Kissingen, to S. Willibrord, as already mentioned, was the foundation of a monastery. Hethan s overthrow, and the troubles that succeeded it, prevented this intention being carried out, and the land remained in the possession of two brothers, Detdic and Dierolf, who are supposed to be identical with the two counts, Siegeric and Cato, who signed as witnesses the original deed of gift. These brothers had fallen into the sacrilegious custom, then so prevalent, of uniting Pagan rites with Christian worship. Winfred having converted them from this horrible impiety, obtained from them possession of the abovementioned land, the ownership of which had, no doubt, been transferred to him by S. Willibrord at his departure from Friesland. He now carried out Duke Hethan s intention, and built a monastery with a church dedicated to S. John Baptist, on which foundation the oldest parish church in Central Germany, was afterwards erected. Here he placed some of the numerous disciples whom he had collected in Friesland and Thuringia, thus gaining at once a firm footing in the land, and a nursery for future laborers in the vine yard.

After founding this monastery Winfred turned his steps to the north, and entered Hesse. The Hatti, Hette, or Chatti, since softened into Hesse, were a tribe of the Sons of Isto, much dreaded for their ferocity. They are first heard of in the first century, when they were confederated with the Suevi, and again in the middle of the fifth, when they were in alliance with the Franks. From this time they disappear from history, till Winfred again brings them to light. During this interval their land had been the common battlefield of Franks, Thuringians, and Saxons, with one or other of whom in turn they would ally themselves, though they were generally tributary to the Franks. During the late disorders they had been subject to the Saxons; but Charles Martel now drove out the latter and divided the country into Frank and Saxon districts, to the former of which the name of Hesse was generally given.

No attempt had ever been made to convert them, for there is no good foundation for the traditions that S. Lubentius in the fourth century, S. Goar in the sixth, and Dagobert I in the seventh, had each built a church in Hesse. Thus they were totally Pagan when Winfred, following in the track of Charles Martel's army, first came among them. He preached with his accustomed fervor and even more than his usual success; for, as his biographer says with expressive brevity, "God was his companion throughout his journey." His stay in Hesse, however, was not long, and no opportunity offered itself to build either oratory or cell.

So long as Winfred was in Friesland, under S. Willibrord s jurisdiction, it was not necessary that he should keep up direct communication with the Holy See. But now that he was in Pagan lauds without an episcopal superior, the case was different. A. large Church had suddenly sprung up, and many important questions had necessarily arisen for Pagan idolatry was so closely interwoven with the whole life of the Germans, that it was not easy to draw the right line between those demoniacal superstitions and rites with which the Church permits no compromise, and mere national customs which she has always looked on with indulgence. The solution of these difficult points, and also many others connected with the discipline of the infant Church, lay beyond the province of a simple priest like Winfred. He therefore sent Bynuan, one of his disciples, to Rome with a letter to the Holy Father, narrating the course of his proceedings during the last three years, and asking for further direction. Bynuan executed his commission with fidelity and dispatch and staying only a few days in Rome, hastened back to Winfred with the Pope's answer. Unhappily, neither of these letters is now extant.

Winfred received the Pope s letter with joy. From its general tone he gathered that S. Gregory II would be glad to confer personally with him, so as to make the most of the present favorable crisis and avoid mistakes, which might mar the success of the great work they had in hand. Winfred accepted the Pope's wish as a command, and selecting a few companions from among his disciples, he joined a party of monks on their way to the Apostolic shrines. France and Italy were covered with armies and military encampments; but the pilgrims passed through them without molestation. On coming within view of the walls of Rome Winfred was overcome with emotion, as if foreseeing what awaited him. But he renewed his offering of himself to God s will, and placed himself under the special patronage of the Apostolic Princes.

CHAPTER VII.SECOND VISIT TO ROME

As on the former occasion, Winfred s first visit was to the tomb of S. Peter. He then announced his arrival to the Pope, who received him graciously, and assigned him a lodging in one of the many hospitals provided For the reception of poor pilgrims.

Before many days had elapsed, S. Gregory II summoned Winfred to meet him at S. Peter's. After the interchange of a few friendly words, S. Gregory began to question Winfred the Creed and the Catholic and Apostolic traditions of the Church. But he had not proceeded far, when Winfred said with great humility, "Holy Father, I am a foreigner, and am not skilful in expressing myself on such important subjects in common and familiar language. I therefore pray your Holiness to give me time to commit my ideas to writing, so that by mute letters I may make confession of my faith." The Pope readily consented, bidding him draw up his confession with as little delay as possible. Accordingly, in the course of a few days, Winfred sent in a full profession of the Holy Catholic faith, expressed in the most lucid and eloquent language that he could command.

Some days elapsed during which he heard nothing about his paper, till at length he was summoned to the Lateran. It was a solemn and anxious occasion, and on entering the Pope's presence, being filled with awe and fear lest he should have erred on any point, he prostrated himself at the Holy Father s feet and asked his pardon and his blessing. But S. Gregory kindly raising him and reassuring him, made him sit down beside him. Then returning him his paper, he exhorted him always to hold and diligently teach the pure faith which was therein fully set forth. After this he kept him in conversation almost the whole day, discoursing on various subjects connected with the faith and the spiritual life, and asking many questions about the tribes to whom Winfred had preached, and about his mode of drawing them from their errors to the truth.

When S. Gregory had thus satisfied himself as to Winfred s orthodoxy and fitness for the missionary work, he told him that he intended to make him a bishop and place him over those poor people, who had hitherto been wandering without a shepherd. As an inducement to overcome his humility, he explained how the grace of the episcopal office would give him more power over souls and add unction to his preaching, since all his words would be reinforced by the authority of the Apostolic Chair, from which his consecration proceeded. Winfred did not dare to oppose the Holy Father and remembering the words of Scripture. He would not have the blessing, and it shall be far from him he humbly accepted the proffered dignity.

Accordingly on the feast of S. Andrew, November 30th, A.D. 723, Winfred was consecrated in the Church of the Vatican, by Pope S. Gregory II, who at the same time gave him the name of Boniface. Then, in order to bind him more closely to obedience to the Holy See, S. Gregory required him to take the following oath on the body of S. Peter.

"In the name of our Lord God and Savior Jesus Christ, in the reign of the Emperor Leo, the seventh year after his consulate, and the fourth year of his son, the Emperor Constantine, the sixth Indiction, I, Boniface, by the grace of God Bishop, promise to thee, Blessed Peter, Prince of the Apostles, and to thy Vicar Blessed Pope Gregory and his successors, by the Indivisible Trinity, Father, Son, and Holy Ghost, and by this thy sacred body, that I will profess the true and pure holy Catholic faith, and by God s grace will persevere in the unity of that same faith, by which, without doubt, Christians are saved; and I will never consent, at the persuasion of any one whomsoever, to do aught that is contrary to the unity of the one Universal Church; but as I have said, I will in all things give my allegiance, fealty, and service to thee, to whom the power of binding and loosing has been given by God, and to the service of thy Church, and to thy aforesaid Vicar and his successors. And if at any time I should know that a bishop acts contrary to the ancient canons of the Holy Fathers, I will not associate or communicate with him but if I can prevent him I will do so, or at least I will immediately inform my Apostolic Lord. Should I ever be tempted, which far be from me, either by my own mind or by circumstances, to do any thing in any way contrary to this my promise, may I be found guilty in the eternal judgment and incur the punishment of Ananias and Sapphira, who also presumed to defraud thee of what belonged to thee. This record of my vow, I, Boniface, an unworthy bishop, have written with my own hand, and placing it on the most sacred body of S. Peter, God being witness and judge, I have taken the above written vow, which I now also promise to keep."

After Boniface, as he must now be called, had taken this oath, Pope S. Gregory promised on his part always to help, support, and protect him. He also gave him a book containing the rules and canons of the Church, to be a guide to him in governing his diocese and by a special privilege, he received him and all who were subject to him into perpetual friendship and union with the Apostolic Chair. There is still to be seen in the library of the cathedral of Wurzburg, a MS. book containing the Apostolic Canons and the decrees of the first Councils, written in an Anglo-Saxon hand of the eighth century, which is supposed to be the one given to S. Boniface by Pope S. Gregory II. The special union with the Holy See here mentioned, is considered to be the earliest record of those pious confraternities which have since spread so widely through the Church, forming a close network of spiritual intercommunion between the Head and the members, and between the members with each other. S. Boniface highly prized this privilege, and on the accession of each successive Pope was careful to renew the tie.

Boniface spent the winter in Rome, and on the opening of spring, A.D. 724, made preparations to return to Germany. The Pope gave him six letters of recommendation addressed respectively to Charles Martel, to the German bishops and dukes, to the German clergy and laity, to the Thuringian nation, to five Thuringian nobles and all other Thuringian Christians, and lastly, to the Old Saxons. These letters taken collectively, sketch out a wide field for almost unlimited missionary labor. The letter to the Old Saxons, inviting them with loving, paternal solicitude to listen to the exhortations of Boniface, proves that the conversion of his kindred in the old country was the chief object of Boniface s most fervent desires.

When Boniface went to take leave of the Pope, the latter said to him, "Thou hast heard, brother, and thou hast thyself seen, how many thousands in Germany are held captive in the old Pagan idolatry, and of how many children our Holy Mother the Church is defrauded. Now, then, since thou art a just man and well instructed in our holy religion, do thou draw this multitude to salvation that the talent which has been committed to thee, thou mayst return doubled to our Lord. Take, therefore, the pastoral staff with the smooth stones of the Divine law, that when the giant who began to destroy all Israel, shall boast of his certain victory, thou mayst, like David, meet the enemy of the human race in battle. And if in that combat the martyr's crown be offered thee, accept it willingly, nothing doubting, that through that transitory suffering thou wilt gain eternal wealth." With these prophetic words and the kiss of peace, S. Gregory gave Boniface his blessing and dismissed him.

CHAPTER VIII.BISHOP BONIFACE IN HESSE

Hitherto Boniface s life had been only the fitting preparation for his future work. In the cloister and school of Nutscelle, at the court of S. Ina, and at the foot of the Apostolic Chair, his special education for it had been completed; then he had visited the whole field of his future labors and in his journeys through France and in the track of Charles Martel s army, he had witnessed those ecclesiastical abuses which he was hereafter to correct. Now, in the year 724, he entered on this vast sphere of action as an episcopus regionarius, or bishop without a fixed see, unshackled by any territorial limits, supported by the Apostolic authority, and endued with the episcopal grace to confirm his weak converts, and ordain fresh laborers for his vineyard.

Boniface first turned his steps to the court of Charles Martel. For he had learned from his former experience, as he wrote to his old friend, Bishop Daniel of Winchester, that "without the support of the Frank prince, whose word inspired universal fear and respect, he should be unable to govern his flock, to defend priests and deacons, monks and nuns, or to prohibit the celebration of Pagan rites and sacrilegious idolatry." But here an unforeseen difficulty met him. He found the court full of wicked priests, some of them homicides and immoral, living openly in their sins, and yet presuming to exercise priestly functions; others not only neglecting to water the seed that had once been sown, but pulling it up, sowing tares in its stead, and forming new heretical sects and all combining to create endless scandal and seduce the people into mortal errors. In such society Boniface had no rest with "combats without, fears within." He remembered that at his consecration he had sworn on the body of S. Peter to avoid all association and communion with such men as these and yet he was now compelled to meet them in the prince s hall, to interchange courteous salutations, and even to eat at the same table with them. And if he should resolve to fly from this contaminating intercourse, he feared lest he should incur a more grave condemnation for neglecting to press the interests of his flock with the Frank prince. In this painful dilemma, he came to the conclusion that he had better tolerate the ordinary social intercourse with them, but carefully avoid communicating with them at the altar. So much however was he distressed, so tender was his conscience, and so great his humility, that he sought consolation and advice from Bishop Daniel, in whose wisdom and paternal affection he had so long been accustomed to confide. This letter closes like almost all which Boniface wrote to his friends in England, with a request for books. He now asked for a certain MS containing six of the prophetical books of Scripture, which had belonged to his former abbot, adding, that he could not procure these where he now was, and this MS being in a large and clear hand, it would be very useful to him, because his failing sight disabled him from reading small characters. In return he sent to Daniel, by Forthere, a priest, who was the bearer of his letter, a towel made of goat s hair and wool to dry his feet. Bishop Daniel in his answer, not only approved of the line of conduct which Boniface had drawn out for himself, but encouraged him by our Lord's example, not to shrink from social intercourse with these wicked priests, in the hope that by patience and gentleness he might lead them to repentance.

At first these men prejudiced Charles Martel against Boniface but the Pope's letter quickly put that to rights. For though Charles would not let himself be shackled in his ambitious career by the Church, he was glad to gain her support by appearing before his subjects as her friend and protector, whenever he could conveniently do so. He was, moreover, fully aware of the aid which Christian missionaries could lend him by converting the frontier tribes. For wherever Christianity took root in a Pagan province, the Christian part of the nation naturally looked to the Franks for protection and favored their domination and thus the national union was broken, and the strength of resistance was weakened. Soon after his accession to power Charles had reduced the Allemans, Bavarians, and Frisians to tributary dependence but the strong Pagan confederacy in Saxony, with its outworks in Hesse and Thuringia, resisted all his efforts, and was a constant obstacle to the consolidation and prosperity of his empire. Notwithstanding the calls made on him from various other quarters, he managed to invade Saxony no less than six times between the years 718 and 739. But all in vain. For each time the waves of Pagan barbarism, which recoiled before his victorious arms, closed in behind him as he retired, and presented as firm and unbroken a front as before. Under these circumstances the missionary who would bring him friends and allies from the ranks of his foes, who would transform Pagan blood-thirsty restlessness and fury into Christian peace and charity, and literally turn the sword and axe of the barbarian into the plough and reaping hook of civilized society, would be a valuable coadjutor.

He therefore received Boniface graciously, and gave him a letter of recommendation to all the principal persons in his dominions, ordering them not to molest, nor hear any complaint against Bishop Boniface, whom, at the Holy Father's request, he had taken under his protection, but to refer all complaints to himself.

Furnished with this valuable passport Boniface set out for the part of Hesse where he had formerly preached. Great was his anxiety about this little flock, which he had left without a shepherd in the Pagan wilderness. Some of his children he found firm in their faith and uncompromising in their conduct; while many others were weak and vacillating. But the number of the promising converts was few, in comparison with those who had fallen away more or less completely. Some openly sacrificed at sacred trees and fountains, consulted auspices, and diviners, and practiced incantations and various Pagan rites; and others did these things secretly, while they still made public profession of Christianity.

This tendency to mix up Pagan and Christian rites has been always one of the greatest difficulties with which missionaries have had to contend. Not only are these Pagan practices supported by the instinctive leaning towards the supernatural, which is so deeply imbedded in human nature, and by all the countless associations of personal and national life, but they are based on a reality, being, in fact, the fulfillment of the delusive promise to Eve, "You shall be as gods, knowing good and evil." The Fathers of the Church have always taken the view that they were a kind of demoniacal sacrament, by which the worshipper was brought into communication with the evil being who was worshipped. In this they followed the authority of S. Paul, who exhorts Christians not to be "partakers of the table of devils." It would be in vain to contend with this Pagan worship on the ground of its being simply null, for its votaries appealed to the broad fact that their ancestors for long ages believed the contrary, and rested their belief on their own personal experience.

Christian missionaries never denied that the demon might make use of the limited power which God still allows to "the powers of the air," in favor of their votaries. At the same time they worked on the rude minds with whom they had to deal, by pointing to the superior prosperity of Christians, and only contended that the help of demons would turn to their ultimate ruin, and certainly to the loss of their souls. Boniface soon found an opportunity of proving the superior power of the One Almighty God.

There stood at Geismar, not far from Fritzlar and Buraburg, an oak of extraordinary size, which was dedicated to Thor or Thunar, "the God of Thunder" and was called Thunar's oak, or Donnereiche, i. e. Thor s oak, or the Thunder oak. Here from time immemorial the Hessians were wont to assemble for the worship of Thor. In the immediate vicinity was Wuodensberg (afterwards called Udenesberg, and later still Gudensberg), a conical hill, on the top of which was a circle of stones, within which the worship of Woden was carried on. Thus the place was the chief sanctuary of the Hessians, and had a character of peculiar sanctity. And as the principal town of the province, Maden or Mattium, where the national assemblies met, was in the neighborhood, it was the most fitting place that could be selected for an open attack on the popular worship.

Having made up his mind to fell this oak, Boniface repaired to the spot with his monks, not carrying as usual the Holy Scriptures in his hand, but armed with the formidable German axe. He made no secret of his purpose, and the report of the intended sacrilege quickly spread around. Thousands of Pagans flocked to the place, a few of the most zealous bent on preventing the offence to the god, but by far the greater part trusting to the god to revenge himself by striking his enemy dead on the spot while others, whose belief in the gods had been shaken, watched anxiously for the result on which their faith was suspended and others again, looked confidently for the triumph of their newly found religion. Every eye was riveted on Boniface as he approached the sacred spot and amid solemn, breathless silence raised his arm, and struck a vigorous blow. The mighty trunk quivered, the branches shook, and a deep groan burst from the excited crowd. Then the monks fell to. Blow followed blow, and the trunk was well nigh half cloven, when suddenly, in the topmost branches, was heard a rushing sound as of a whirlwind, and the giant of the forest toppled over, fell to the earth with a thundering crash which shook the whole forest, and echoed again and again from the Wuodensberg, and in the fall its whole length split into four parts. But Boniface and his little band stood unharmed, giving thanks to Him through whose strength they had triumphed over the thunder god. The crowd wonderstruck, acknowledged the power of the one true God, and numbers of Pagans were baptized.

Nor was this the only fruit of the victory. For Boniface remembered the traditions of his native land, and resolved to convert the Pagan sanctuary into a dwelling-place of the true God. He and his monks hewed the prostrate oak into planks, with which they built an oratory dedicated to S. Peter. A beautiful chapel attached to the great church at Fritzlar is still pointed out as the site of the original wooden shrine. Wherever it was, however, this oaken chapel was the first church in Hesse, which is mentioned in authentic historical records; and close by Boniface built cells for a few monks, whom he appointed to minister in it, to preach to the Pagans, and to instruct the Christians in the neighborhood.

This was not the only Pagan shrine which Boniface overthrew. His early biographers give few details of his life, but content themselves with recording the general course of his movements, and the broad fact that as he passed along he baptized thousands of the Pagans, destroyed many idol temples, and erected Christian churches and monasteries in their stead. To fill up the gaps that they have left, recourse must be had to the popular traditions, which, in spite of Protestant influence, are still to be found in every mouth, and are connected with the names of hills and towns all over the field of his labors. These are most valuable as living testimonies to broad facts, though as strictly historical records, they cannot be traced back farther than the fifteenth century.

Following the guidance of these traditions, it would appear that before Boniface felled Thor's oak he visited Kestersberg, between Marburg and Frankenberg, where he destroyed the altar of Castor, or some say of Woden, built a church, and changed the name of the hill to Christenberg.

Thence ho probably passed on to the river Werra, where he built a church in honor of S. Vitus, and a small house in which he took up his abode for a considerable time. Round this church sprang up a small town, which, even to the present day, is called Wannfried, from his old name. Near Wannfried, between Heiligenstadt and Eschwege, rose the Stuffenberg, on which stood an image of the god, Stuffo, which was much resorted to as an oracle. On the spot which the god had occupied Boniface built an oratory, in which he left a priest. Fifty years later, A.D. 774, Charlemagne visited this place and restored the Cross which the Saxons had carried off. In thanksgiving for the victory which he had just gained over the Saxons at Trefurt on the Werra, he made a rich offering to enlarge S. Boniface s chapel, at the same time chang ing the name of the hill from Stuffenberg to S. Gehulfensberg. The Emperor s will seems, however, not to have been strong enough to eradicate the old Pagan tradition, for in documents of the fourteenth century the name Stuffenberg is found, though now the hill is called Hulfensberg; and on it is a large church with a chapel and well of S. Boniface, which still make it a favorite place of pilgrimage.

From the Stuffenberg Boniface went about midnight to the place where Gottingen now stands, intending to destroy the image of Fortune which was erected on a desert hill, now occupied by the village of Hardegsen, but such a crowd assembled to defend their god that he was compelled to spend the night on the moor, and to return the next morning to Eichsfeld. A chapel was afterwards built on the spot where he turned back, and was called Weende, from the verb wenden, to turn. Thence he would probably have gone to the Retberg, in the principality of Gottingen, where there was an image of Eeto, and to Vielshohe on the Rhume, now Katlenberg, where there was an image of Viel, both of which he overthrew. But the Saxons having carried off the image of Viel and erected it at Ilefeld, he hastened after them, and shivered the image to pieces. Where Osterode on the Hartz now stands, he destroyed the image of Astaroth; on the site of the castle of Lohra, he demolished the Lar, which was in a temple on a hill in the middle of a grove and in the Principality of Schwarzburg-Sondershausen he overthrew the image of the goddess Jecha, which stood on the site afterwards occupied by the castle of Jechaburg. There is no mention of these gods in the most ancient writers, whence it would appear either that they were local deities, or that these were the local names of the national gods, which, it is well known, were worshipped by various names in different places.

It was not, however, only by open attacks on Pagan shrines, that Boniface sought to convert the Hessians. In a previous chapter it has been shown, that the old German religion though a rude and simple creed, yet manifested traces of profounder questions. The Germans were naturally so reflective, that the deeper parts of their religion seem to have been familiar to all classes, instead of being concealed, as with the Greeks and Egyptians, in mysteries, which were understood by only a few philosophers; and hence, Boniface was often called on to discuss deep truths with these unlettered barbarians.

Under these circumstances, mistrusting his own powers, he wrote to ask Bishop Daniel s advice. His letter is lost, but its purport may be surmised from the bishop's answer, which throws much light on the intellectual and religious state of the Pagans of Central Germany. "Do not begin" he writes, "by advancing any arguments against the genealogies of their fallen gods but allow them to assert that some of their gods are begotten of others in the ordinary way of human nature, so that you may afterwards prove to them, that gods and goddesses, born like men, and beginning to exist out of non-existence, are men rather than gods. But if the gods had a beginning, inasmuch as some were begotten by others, then ask whether this world had a beginning, or if it always existed? If it had a beginning who created it? For without doubt, before the creation of the world there was no place for those begotten gods to exist in or inhabit. By the world I do not mean only the visible heaven and earth, but the whole extent of universal space, which even these Pagans can imagine or conceive. If they say that this universe always existed, refute them by the following arguments. Ask who governed the world before the gods were born? Who regulated it? How did the gods bring under their own dominion or laws this world, which had always existed before them? Also, where, from whom, and when, was the first god generated? Or was a goddess the first? Also, do they suppose that gods and goddesses up to the present time beget gods and goddesses? If they do not, when and why did they cease to do so? But if they still do so, then the number of the gods must be infinite. And among so many gods, men must be uncertain which are the most powerful; and great caution must be necessary, lest one should offend the most powerful. Again, is it for temporal and present blessings, or for eternal and future ones, that the gods are to be worshipped? If for temporal, in what are Pagans better off than Christians? Again, what benefit do they think that their sacrifices confer on those gods, who possess all things? Or why do these gods permit those who are subject to their power, to retain the things which they offer? If they need these things, why do they not take them and better ones too? If they do not need them, it is vain to think of propitiating the gods by such sacrifices. These and much other similar reasoning which would be too long to mention, you should bring before them, not by way of insulting and irritating them, but with great calmness and moderation. And from time to time you should compare their superstitions with our Christian dogmas, in such a way, that when they see them, so to say, side by side, being ashamed rather than provoked, and blushing for their own absurd opinions, they may boiled to confess that these are foolish and wicked fables. Further, it is to be inferred, that if the gods are omnipotent, beneficent, and just, they not only reward their own worshippers, but also punish those who despise them? And if both of these they do in this present time, why do they spare the Christians, who, throughout the whole world, turn men from their worship and throw down their images? And why do the Christians possess all the fertile regions, abounding with wine and oil, and all manner of wealth, while the Pagans and their gods, being now wrongfully driven from the best parts of the earth, are left only those frost bound lands, in which alone they are supposed to reign? And lest they should boast of the dominion from the beginning of time of these gods over their own nation, they should be told how the whole world was given up to the worship of idols, till, being brought by Jesus Christ to the knowledge of the one true, omnipotent Creator, Ruler, and God, they were restored to life, and reconciled to God."

It is very curious to find an unlettered nation, whose chief occupation was war, thus occupying itself with speculative questions and genealogies of gods not unlike the Gnostic theories, which, emanating from the East, long agitated the learned schools of Alexandria, Antioch, and Greece. It is evident, too, that the Thuringians and Hessians, still living amid their national sanctuaries and ancient Pagan associations, Jutes and Angles, to whom S. Augustine and S. Paulinus first announced the Gospel, but on whom their traditional faith had in some degree lost its hold, through their removal from the objects in nature with which it was most closely linked.

CHAPTER IX.BISHOP BONIFACE IN THURINGIA
After spending some months in Hesse, and strengthen ing his converts by the Sacrament

of Confirmation, Boniface passed into Thuringia. His episcopal dignity and the support of the Pope and Charles Martel enabling him to act more decidedly than had formerly been possible, he summoned the principal persons of the province to meet him. When they were assembled he spoke to them with deep earnestness and loving anxiety, beseeching some to turn away from the idolatry into which they had relapsed, and others to give up the false doctrines and scandalous practices into which they had been seduced by immoral and heretical priests, who wandered about the country corrupting the Christians and hindering the conversion of the Pagans, in whose idol worship they often joined.

But his eloquence was thrown away. For the wicked priests, the principal of whom were Torchtwine, Berchthere, Eanbrecht, and Hunred, fearing to lose their position with the people, united together and formed themselves into a sect, rallying their friends around them, proclaiming their own opinions to be the true Catholic faith, and denouncing Boniface as a stranger and innovator. Nor was this the only opposition that he encountered. For a neighboring bishop, apparently the Bishop of Cologne, after long neglecting this Pagan region, now laid claim to it as a part of his diocese, and treating Boniface s authority as an intrusion, indirectly strengthened the party of the heretics. In vain did Boniface appeal to the Papal briefs and to ecclesiastical canons and discipline. His opponents were deaf to reason, and stirring up the passions of the people, raised a storm which threatened for a time to bar his progress.

In this emergency Boniface wrote to the Pope about the pretensions of the Bishop of Cologne, and S. Gregory II in his answer, dated 4th December, A.D. 724, promised to write on the subject to Charles Martel, who, he had no doubt, would forbid the bishop to interfere with Boniface. This probably put an end to that difficulty. As to the heretical and immoral priests, after making every effort to reclaim them, he formally excommunicated them; after which all those of their followers who were at all well disposed, forsook them, their influence died out, and their very names were forgotten.

How painfully this discord jarred on Boniface's loving nature, which instinctively sought sympathy with those around him, appears in his correspondence with his English friends. In his letter to Bishop Daniel, he complains of "the anguish of his weary spirit, for which he seeks advice and consolation from his friend's compassion." His sufferings are also forcibly depicted in his letters to the Abbess Eadburga, supposed to be an abbess of Wimburn, for whom he seems to have felt a warmer friendship than for any of his female correspondents except S. Lioba. In one of these letters addressed to the "Most reverend and in Christ most dear Abbess Eadburga," he says, "I earnestly beseech you to remember me in your holy prayers, as your charity led you to promise by our brother on his return. I press this petition the more urgently in order that my bark, which is now tossed about amid the whirlpools and storms of this world, may be protected from the poisoned darts of the old enemy by your constant prayers. I send you, my revered and beloved, a small present; namely, a silver pen and some storax and cinnamon that you may know from these trifles how acceptable were your gifts and salutations to me. And if you will order aught of me, whether by the bearer of this letter or by any one else, be assured that the charity which unites us in a spiritual brotherhood, will make me fulfill your wishes to the best of my poor power. Meanwhile, I pray that you will not refuse to send me your sweet letters." In another letter, addressed to his sister the Abbess Eadburga, whom he embraces in the golden bond of spiritual love, and presses with the holy and virgin kiss of charity he says, "We earnestly beseech your loving pity to intercede for us with the Creator of all things. That you may not be ignorant why we thus pray, know that for our sins the course of our pilgrimage is agitated by many storms. On all sides labor, on all sides sorrow, combats without, fears within. But what weighs heaviest of all, is, that the snares of the false brethren surpass the malice of the Pagans. Pray, therefore, the merciful Defender of our lives, the only safe Refuge of those who labor, the Lamb of God who taketh away the sins of the world, that purifying and protecting us by His right hand in this den of wolves, He may keep us unhurt, so that the dark footsteps of wandering apostates may not be found where the beautiful feet of those who bear the light of the Gospel of peace, ought to be. Meanwhile, I pray you of your pity to intercede for these Pagans, who are committed to us by the Apostolic See, that the Savior of the world may withdraw them from the worship of idols and collect them together as sons of the one Catholic Mother Church, to the praise and glory of His name, who wills that all men should be saved and come to the knowledge of the truth. Farewell." Another letter, supposed to be addressed to Eadburga, though her name is not mentioned, runs thus: "I beseech your charity and clemency to intercede with God for us sinners, because we are shaken and agitated by many and various tempests and whirlwinds, whether by Pagans, or false Christians, or immoral clergy, or pseudo-priests; and chiefly are we troubled because we fear that these things are deserved by us. But we pray that we may be consoled and delivered through your supplications and we have confidence in Our Lord Jesus, that through your charitable prayers we shall obtain pardon of our sins and the calming of the tempests. Be not displeased that I always ask the same thing; because I must evidently ask what I never cease to desire. For my daily tribulations admonish me to seek spiritual consolation from my brothers and sisters."

But it was not by prayer alone that Eadburga helped her saintly friend for she seems to have been very skilful in the arts of writing and needlework, and her pen and her needle as well as her heart and spirit, were given to Boniface s service. How much he prized her gifts appears from one of his letters, in which he says, "May the eternal Bewarder of good works make my dearest sister rejoice with the angelic choir, because, in sending the gift of those Holy Scriptures, you have consoled the German exile with spiritual light. For he who is called to purify the dark corners of the German nation, will fall into the snares of death, unless he have the Word of God as a lantern to his feet and a light to his steps. Therefore, confiding in your charity, I beseech you to pray for me, who, on account of my sins, am agitated by the tempests of this dangerous sea, asking Him who dwells on high, but regards the humble, that pardoning my offences, He will grant that through my word the Gospel of the glory of Christ may run and be glorified among the Pagans." And in another letter in which he beseeches God to reward her for "all the benefits" she has conferred on him, he adds, "For often your pity has consoled my sadness by the solace of books and the help of garments. I pray you now to add to what you have begun, and to write for me in gold the Epistles of my master S. Peter the Apostle, in order that when I preach, the Holy Scriptures may have honor and veneration in carnal eyes, and because I wish greatly to have in my sight the words of Him who sent me on this journey Dearest sister, grant this my petition, as you kindly are accustomed to do all my requests, that this work of yours may shine in golden letters to the glory of our Heavenly Father."

But notwithstanding the almost feminine tender ness and the distressed tone of these letters, no trace of weakness or discouragement was visible in Boniface's actions. Steadily and calmly he pursued his course, sharing the poverty and hardships of his suffering flock, and constantly traveling about and preaching to both Pagans and heretics. The purity of his life, his humility, and his gentleness, contrasted strongly with the pride and vices of the heretics, while his eloquence was most attractive. The Pagans came by hundreds and thousands to listen to him, and great numbers were converted.

Here, again, the old biographers fail us, and recourse must be had to the local popular traditions, to trace Boniface s footsteps in Thuringia. One of the best authenticated of these traditions, which is supported by almost all the Thuringian chronicles, says that he built, A.D. 724, a church, dedicated to S. John Baptist, and a dwelling house, on the high hill on which the village of Altenberga, near Ohrdruf, now stands. Here such crowds of Thuringians came to listen to him, that he would often be obliged to leave the church and preach in the open space before it. But so many ravens, cranes, and jackdaws congregated round the spot, and kept up such a constant cawing and chattering that his voice was drowned and his audience could not hear what he said. When this had happened frequently, Boniface complained to God of this uproar and bidding his people pray with him, he besought God so earnestly to send away these birds, that from that time forth not a single one of them was to be found there.

Great interest and pride was taken in this church by the Thuringians, for it was generally believed to be the oldest church in the province, or at all events in that part of it. It was for many centuries the parish church for the four villages of Altenberga, Engelsbach, Finsterberga, and Catterfeld, which last is said to have taken its name from a woman called Katharina, to whom Boniface gave a house and a field close to the well in the valley. At length in the year 1662, the inhabitants of Finsterberga built a church for themselves. But the three other villages continued to use S. Boni face s church till A.D. 1712, when, it being very dilapidated, they built the existing Immanuel s Church in the valley between Altenberga and Catterfeld. After this the old building was allowed to go to ruin, and the waste ground adjoining the churchyard on which it had stood, being purchased by the commune, A.D. 1805, all trace of this interesting memorial was on the point of being effaced. But the public spirit of a poor wood cutter of Altenberga, called Nicolas Bruckner, averted this disgrace. In his will he left a small sum of money to be spent in erecting and keeping up a stone to mark the spot on which the church had stood; and his example reviving the general interest in this national monument, a subscription was set on foot and a hand some lamp mounted on seven steps, was erected on the site, A.D. 1811.

Besides this church at Altenberga, Boniface is said to have built in the vicinity of the Unstrut, a church at Tretteburg, oratories at Teddenborn and Ebeleben, which afterwards became monasteries; a beautiful church at Langensalza, where S. Boniface s well is still found churches at Herbsleben, Thamsbruck, Great and Little Uhrleben, Greussen, Monra, and Salza, and a monastery at Humburg, which was afterwards totally destroyed. Also on the Werra he is said to have built a monastery in honor of S. Peter on the hill near Kreuzberg, hence called S. Petersberg, and also at Falken near Trefurt, and at Heiligenstadt, in which last he placed the relics of S. Aureus.

In connexion with the church at Tretteburg there is the following legend, which may be traced back to the time of Charlemagne. When Boniface arrived in this neighborhood, he found all the inhabitants assembled on the hill of Tretteburg, at the base of which was a quagmire extending to the banks of the river Unstrut. They were expecting to be attacked by the King of Hungary, who was in the habit of exacting from them the tithe of all their possessions, including their women and children, or as an equivalent, three hundred swine and five hundred and seventy-two webs of cloth. They had resolved to resist this oppression, and there being no fortified town in the district, they intended to make their stand on this hill.

Boniface invited their chief men to a conference and told them how God for love of men had Him self become a man and died, in order to bestow justice, peace, and all blessings here and hereafter, on all, rich and poor alike, who would believe in Him and be baptized, which he earnestly pressed them to do. After some parley the Thuringians answered, "If God has indeed been born and died for us. He can easily deliver us from the King of Hungary. If He will do so, we will believe in Him. But if not, why should we forsake the customs and laws of our fathers?" Boniface hesitated how to reply, for he knew the great power of the King of Hungary, but he promised to give his answer on the following day.

That night as he lay in bed, he heard a voice which said, "Boniface, thou of little faith, why didst thou doubt? Hast thou never read, he slew mighty kings? If thou doubtest, what must the Pagans do? Because I became man and redeemed men with my blood, it is my will that henceforth no man shall be in servitude to the devil, or give a tenth from his own body to another. I therefore free this people from the tithe and the tyrannical power of the King of Hungary."

The next morning Boniface summoned the Thuringians to him, and in Christ's name he solemnly absolved them from all future payments of tithe to the King of Hungary, promising not to leave them till they had seen the power of the Most High. Then he instructed them in the faith, which great numbers of them accepted and were baptized.

Before long the King of Hungary came to enforce the payment of the tithe. On beholding his vast army, Boniface, raising his eyes and hands to heaven, prayed aloud, "Lord, of whom it is written, He slew mighty kings show Thyself today, and help this small, weak flock of Thine." Boniface and the Thuringians were on one bank of the Unstrut, the ground all around being marsh and quagmire, and the Hungarians were on the other bank. The latter heeding not the river nor the soft ground, rushed like mad dogs on the Thuringians, but slipping in the mud and pressing on each other, they fell into confusion, when the Thuringians attacking them boldly, precipitated both the horses and their riders into the river. So great was the carnage that the Thuringians waded in blood up to their ankles, and the river ran with blood for three days. Only two of the Thuringian chiefs were killed; and on the spot where they fell, two stone crosses were erected. Thus were the Thuringians freed from the tithe to the King of Hungary, and converted to the faith.

Whatever be the foundation for this legend, it is undoubted that Charlemagne did not require of the Thuringians the tribute of swine, which they had been accustomed to pay from the earliest times and at a later period, in the disputes between the Archbishops of Mayence and the Abbots of Fulda about the tithes of Thuringia, it used to be said, "As far as Boniface came, no man pays title."

It must not be supposed that the churches and monasteries which Boniface now founded in Thuringia and Hesse were solid and permanent erections. They were only huts of wood wattled with mud, and roofed in with planks or branches. In many cases every vestige of them has disappeared while in others, a stone church built sooner or later, either on the same site or in its close vicinity, has served as a memorial of S. Boniface's work. For the same circumstance, such as a river or spring, or a salubrious hill, or the vicinity of a great thoroughfare, which originally recommended the site to him, gave it equal claims to the preference of his successors. In fact, so carefully and wisely did S. Boniface and his successors choose the ground on which they built, that even to the present day there is to be found in Germany scarcely a town or village of any importance, which was not originally connected with ecclesiastical foundations.

CHAPTER X.PROGRESS

S. Gregory II, in his letter last December 4th, A.D. 724, already quoted told Boniface that he had written to his German converts, and directed them to build churches and dwellings for their bishop and his clergy. This hint led Boniface to seek for an opportunity to erect a church and monastery, of a more permanent character than had hitherto been in his power; and the following circumstance decided his choice of a site.

In the course of his journeys through Thuringia, it happened that he pitched his tent one evening at Ordorp, or Ohrdruf, on the banks of the river Oraha. Throughout the night a bright celestial light was seen shining round the spot on which he lay; and in the midst of this light the Archangel Michael appeared to him, talking to him, and strengthening him in the name of God. When morning dawned he arose, and said Mass with more than usual joy and fervor and after Mass he told his disciples that he would dine where they were now encamped. But the brother, whose business it was to prepare their meals, answered, that he had not got their usual supply of food. Where upon Boniface replied, "He who for forty years could feed His people in the wilderness with manna from heaven will not He be able to provide me, His unworthy servant, with food for a single day?" And he bade the brother lay the table. While this was being done, a bird carrying in its beak a great fish flew over the place, and as it passed it dropped the fish. Then Boniface gave thanks to God, and taking up the fish, ordered the brother to cook it. And they all dined off it, and the fragments that remained they threw into the river.

Afterwards as they journeyed slowly along, Boniface took pains to ascertain to whom belonged the place in which the Archangel had appeared to him. Finding that it belonged to Hugh, or Haug, a noble of high station whom he had lately baptized at Altenberga, he went to him and asked him for it and Hugh gladly granted his request, thus winning the honor of being the first Thuringian who gave land to S. Boniface. His example was followed by Albot, supposed to be the same as Albordo, one of the five Thuringian nobles to whom the Pope had written, who added to Hugh's gift several meadows which adjoined it.

As soon as Boniface had got the land, he set his monks to work to clear away the forest, bring the ground into cultivation, and lay the foundations of the church and monastery. As these were intended to be permanent erections, they were not finished till A.D. 727; and when they were completed, Boniface placed in the church a book, in which was written an account of the vision which had determined his choice of the site. The foundation of this monastery was a great event, not only as marking the advance of Boniface s work, but from its results to the whole neighborhood. For this place, which had hitherto been a wild uncultivated waste buried in the forest, was soon brought under cultivation, wide clearings were made, a Christian village gathered round the church and in course of time a town sprang up.

The subsequent history of this church and monastery is uncertain. It was probably destroyed with many others in the terrible invasion of the Saxons, A.D. 743 and no doubt it suffered during the subsequent incursions of the Serbs. But these heroic monks were not to be vanquished by such trials. As the invaders retired they would return to their homesteads, collect their scattered flock, and labor with such spirit and industry, that scarcely were the smoldering fires extinguished and the charred ruins removed, than fresh crops were planted, new buildings were erected, and the landscape resumed its aspect of peace and fertility. Thus Ohrdruf outlived all casualties. In the year 777, Lullus, S. Boniface's successor at Mayence, built a new church on the old site. Another was erected there, A.D. 980, by Gotzbert, Abbot of Hersfeld which was still in existence when Othlo wrote in the eleventh century.

Up to this time Boniface had had but few helpers in his work. When he set off from England on his pilgrimage to Rome, he was probably accompanied by two or three monks, as he had been on his first visit to Friesland. During the three years that he after wards spent in Friesland, several of his converts had devoted themselves to his service but the name of only one of these, Gembert, has been recorded. After wards, on his journey back to Thuringia he picked up Gregory at Pfalzel. Then, Ceola is mentioned as the bearer of a letter to Eadburga, and Forthere, of one to Bishop Daniel, and Binnan, of one to the Pope. Probably some of his converts in Hesse and Thuringia, also, gave themselves to him and as his fame spread, others may have come to him from France and Burgundy; for he could not have accomplished so much as he had already done, unless he had had priests and monks whom he could leave at Hamelburg, Geismar, Altenberga, and all the churches which he had founded on the Werra and Unstrut, and here and there all over Hesse and Thuringia. But of all these early disciples, the only one who was distinguished by saintliness, or rose to high office in the Church, was Adela's grandson, S. Gregory, who became Abbot of S. Martin s at Utrecht, and succeeded Boniface in the government of that see.

Whatever may have been the number of these disciples, there is, however, no doubt that they were far too few for the harvest that they were called to reap. The want of laborers in the vineyard, became from day to day more and more evident. At length, immediately after the foundation of Ohrdruf, Boniface took steps to supply his need.

During all these years of long journeyings amid dangers, weariness, and the daily pressure of care to find food for himself and his companions, Boniface had carried on an extensive correspondence with his friends in England. It is easy to imagine how great an interest his letters from Old Germany must have excited. The deep enthusiasm, not only of abbesses and nuns, but of kings and bishops, and especially of the old friends and pupils by whom he was so loved, was stirred up. Prayers and Masses were constantly offered for his work, and books, money, vestments, clothing, and other necessaries, were generously contributed to its success. But it should be noticed, that prayers and books were the only things for which he asked, the rest being the overflowing "offerings of warm English hearts for all his other wants seem to have been amply supplied by the Germans. As Pagans they had been wont to offer their richest spoils of war to their gods, burying or burning them, or throwing them into the rushing river or the ocean waves, in the hope of receiving them again in a future life. This grand, natural instinct being now supernaturalized, their generosity to Boniface had no limits. Land, forests, food, and ail else that they possessed, were at his command and the industry of his monks turned these gifts to such good account, that more laborers were the only want that Boniface experienced.

He now wrote to his English friends, inviting them to come and help him in the conversion of their kindred in Old Germany. His invitation arrived at a most opportune season. For only three or four years later, A.D. 731, Bede wrote, that "the times being calm and peaceable, many, as well of the nobility as private persons, laying aside their weapons, rather incline to dedicate both themselves and their children to the tonsure and monastic vows, than to study martial discipline. What will be the end hereof the next age will show. The response which met Boniface s invitation had already begun to clear up Bede s doubt. For the remaining five and twenty years of Boniface s life, and for many years after his death, a constant stream of monks and nuns flowed from England to Germany and Scandinavia and in the conversion of their German kindred, which during this period was effected with such remarkable rapidity and completeness, the strong attraction of the English nation to missionary and monastic life, found its true object and end. Boniface s early biographers give no detail of the names and numbers of those who responded to his call, at what time they severally joined him, or from what convents they came, the names of only a few who rose to celebrity being preserved. Among Boniface s letters, there is one addressed to the Abbess Kanebada, by Lullus, Burchard, and Denval conjointly, which places them among the early arrivals. Who this abbess was, is unknown, but she was of royal race, and the writers style themselves "her sons and servants," "who, from the depths of their hearts, embrace her above all other women with love." They tell her that "after the death of their father, mother, and other relatives," they had gone into Germany, and were now all together in one of Archbishop Boniface's monasteries a title which shows that the letter could not have been written earlier than A.D. 732, when Boniface was made archbishop. They had, however, all joined Boniface separately, and at different times. Denval appears from a letter of Abbess Cangyth, to have been on a pilgrimage abroad, and he came to Boniface previous to A.D. 726, when he was the bearer of a letter to the Pope Burchard, too, had long been a pilgrim in France, when he was irresistibly drawn by an interior impulse and the fame of Boniface s sanctity to go to him. As for Lullus, he entered the Abbey of Malmesbury when he was only seven years old, and he went thence to Germany at Boniface s invitation, about A.D. 732. Both he and Burchard are said by some writers, to have been related by blood to Boniface.

But it was not from England alone that help came to Boniface. His fame was now widely spread, and disciples knocked to him from France and Ireland. Some from all three countries were very learned men, others were skilful writers, and others again, expert artisans of various kinds. Thus, hand in hand with Christianity, were learning, education, and the arts of civilized life, transplanted into the German wilderness.

As Boniface s work increased, fresh points for consideration and decision were constantly arising. On many of these, such as the validity of baptisms and the non repetition of Confirmation, which are familiar to every educated Catholic, he could not have required instruction. But his humility and faith both alike, made him shrink from establishing precedents for the Church of Germany on his own poor authority alone, or on aught else than the infallible word of S. Peter. He was therefore in the constant habit of referring to the Pope for minute directions on a great variety of subjects. That S. Gregory appreciated his motive, is evident from a letter of his, dated November 22nd, A.D. 726, in which he says, "To these letters thou hast annexed certain questions, inquiring what this Holy Apostolic Roman Church holds and teaches. Thou hast done well, because the blessed Apostle Peter is the foundation of the Apostolate and Episcopate, and in advising thee concerning ecclesiastical matters, we tell thee, not from ourselves, as if of ourselves, but by His grace, who open the mouth of the dumb, and maketh the tongues of infants eloquent, how thou shouldst hold the doctrine of Apostolic power."

The Pope then proceeds to give instructions on the following points: 1. That though it would be desirable that marriage should not be contracted between persons who are known to be related, yet, to avoid over strictness, especially among barbarians, it may be allowed after the fourth generation. 2. Under what circumstances a marriage is null. 3. That if a priest be accused of a crime without sufficient evidence, he shall clear himself publicly by an oath, and produce such proof of his innocence as shall make it plain to all; after which he shall retain his office. 4. That the Sacrament of Confirmation must not be repeated. 5. That two or three chalices ought not to be placed on the altar at Mass. 6. That meat said to be offered to idols, even though blessed by the sign of the Cross, ought not to be eaten. 7. That parents who have offered their children in infancy to be trained to a religious life, shall not be at liberty when they are grown up, to take them out of the monastery and give them in marriage. 8. That if persons have been baptized by immoral and unworthy priests without being questioned in the Creed, the ancient custom of the Church should be observed and provided they were baptized in the name of the Father, Son, and Holy Ghost, they must not be rebaptized. 9. But when it is uncertain whether children have or have not been baptized, they ought to be baptized conditionally, according to the traditions of the Fathers. 10. Lepers, who are Christians, may be admitted to Holy Communion, but they ought to be prohibited from eating at table with healthy persons. 11. If a mortal pestilence breaks out in a church or monastery, it would be very foolish of those who have not been attacked, to fly from the place, hoping to escape the danger, for no one can fly from God's hand.

Finally, as to the unavoidable intercourse with wicked priests, about which Boniface had already consulted Bishop Daniel, S. Gregory adds, "We say, that thou shouldst admonish them by the Apostolic authority, and bring them back to the purity of ecclesiastical discipline. If they obey, they will save their souls and thou wilt gain thy reward. But in any case, do not refuse to converse and eat with them. For it often happens that those who are slow to receive the truth through the correction of discipline are led to the way of righteousness by gentle admonitions and social intercourse. Thou shouldst act in the same way towards those nobles who give thee help. This, then, dearest brother, written with the authority of the Apostolic See, will suffice."

This is the last letter from S. Gregory II to Boniface, still extant. The same year that the Pope thus occupied himself with petty details connected with the foundation of the German Church, he sent a legate to Constantinople, with letters threatening the Emperor Leo, the Iconoclast, with excommunication, and encouraging the Patriarch Germanus to persevere in his noble defense of Catholic traditions. Thus did S. Peter's successor stretch out his arms at once to the East and the West, and enclose in his Apostolic embrace both the wild forests of barbarian Germany and the centre of luxury and civilization at Constantinople.

On the 11th of February, A.D. 731, S. Gregory II expired. The conversion of Germany immortalizes his name, as that of England does that of his great name sake. And as the first

Gregory, through his zeal in confirming and promulgating the Benedictine rule, has been called its second founder; so the second Gregory has the honor of being the second founder of the Abbey of Monte Cassino, the cradle and paternal home of the Benedictine order. This abbey having been destroyed by the Lombards, as S. Benedict had foretold, the monks retired to Rome, and the abbey lay in ruins for about one hundred and forty years, till S. Gregory II sent S. Petronax to rebuild it, A.D. 718.

CHAPTER XI.ARCHBISHOP BONIFACE

Thirty five days after the death of S. Gregory II, a Syrian priest, who was present at his funeral, was placed on S. Peter s Chair by the unanimous voice of the Roman clergy and people, and took the name of Gregory III. No doubt Boniface sent him without delay the usual letter of congratulation on his election. But the following year, A.D. 732, he wrote to him again, soliciting a renewal of the special privilege of friendship and union with the Apostolic See, which his predecessor had granted to him and his flock, renewing his vow of obedience to S. Peter s successor and submitting certain questions to his decision. S. Gregory III. in answer, made him an archbishop and sent him the pall; and further directed him as the number of the faithful increased, to "ordain bishops by the power of the Apostolic See" to "teach and provide all that was necessary for their salvation."

S. Gregory then proceeded to answer Boniface's questions, which show what were the customs and crimes common among the barbarian converts, and against what difficulties Boniface had to contend. They prove how hopeless would have been his struggle in this chaos of Paganism, heresy, crime, and vice, had there not been a centre of unity in the Church, to which all divergent opinions and practices could be referred or had he not wisely taken the precaution to keep himself in the closest union with that centre. Unhappily, Boniface s letter to which

Gregory's is an answer, is lost, so that there is no means of elucidating a few obscurities which occur in the latter, about eating horseflesh, Pagan baptisms, and greater strictness as to marriage.

It appears from S. Gregory s letter, that a priest, whom Boniface had degraded for his criminal life was defying his authority by boasting that he had been to Rome, where he had confessed to the Pope, by whom he had been absolved. But S. Gregory writes that the man had indeed come to him, professing to be a priest and asking for a letter of recommendation to Charles Martel, but that he had not confessed to him, nor been absolved by him, nor received the least sanction for the indulgence of his passions. Wherefore, he orders Boniface to proceed against him and all other offenders with the authority of the Apostolic See.

He then forbids the eating of horseflesh, probably because feasts of horseflesh were connected with Pagan rites. And he orders that those who had been baptized by Pagans or by a priest who offered sacrifice to the Pagan gods, no doubt in the name of a Pagan god, or who did not know whether they had ever been baptized, should be baptized in the name of the Holy Trinity. Masses and prayers for the dead were not to be offered for any except Catholics, to the exclusion of impious Christians. Those who had killed their father, mother, brother, or sister, were to receive Holy Communion only on their death-bed and as penance, they must never eat meat or drink wine, and must fast three days in every week. Christians who sold their slaves to Pagans to be offered as sacrifices, were to do penance as homicides. Marriages within the seventh degree of kindred were forbidden, as was the general rule of the Church and it was recommended that persons should not marry more than twice. Then followed the usual rule that at the consecration of a bishop, two or three bishops besides the consecrator were to be present. And, finally, the special privilege of communion with the Holy See, was renewed to Boniface and his flock.

Though Boniface had been made an archbishop with the express object of enabling him to consecrate bishops for his increasing Church, yet none of his disciples were at this time prepared for the episcopal office and nine years elapsed before political circumstances permitted him to establish four dioceses in Thuringia and Hesse, though probably before that time he had made Burchard and Wizo bishops without fixed sees.

As soon as Boniface s messenger returned with S. Gregory s answer, he set to work to build two large monasteries at Amoneburg and Fritzlar in Hesse, of the same permanent character as that at Ohrdruf.

Amanaburg, now Amoneburg, on the river Amena or Ohm, was in Upper Hesse. Adalgar, one of Boniface s converts, had a good deal of land in this neighborhood, and as he devoted himself to Boniface s service and became a priest, it is supposed that the land on which the monastery was built, was given by him. Many years after, when Boniface was Archbishop of Mayence, Adalgar being on his death-bed, made over to S. Martin, the patron saint of Mayence, all the rest of his patrimony in Amanaburg and the adjacent villages of Bretteubrunum, now Breidenborn, and Seleheim or Seelheim, where Boniface often resided. But after his death his brothers, Asperth and Trutmund, claimed the land as their own and offered to prove their right to it by oath. Boniface accordingly required them to take the oath in his presence, and before they did so he warned them of the sin and danger of perjury. Notwithstanding, they persisted and swore the false oath; whereupon Boniface told Asperth that he would be killed by a bear, and Trutmund that he would derive no profit from the land. Some little time after it happened one day, that as Asperth sat at table his servants told him that a large bear was in a field close by. He immediately rose, seized his spear, and mounting his horse, gave chase to the beast. But when his servants, hastening after him, came on his track, they found him lying on the ground quite dead. Trutruund was so terrified by his brother s fate, that he gave back his ill-gotten possession to S. Martin s altar, thus fully verifying S. Boniface's prophetic words.

On getting possession of the land at Amanaburg, Boniface began, A.D. 732, to build on it a church, which he dedicated to S. Michael the Archangel, and a monastery of sufficient size to accommodate a large community, who would be able to carry on both the missionary work and the observance of monastic discipline more fully than had hitherto been possible. The stillness of the primeval forest, which for long centuries had resounded with the savage war cry or the abominable revelry of the Pagans, was now broken only by the sweet and solemn chants of praise and prayer, mounting night and day to God; while the daily celebration of Mass, the unbroken round of fasts and festivals, of vigils and penance, purified and sanctified that dark wilderness, which had hitherto been abandoned to demons and their fiend-like votaries. Then there was the daily manual labor, the monks living by the sweat of their brow, clothing themselves by their own industry, creating around them, by their skill, the comforts of civilized life, and transforming the desert into a rich and beautiful garden. Nor were the daily hours of study omitted. For there were barbarian novices to be taught to read, as was indispensable to every monk, and others -to be prepared for the priest hood, or trained to learned studies, and books to be multiplied by expert writers while all, after the fatigues of hard work, found rest and strength from reading, or listening to the pages of some saintly Father of the Church.

Here Boniface took up his abode from time to time, and hence he and his monks made missionary excursions. Round the abbey, too, clustered converts, who had been disowned by Pagan kindred, or who fled from the contamination of a Pagan home. The peculiar methodicalness and love of order, the habit of performing all their actions as untold generations of ancestors had performed them, which still distinguish the German, had been a snare to the converts in the midst of Pagan society and life-long associations. But when they placed themselves under the wing of their holy pastors, and were initiated into a new round of daily life, new arts, new modes of agriculture, new trains of pure and pious thought, and undreamt of aspirations for time and eternity, this national habit came to their aid, and quickly and almost insensibly, they were transformed from blood-thirsty, restless barbarians into the thoughtful, industrious, and deeply religious Christians, who are still to be found in Germany. Gradually the few scattered huts of these converts formed a village and as time passed on, the village grew into the town of Amoneburg, which, after above eleven centuries, stills stands as a monument to S. Boniface s honor. Such is the history of Amoneburg and of the principal towns of Germany, all of which have sprung out of religious foundations; and thus was it that Christian thought and feeling infiltrated through Old Germany.

Though the Abbey of Amoneburg never rose to such celebrity as other foundations of the period, yet its influence told on its immediate neighborhood. It continued to exist till the twelfth century, when, the abbey having fallen into ruins, its property was transferred to the Cathedral of Mayence. The church, however, remained; and in the fourteenth century, Gerlach, Archbishop of Mayence, attached to it a college dedicated to S. John Baptist.

The Abbey of Fritzlar, which Boniface built at this time, soon became the principal monastery in Hesse. It stood in a rich country near the river Eder, and the position was very central, close to the old Pagan sanctuaries of the Donnereiche and Wuodensberg, and the village of Maden, where the national assemblies of Lower Hesse were held. The monastery was finished about A.D. 734 but the church, which was dedicated to S. Peter, was a more elaborate edifice, and was not completed till A.D. 740. It is a disputed question whether there existed a village called Friedeslar before the abbey was built, or whether Boniface gave it this name from Friedeslehre, i. e. Doctrine of peace. In the crypt of the great church above the now empty tomb, which once contained the body of Abbot Wigbert, there is an ancient inscription on the wall, purporting that the name was bestowed upon the place by the apostle, who brought to it the good tidings of the Gospel of peace. It appears probable, however, that the spot was considered sacred by the old Hessians in Pagan times and hence received its name. But there is no doubt, that in any case the site was previously an uncultivated wild, and that the town of Fritzlar, which sprang up round the abbey, owes its origin to Boniface s monks.

For a time Boniface kept the government of this abbey in his own hands, and made it his principal place of abode. But he found that his frequent absence interfered with the regularity of the discipline, and as his circle of work was daily widening and calling him away more frequently, he sent an invitation to Wigbert, a monk of Glastonbury, to come and take charge of the monastery. Wigbert was advanced in years, and it was no little sacrifice to ask of him at his age. Notwithstanding, that heroic love of souls which animated every English cloister of that time, compelled him to accept the invitation. But how hard a trial it was to the old man to leave his sweet English home and those dear brethren with whom he had spent his life, and how strange was his new position to him, appears in the letter in which he tells his abbot how God "had given him a prosperous journey across the sea and through the perils of this world" adding, "Be assured, brethren, that no space of earth divides us, whom the love of Christ unites, and that your revered brotherhood always abides with me in my prayers to God for you. Almighty God, of His mercy and through your merits, gives success to our work, though our abiding here is dangerous and laborious in all things, in hunger and thirst, in cold, and the incursions of the Pagans."

When Boniface heard that Wigbert was coming, he traveled some distance to meet him, and greeted him most joyfully. Truly fortunate was he to have secured his help; for Wigbert was no ordinary man. He had long been remarkable as a pattern of monastic virtue and discipline. His whole bearing and conduct, his every look, word, and act, all bespoke the true monk. In all his actions, whether great or small, the same monastic perfection was visible. If he was summoned to shrive the sick, he hurried along with speed, spoke to no one by the way, but kept himself recollected for the solemn office that he was about to perform. If he was with others he was cheerful and affable, keeping silence if the conversation turned on light or worldly matters, but seizing every opportunity to direct it to spiritual subjects, and skillfully managing to turn even the smallest trifles to profit for awakening the conscience or exciting the zeal of his hearers. To him Boniface committed the Abbey of Fritzlar, and soon a marvelous spirit of piety and love of learning pervaded the place. Regular discipline was strictly observed; the fame of the school spread far and wide barbarians sent their children to be educated, or came themselves to be instructed, or even trained as monks and priests. Under Wigbert s rule were the most distinguished of the English missionaries, Lullus, Burchard, Magingoz, and "Wizo after a time the young Bavarian, Sturm, of whom more will be said hereafter, was committed to his care and besides these there were numbers of others, whose names, lost on earth, are registered in heaven, through whose saintly influence and zeal the spirit of Christianity was infused through the whole length and breadth, and into every dark corner, of that Pagan land."

The presence of such a man as Wigbert formed an epoch in the conversion of Germany. After he had been some years at Fritzlar and had brought the community and school into a flourishing state, Boniface removed him to Ohrdruf, where he recommenced the same work, and with like success. Thus, under S. Wigbert s fostering care, these two monasteries became the nurseries of monastic discipline in Old Germany. In the course of years, the infirmities of age growing on him, he asked and obtained leave to return to his first German home at Fritzlar, where he closed his life on the 13th of August, A.D. 747.

S. Wigbert s tomb is still to be seen in the crypt of the church at Fritzlar; but as Fritzlar was much exposed to the Saxons, Charlemagne caused his body to be removed, A.D. 780, to Hersfeld, where a church was built in his honor, A.D. 850. The Abbey of Quedlinberg also was dedicated to him and S. James the Apostle, A.D. 980, by Matilda, the wife of Henry the Fowler. In the tenth century the Abbey of Fritzlar was secularized and turned into a college, which long maintained the reputation that the school had acquired under the monks.

Many a tradition still lingers about the place, and amongst others the peasants relate a prophecy of S. Boniface. At that time the opposite hill of Buraburg was covered with a hill-fort, a church, and a town. The Saint was one day walking on the hill with some of his disciples, when he stopped, and, looking across the low ground through which the river Eder flows, fixed his eyes on the solitary height where the roof of the monastery of Fritzlar could be seen amidst the oaks of the forest. He then said that the time would come when Buraburg would be bare of houses and yonder hill would be covered by a fair town. He also foretold that the church of Fritzlar would never be burnt by fire. Both these prophecies have come true. After the subjugation of the Saxons by Charlemagne, Buraburg lost its value as a frontier fortress, and its inhabitants began to migrate to Fritzlar. The plough now some times strikes on the foundations of old buildings, but the town has disappeared. Only a lonely chapel, still a place of pilgrimage, marks the spot where Boniface once said Mass and of what afterwards, as we shall hear, became a bishop s see, nothing is left but the poor little village of Ungedanken at the foot of the hill. On the other side of the river, however, may be seen the hill still covered with the mediaeval walls and turrets of Fritzlar; and over all rises S. Wigbert s church, with one of its towers tragically maimed but untouched by fire.

In the year 774, the Saxons having broken into Hesse, the monks of Fritzlar, laden with the precious relics of S. Wigbert, fled across the river Eder, and took refuge in Buraburg, which was strongly fortified. The Saxons ravaged the surrounding country, and, heaping up a quantity of wood round the church of Fritzlar, tried to set it on fire; but as the flames rose and encircled the walls, two youths in white garments were seen to float over it. At this supernatural sight the Saxons fled in terror; and when the Christians returned, they found the church uninjured, and amid the charred wood knelt a Saxon warrior, as if in the act of blowing up the flame, but quite dead.

Since then the Landgraves of Thuringia in the middle ages, the Swedes of Gustavus Adolphus, and the French in the Seven Years War, have given Fritzlar to the flames, but the church has always come out unscathed by the fire which girt it round. But it is even more remarkable that while the Landgraves of Hesse have succeeded in infecting with heresy even S. Elizabeth's Marburg, and the country all around is Lutheran, the townsmen of Fritzlar and the poor peasants of Ungedanken are still faithful to the religion of S. Boniface. Thus the faith even now shines brightly where first it dawned on the forests of Hesse.

Another monastery which Boniface founded at this time was that of Amorbach in Odenwald, two leagues north of the Main. This foundation originated with S. Pirminian, one of those heroic men whose country and lineage are forgotten, and whose memory lives only in the work which they did for love of Christ and of souls. He first made a journey to Rome, to obtain the Pope s authority for his labors, and then went into Allemania, where, about A.D. 724, he founded the Abbey of Reichenau on an island in the Rhine, near the place where it falls into the lake of Constance. Afterwards on the invitation of a Frank noble, Werinherus or Rudhard's, he went into the Odenwald, where he built a few rude cells for himself and his companions on a high hill to the north of the present town of Amorbach, and a chapel dedicated to our Blessed

Lady on the spot where the chapel of Amorsbrunn now stands. He preached in the Odenwald with remarkable success, till at the end of some years, being about to go to Count Rudhard's estates in the Vosges, he made over his rude cells and chapel to Boniface. The latter built at a little distance a monastery and church, which he dedicated to our Blessed Lady in September, A.D. 734. The abbey was long known as the Minster of our Blessed Lady in the Odenwald but it was afterwards called Amorbach, from S. Amor, one of S. Pirininian's monks at Reichenau, who was the first abbot.

After thus providing fully for the spiritual wants of Thuringia and Hesse, Boniface seems to have made some effort to penetrate into Saxony, and to have met with such success as sufficed to excite his most sanguine hopes. This is evident from a letter 6 written to him about this time by Torthelin, an English bishop, who says, "We have received your wished-for letter, by which we learn that you meditate day and night how, through God s help and for the salvation of your own soul, you may convert the Saxons to the Catholic Apostolic faith. Who will not be glad to hear this joyful news? Who will not exult and rejoice that our kindred, through these means, shall believe in Almighty God? Hasten then to gather in and dedicate this new nation to Christ for your protector is our Lord Jesus, the Redeemer of mankind."

Also about this time, Boniface addressed a letter to "all the bishops and priests, deacons and clerics, abbots and abbesses, monks and nuns, and all God-fearing Catholics of the English race" beseeching them to remember him in their prayers and to entreat "God and our Lord Jesus Christ to convert the hearts of the Pacran Saxons to the Catholic faith." "Have compassion on them/ he continues" because they are wont to say that we and they are of one blood and bone. Remember that they are going the way of all flesh and there is no one in death that is mindful of God and who shall confess to Him in hell? Know also that I have received the support, consent, and blessing of two Roman Pontiffs. Grant then our petition, that your reward may be great and glorious in the supernal choirs of Angels. What were the circumstances which called forth these letters is not known. But the time for the conversion of the Saxon was not yet come, and the hopes of Boniface and his friends were soon seen to be fallacious.

After this disappointment Boniface turned his steps to Bavaria, which naturally fell within his province, since he was the only Archbishop in the wide east of the Rhine.

It will be remembered that Duke Theodo had gone Rome to place the Bavarian Church under the protection of S Peter; that after his death the dukedom was divided between his sons

Theodebert and Grimoald; and that S. Corbinian had been compelled by the persecution of Piltrude to retire to the monastery which he had in the wild solitude at Mays.

On Theodebert s death, A.D. 724, a civil war having broken out between his son Hucbert and Grimoald who claimed the whole dukedom, the Lombards a Charles Martel seized the opportunity to make themselves masters of portions of the Bavarian territory. In the year 729, Charles Martel again invading Bavaria, Grimoald and all his children perished; Piltrude followed Charles into France, whence she was expelled for her crimes, and died in great poverty in Italy and Hucbert came into possession of the dukedom, now diminished in extent, as a tributary to the Franks. He recalled S. Corbinian to his see at Freisingen, made large gifts to the churches of S. Eupert at Salzburg and S. Emmeran at Ratisbon, of which last Wicterp was bishop, and labored by every means in his power to reform the abuses which had multiplied during the late wars.

When Boniface arrived in Bavaria both S. Corbinian and Wicterp were dead, and the only Catholic bishop in the duchy was Vivilo, who had lately gone to Rome to be consecrated Bishop of Passau by Pope S. Gregory III. Whether Boniface came by Hucbert s invitation is uncertain, but in any case he was most cordially received. He made the circuit of the province, boldly reproving heretical and immoral priests, preaching diligently to the nobles and people, and zealously correcting abuses so far as he could. He excommunicated Eremwulf, the head of an heretical sect, and converted many of his followers. He also made himself fully acquainted with the state of religion in all parts of the duchy, and probably planned with Hucbert the measures which he carried out a few years later for the establishment of unity and discipline in the Bavarian Church. But he could not now remain long in Bavaria, for he had a great desire to be again with his monks, and at the close of the year 737 he returned to Thuringia and Hesse.

In the course of this visit to Bavaria, Boniface picked up many disciples, and, among others, a youth, called Sturm, was given to him by his parents, who were Christians of noble birth in Noricum. Sturm joyfully confirmed the pious gift, and, bidding farewell to his home and family, followed Boniface in his journeyings, till they arrived at Fritzlar, when he was transferred to S. Wigbert s charge.

CHAPTER XII.THIRD VISIT TO ROME

While Boniface was thus pursuing his peaceful career of bloodless victories the most critical events were occurring. S. Gregory III having excommunicated the Emperor Leo for his sacrilegious iconoclasm and furious persecution of Catholics, all connexion between the Roman see and the Eastern Empire was finally severed. Home, thus left of the aid, small and uncertain though it had been which the Imperial armies had rendered, was at the mercy of Liutprand, King of the Lombards, who frequently ravaged the Roman States, and even threatened the city.

But even a greater danger was imminent. For the Saracens, flushed with the pride of their unbroken career of victory in the East, Africa, and Spain, had resolved on the conquest of France and Italy and the subjugation of either would have been quickly followed by the overthrow of the Greek Empire and the expulsion of Christianity from the civilized world. In the year 719, they reduced Septimania into a tributary province. In 721, and again in 725, they invaded Aquitaine, and Duke Eudes obtained peace only by giving his daughter in marriage to the Caliph's lieutenant, Munuza. But at length, A.D. 732, Abderrama, taking advantage of a civil war between Charles Martel and Eudes, crossed the Pyrenees with an innumerable host, who, accompanied by their families, resolved to settle in France. Half of the army passing on to the east along the Rhone and Saone, took Avignon, Valence, Vienne, Lyons, Chalons, Besangon, Dijon, and Auxerre, and carried all before them till they reached Sens, where they were repulsed by S. Ebbon, the bishop. The other half of the invaders advanced through Gascony and Aquitaine, took Bordeaux, Saintes, Poictiers, and many other towns, burning all the churches and abbeys on their route, till they encamped before Tours, where the two parts of the host reunited.

Meanwhile Charles and Eudes quickly made up their quarrel at the approach of the common foe. Charles collected all the troops he could muster in the north of France, Friesland, Bavaria, Allemania, and Germany, and met the vast Saracen host between Poictiers and Tours. Seven days were spent in skirmishing. But on a Saturday in October, A.D. 732, a great battle, on which hung the fate of the world, was begun at early dawn and lasted till nightfall. The next morning the Franks prepared to renew the fight, but the Saracens did not appear; and before long spies brought the news that they had deserted their camp and fled during the night. Contemporary historians say that 375,000 Saracens fell in the battle.

This great victory saved Europe from the Saracen yoke, but it well nigh ruined the Church. While it added greatly to Charles Martel's power and prestige, it imposed on him the necessity of rewarding the retainers, who had gathered round his standard in the hour of danger. He had always been unscrupulous in the disposal of ecclesiastical benefices. He had already expelled S. Rigobert, Bishop of Rheims, from his see, and given it to Milo, a tonsured cleric, who held also the bishopric of Treves; and he had bestowed many other bishoprics and abbeys on his military followers. But after the battle of Poictiers this sacrilegious policy was more fully carried out and the principal benefices were occupied by either laymen or blood-stained clergy, ruthless, avaricious immoral men, who basked in court favor by virtue of their deeds of arms and their subserviency to the vices of the great.

The Saracens had burnt all the churches and abbeys on their route, and killed all the clergy and monks who had not fled. But when the scattered fugitives returned to their ruined homes, they found that they had to deal with even a worse enemy than the passing bands of Saracens. Charles, instead of helping them to collect the wrecks of their property, rebuild churches and monasteries, and fill up the vacancies in the ecclesiastical government, gave their lands to his adherents, and thus perpetuated the ruin which the infidel sword had begun. Under the dominion of military chiefs or sacrilegious clergy, religion stood no chance. The devastated lands, torn from communities of laborious monks, remained untilled. The bishoprics were not filled up. The religious communities were scattered. Luxeuil was without an abbot for fifteen years; and long vacancies are to be seen in many of the rolls of bishops and abbots, even in some cases till the beginning of the next century. Barbarism was quickly reasserting its sway over France, and Paganism was following close on its track. Nor was the danger from Mahometanism quite extinct. For the Saracens entered France A.D. 737, went up the Rhone, and took Avignon; and again, A.D. 739, they took Aries, Avignon, Marseilles, Embrun, Vienne, and many other towns in that neighborhood. And though Charles Martel retook all these places, reconquered Septimania, and drove the Saracens back behind the Pyrenees, yet it was only by constant vigilance and the most energetic efforts, that this ever imminent peril was averted from France and Italy.

Such was the state of Christendom, when, in the autumn of the year 738, Boniface went for the third time to Rome. On the two former occasions he had visited the Apostolic threshold as an obscure priest, in the company of poor pilgrim monks like himself. But now he came as a high dignitary of the Church, of wide-spread reputation, as being one of the greatest men of his age, and attended by a numerous retinue, English, Irish, Bavarians, Franks, Frisians, and converts from many a wild German tribe. His companions were young men of fine intellect, heroic spirit, and unlimited devotedness, either the fervent votaries from England and other Christian lands, or the choice first fruits of his own mission and no rich gifts of gold and silver at the Apostolic tomb were so prized as the offering of these noble soldiers of the Cross, the chosen instruments of the Church s future work.

Our Holy Father has told us, "that out of the very tomb where the ashes of Blessed Peter rest, for the perpetual veneration of the world, a secret power and healing virtue go forth to inspire the pastors of the Lord's flock with daring, courage, and nobleness of mind and through this renewal of their strength, the bold audacity of the enemy, which is no match for the virtue and power of Catholic unity, sinks and falls in so unequal a conflict." Such was the motive that now drew Boniface to Rome, and made him bring his sons to receive the grace of the Apostolate at the Apostle's tomb, before he ordained them bishops, abbots, and pastors of his flock.

Soon after his arrival in Rome, he wrote to his "most beloved sons, Geppan and Eoban, Tatwin and Wigbert, and all his brothers and sisters" that the Pope had received him most graciously and joyfully, and given a favorable answer to the object of his journey, with counsel and directions as to the future progress of his work. He added that he would wait in Rome for the meeting of a synod, though he knew not when the Pope would summon it; and as soon as it was over he would return to Germany. There is no record of a synod having been held in Home at this time; but tins letter leads to the conclusion, that there must have been some ecclesiastical assembly which answered his purpose.

What was the special object of the journey above referred to, and what the subjects on which Boniface received advice and direction in those frequent conferences which he had with the Holy Father during the year that he remained in Rome awaiting the synod, is not recorded. But in the critical position of the Church, his personal knowledge of Charles Martel and the state of affairs beyond the Alps must have been a great assistance to the Holy Father. The events which followed this visit of his to Rome have given rise to the supposition, that not only the foundation and reconstruction of the Churches of Germany and France, but also the transfer to the Carlovingian family of the Church s protectorate and the sovereignty of the West, formed the main subject of their consultations; and that soon after these conferences S. Gregory III sent to Charles Martel the keys of S. Peter's tomb, into which some filings from the Apostle's chains had been wrought.

During the year that Boniface spent in Rome, he found ample occupation in going the round of the churches with his sons, inspiring them with courage and fervor at the tombs of apostles and martyrs, and making them familiar with Roman customs and discipline. There were also many, living saints and many old friends to be seen. There was the royal S. Ina in his monks habit and cowl, who, no doubt, was glad to have the opportunity of consulting Boniface about his Saxon school. There was also Boniface's old correspondent, S. Eadburga, or Bugga, Abbess of Thanet, of whom more will be said hereafter; and her hostess Wiethberga, with whom also Boniface corresponded. And who can say how many more saints and old friends he found in that multitude of his countrymen, "noble, and ignoble, clergy and laity, men and women," who at this time left England, and lived as pilgrims in Rome, in order to be more easily received by the saints in heaven. But of all whom he met, none claimed his love like his nephew, S. Winibald.

It has been already mentioned that Boniface s sister Winna had married S. Richard, one of the under-kings of the West Saxons. They had two sons, Willibald and Winibald, born respectively A.D. 701, and A.D. 704. S. Richard had also a daughter, Walburga, and another son, who, being considerably younger, are supposed by some writers to have been the children of a second marriage.

When Willibald was three years old he fell dangerously ill, and being at the point of death, his parents placed him at the foot of the Cross, which stood in the centre of the village, and vowed him to God s service if his life were spared. Scarcely were the words uttered when he was perfectly cured. Accordingly, when he was five years old he was sent to the Abbey of Waltham, near Winchester, where he was trained to monastic life by Abbot Egbald. From his earliest years he was remarked for his modesty, wisdom, and love of study. The Psalms were his constant meditation, and his thought day and night was how to conquer self and fulfill more perfectly the duties of his vocation. As he grew to manhood there sprang up in his heart the desire to go on pilgrimage to the tombs of the Apostles; but not content to win this privilege for his own soul, he could not be satisfied unless his father and brother shared his merit. S. Richard at first objected to leave his wife and younger children unprotected. But Willibald spoke so eloquently about the dangers of a life of ease, the loving promises of Jesus, and the joys of Paradise, that he carried his point ; and it was finally arranged that S. Richard, with his two elder sons and a large party of friends, should go on pilgrimage to Rome and the Holy Land and that during his absence his wife and daughter should remain in the convent of Wimburn, of which their relative S. Cuthburga was abbess.

In the year 721 the pilgrims embarked at Southampton, and landed at Rouen. Hence they proceeded through France and Italy, till they arrived at Lucca, where S. Richard died. He was buried in the church of S. Frigidian, an Irish monk, who was formerly Bishop of Lucca. The numerous miracles wrought at his tomb excited such devotion to him, that when many years after, the clergy of Eichsfeld wished to place his body in their cathedral, the people of Lucca refused to part with the smallest portion of it, and were with difficulty persuaded to allow some of the dust from the inside of the tomb to be carried away.

After burying S. Richard the pilgrims hurried on to Rome, where they arrived in time for the feast of S. Martin, November 11th, A.D. 722. They took up their abode in a monastery, where Winibald received the tonsure. Though the first twenty years of his life had been spent in the world, yet he embraced his new vocation with such ardor, that he was in no way behind his brother who had been a monk from his childhood; and before long his companions so loved and revered him, that they were wont to look up to him as an example and a master, while he was still only a novice in the monastery.

In the course of the following summer the brothers fell ill and nearly died of intermittent fever; but happily it attacked them on alternate weeks, so that when one was down with it, the other was able to nurse him. However ill they were they never relaxed the strictness of their life, but always recited the daily Office and as soon as they regained the least strength they resumed their study of Holy Scripture.

After spending two winters in Rome, Willibald and two of his friends set out for Jerusalem after Easter, A.D. 723. Many and great were the sufferings and hardships they endured during this long journey. At one time they were imprisoned at another Willibald was ill with fever then again, he was blind for two months and again, he was at death s door with plague. But such sufferings only enhanced the joys of the pilgrimage, the object of which was, not to visit the holy places from mere curiosity, or even with a view to sensible devotion, but to walk in the footsteps of Him who came down from His eternal home in the bosom of His Father, and clothed in flesh as a man, bore every human ill and infirmity, even to the shedding of His Precious Blood. Filled with this holy fervor, Willibald and his companions spent four years in visiting Jerusalem and Judea; then they stayed for two years at Constantinople and at length, in the seventh year of their pilgrimage they returned with the Pope s legates to Italy. Willibald s devotion was now satisfied and he took up his abode in the Abbey of Monte Cassino, which had been rebuilt about ten years before by S. Petronax.

Meanwhile Winibald remained in Rome, a gouty affection, which eventually crippled him, probably preventing his going with his brother to the East. For seven years he followed the usual round of monastic life in Rome, till at length he was drawn to revisit his native land. On his arrival in his paternal inheritance he was joyfully greeted, and love and reverence met him on every side. But his only thought was how to induce his kindred and friends to ascend through this transitory world by close and severe wrestling with the flesh, to the narrow gate of Paradise. With this view he went from house to house and village to village, preaching, and persuading all whom he met to give themselves to God s service. He was so successful, that before long he was accompanied back to Rome by a large band of pilgrims, among whom was his younger brother.

On his arrival in Rome he resumed his former life and seven more years passed on unmarked by outward change, but noted by watching angels for his hidden progress in purity, light, and love. Then all Rome was stirred by the arrival of Boniface, the great Apostle of the north. Nobles and high dignitaries, rich and poor, young and old, gathered round him. His persuasive eloquence and the singular union of authority and sweetness in his air touched all hearts; his exhortations and admonitions were received with reverence and many young men became his disciples, and devoted themselves to his service. But by none was he more joyfully greeted than by Winibald; and when the venerable bishop asked the young monk to be the solace and support of his declining years, because he was tenderly and closely drawn to him by ties of blood, Winibald s warm English heart instantly responded, and he gave himself to his uncle. He followed Boniface to Germany with a number of his friends, among whom was S. Sebald, the

Apostle of Nuremberg. Boniface ordained him a priest, and placed him in charge of seven churches in Thuringia. Then appeared the fruit of his long years of contemplation. The words of Scripture and of the Fathers were, so to say, at his fingers ends; the history of our Lord s life on earth was ever on his lips and by his example he set forth those Divine things which were the theme of his constant meditation. Between him and Boniface there sprang up the closest communion; and they were wont to discourse much together, interchanging holy thoughts, and searching out in Scripture the hidden mysteries of God's love.

The gain of one saintly nephew made Boniface long the more to win the other; and before he left Rome he petitioned the Pope to send Willibald to him whenever an opportunity should offer. Willibald, meanwhile, was leading a hidden life at Monte Cassino. The first year he filled the office of cullcularius; the next that of decanus then for four years he was porter in the upper monastery, and for four years more he filled the same office, which was one of great trust, in the lower monastery ; thus making in all ten years that he spent at Monte Cassino.

At the end of this time it happened that a Spanish monk visited the abbey on his way to Rome and on his departure he asked leave for Willibald to accompany him, which Abbot Petronax readily granted. The fame of Willibald s pilgrimage in the East was wide-spread, and the Holy Father, on hearing that he was in Rome, desired to see him. Willibald at his command told the story of his pilgrimage, when "many shed tears, because there stood a living man who had done so much for the sake of our Blessed Lord, and they themselves had done so little in return for His great love."

When the tale was concluded the Pope told Willibald about his uncle's wish to have him in Germany, and asked him to go to him. At first Willibald shrank from exchanging his peaceful cloister for the world's turmoil. But the Pope said, "Our love to God proved by our love to our neighbor. When our Lord had thrice heard Peter say that he loved Him, then He committed to him the care of His flock. He who has attained to great virtue, and yet preferring his own tranquility to the profit of others, refuses to be a bishop, deserves to suffer all the pains of the lost souls whom, as a prelate, he might have converted." Willibald consented to go if his abbot would give him leave. But the Pope quickly replied, It suffices you to receive the order from me; for if I should bid your abbot himself go any where, he would have neither the power nor the will to disobey. Whereupon Willibald instantly declared, that he was ready to go, not only to Germany, but whithersoever. Holy Father would deign to send him.

After Easter, A.D. 740, Willibald, with three companions, set out for Germany. They visited the tomb of S. Richard at Lucca. Then they passed Bavaria, where they spent a week with Duke Odilo and another week at the castle of Suitgar, Count of Hirschberg. The Count conceived a great friendship for Willibald and on his departure accompanied him to Linthrath, where Boniface then was. The object his visit was to offer Boniface a wide tract of land at Eichstedt, whereon to build a monastery. It was a thick forest of oaks, in which were a few poor huts thinly scattered here and there, and one small church which was dedicated to our Blessed Lady. But the position was central and well suited to be a bishop s see at some future time. Boniface therefore thankfully accepted the gift, and sent Willibald back with the Count to explore the wilderness and choose a site for the monastery.

On the following feast of S. Mary Magdalen, July 22nd, Willibald was ordained a priest by Boniface at Freisingen, after which he returned to his church of our Lady of Eichstedt and set about building the monastery.

CHAPTER XIII.THE CHURCH IN BAVARIA

Boniface's third visit to Rome was a turning-point in his life. Hitherto he had toiled as the Apostle of Germany alone but henceforth his principal work was to be the formation of that Church of the Middle Ages, which freed Europe from the despotism of barbarian soldiers, and transmitted to modern times the blessings of Christianity and the noble inheritance of learning, art, and education, which saints had snatched from the wreck of the ancient world.

Towards the end of the year 739 Boniface received the Pope's parting blessing and set out for Germany. The commendatory letters which he took with him were distinguished in two respects from those of which he had been the bearer on former occasions. In the first place, the letter to the German laity was not addressed to the Thuringians and Germans generally, as before, but to several tribes whose very names had hitherto been unknown, and whom Boniface had brought for the first time into communication with Christian society. In the next place, the letter to the bishops and abbots gave Boniface authority to appoint priests to officiate in places within the jurisdiction of other bishops and abbots, and called on the Bishops.

Bavaria and Allemania to obey him as the Legate of the Holy See and attend the council which he should summon to meet at Augsburg, or elsewhere. Bavaria was naturally the first point to which Boniface directed his steps. He was uncertain what reception he should meet with there because his friend Duke Hucbert was dead, and the orthodoxy of his successor, Odilo, the youngest son of Theodo II, was doubtful. But happily his anxiety was relieved by a cordial invitation from Odilo, which he received during a short stay that he made at Pavia with Luitprand, King of the Lombards.

Boniface's task in Bavaria was to give full effect to S. Gregory II's capitular, addressed to Theodo II. He accordingly examined the orders of the clergy; deposed the bishops and priests who had taken those offices on themselves or whose orders were invalid; conferred true orders on those who had gone astray only from ignorance, and excommunicated the contumacious. He also traveled about preaching the Catholic faith, extirpating idolatry and heresy, and restoring the canonical administration of the Sacraments. He further placed a bishop in each of the four provinces into which Bavaria was divided for all the sees were vacant, except that of Passau, to which S. Gregory III had consecrated Vivilo. He appointed John to Salzburg, which had been vacant since S. Rupert s death, A.D. 718; Eremberclht, brother of S. Corbinian, to Freisingen, which also had been vacant since S. Corbinian s death, A.D. 730; Goibald or Gaubald to S. Emmeran's Church at Ratisbon; and Vivilo he left undisturbed at Passau. These four bishoprics remain to the present day, thus proving Boniface's judicious selection of their sites. He also founded about this time a bishopric at Neuburg, in the eastern part of the diocese of Augsburg which continued subject to Bavaria, though Augsburg and the rest of the diocese had been conquered by Charles Martel. But this bishopric was of brief duration. For when Charlemagne united Bavaria with his empire, A.D. 801, this district became once more a part of the diocese of Augsburg. In 798 Salzburg was made the metropolitan see of Bavaria, and its jurisdiction extended over the above bishoprics, and also over Seben in the Tyrol, a very ancient see, which having been seized by the Lombards, had been for a time under the metropolitan of Aqueleia, but on the reconquest of the Tyrol by Bavaria became subject to Salzburg. This see was afterwards removed to Brixen.

Charles Martel having recently gained a great victory over the Saxons, who were consequently driven out of Thuringia and Hesse, the Pope now wrote to Boniface congratulating him that a hundred thousand souls had been brought into the Church by his labors and Charles arms. He also approved of all that Boniface had done in Bavaria, and ordered him to preside in his stead at a council which he was to hold on the banks of the Danube. This letter touches on two important points regarding the validity of the Sacraments. For while in this and many other places it was forbidden to repeat baptisms, by whomsoever they had been performed, provided only they had been administered in the names of the three Persons of the Holy Trinity, a stricter rule was laid down with respect to priests orders. On this latter point the Pope says, "If those by whom they were ordained are unknown and it is doubtful whether they were bishops, provided these priests are Catholics, well conducted, and instructed in God s law for Christ s ministry, let them receive the priestly benediction and be consecrated by their bishop, and thus be fitted for the sacred office." Finally, he told Boniface not to remain in one place but to go and preach wherever the way was open to him and whenever he had an opportunity he was to ordain bishops in the Pope s stead according to the canonical rule, and teach them to observe the Apostolic and canonical traditions.

No record remains of the place where Boniface held the council in obedience to the Pope's command, nor of the bishops who attended it. But it is supposed that the recently-consecrated Bavarian bishops, Vivilo, Bishop of Passau, and the Allemanian bishops to whom the Pope had written, were present, excepting only Kudolt, Bishop of Constance, who had recently died.

The spirit of Catholic unity which Boniface thus infused into Bavaria, gave new life and vigor to the languishing Christianity of the province. Idolatry, heresy, and schism, quickly disappeared through the steady and united operation of zealous bishops and priests. True sacraments diffused grace far and wide through the land. Princes and nobles, following the example of their duke, vied with each other in magnificent liberality to the sons of S. Benedict. Churches and abbeys rose on every side, and persons of all classes, nobles and serfs, rich and poor, men and women, crowded into them or gave their children to them for the glory and service of God.

This grand awakening of Catholic life and love called into existence in less than forty years, from A.D. 740 to 778, no less than twenty-nine splendid abbeys, which were centers of holiness and learning throughout the Middle Ages, and have left their mark on the Christian and civilized world even to the most distant times. S. Pirininian's name has already been mentioned in connexion with the Abbeys of Amorbach and Reichenau, the latter of which being built on an island or awe of the Rhine near its entrance into the Lake of Constance, received its name from its great wealth. After founding several other monasteries in Alsace and Allemania, he went with twelve monks into Bavaria. Here, through Duke Odilo's generosity, he founded the Abbeys of Upper and Lower Altach, on the left bank of the Danube, Osterhofen on its right bank, Pfaffenmunster to the north of the river, and Monsee on the lake of the same name. Odilo also richly endowed the Abbey of Niedernburg at Passau for women, and a monastery which the Bishop of Freisingen built adjoining the church of S. Zeno on the Isana. There were also the seven abbeys of Benedictbeuern, Schlehdorf, Staffelsee, Kochelsee, Polling, Sandau, Wessobrun, and the church of Pura, built and endowed by the three brothers Lantfried, Waidram, and Eliland, and their sister Gailswinde, the grandchildren of Theodo II's eldest son, Theodoald. When the brothers and their sister had each built one of the four first-named abbeys and the church of Pura, they invited Boniface to come and consecrate their offerings. Gladly he accepted the invitation, and on the 22nd of October, some time subsequent to A.D. 742, he consecrated the church of Pura to S. Benedict and S. James the Apostle, and made Lantfried Abbot of Pura and the three other abbeys which were subject to it. For twenty-five years Lantfried, popularly known as the good Lanzo, governed this fraternal offering as Prince Abbot still wearing his princely robes but distinguished by his monastic virtues and his fraternal love. His two brothers succeeded him in this office. The sons and daughters of nobles and princes begged for admittance within these holy retreats. The unhappy Gisila, wife of the last Merovingian king, sought shelter and consolation with Gailswinde at Kochelsee. And before very long, as the throng of applicants could not find room in the four abbeys, Lantfried added to them the Abbeys of Polling and Wessobrun for men and Sandau for women. The example of this family was followed by their cousins, Adelbert and Ottokar, who after many misfortunes exchanged their military accoutrements for the monk s frock about A.D. 746, and founded the Abbeys of Tegernsee and llumiinster, which they endowed with all their inheritance.

The spirit of S. Benedict soon spread from Bavaria into Allemania. There still lingered the rule of S. Columban in the Abbey of S. Gall. In the year 720, Otmar, an Alleman by birth and of great repute for sanctity, was made abbot by Victor, Count of Rhoetia, and Waltram, the owner of the forest in which the abbey stood. He rebuilt the monastery, restored discipline, and collected together a large community. But they were in great poverty till 4.0. 751, when Pepin le Bref, at the request of his brother Carloman, then a monk, richly endowed the abbey on the condition that it should be placed under the rule of S. Benedict. This S. Otmar accordingly did, and before his death the abbey had risen to a very flourishing state, and the school had begun to take the lead, after Fulda, in the revival of learning and the spread of education.

CHAPTER XIV.THE CHURCH IN THURINGIA AND HESSE

At the end of the year 740, or the beginning of the following year, Boniface having completed his task in Bavaria, went into Thuringia and Hesse. The two years or more of his absence had been very eventful. In 738 Charles Martel had made war for the sixth and last time on the Saxons, and having gained a great victory over them, had finally driven them out of these provinces. From this time they made only incursions into them with the object of plunder, but had no permanent hold on them. This was a fine opening for the missionary work. Another important circumstance was that Charles Martel, having subdued all his enemies, now began to turn his attention to the peaceful settlement of his dominions. And moreover, it was in this same year, that in consequence of two letters from S. Gregory III, which followed each other in quick succession, he promised to defend the Holy See. Thus it was at a most favorable conjuncture that Boniface undertook the task of founding the Church of Old Germany.

It ought to be remarked that though the names Thuringia and Hesse have been used in these pages for convenience sake, yet at this time these distinctive appellations were unknown. The whole of this territory was in the hands of numerous tribes of Thuringian, Hessian, or Frank origin, the limits of whose respective possessions were vaguely defined and constantly fluctuating and it was only through the ecclesiastical organization that Boniface now introduced, that the restless population settled itself permanently, and the provinces of Hesse, Thuringia, and Franconia were formed.

In this vaguely-defined territory Boniface placed three bishops, namely, one at Buraburg, for the northern part of the district, since called Hesse; another at Erfurt, for the central part, since known as Thuringia ; and the third at Wurzburg, for the region which in later times developed into the Duchy of Franconia. There still remained a district unprovided with a bishop. This was the border-land between Thuringia and Bavaria, the Thuringian portion of which was known as the Salafeld, and the Bavarian as the Nordgau. It had long been a bone of contention between the Franks and Bavarians; but as the former advanced their frontier in each successive war, Boniface seems to have purposely excluded it from both the adjoining dioceses of Wurzburg and Ratisbon, in anticipation of the period, now close at hand, when the whole would belong to the Franks, and the bishop whom he hoped to place at Eichstedt, would not be embarrassed by the claims of a divided allegiance.

No place could have been better chosen than Buraburg for the site of the Hessian see. Not only did it stand in the same central position as Fritzlar, but the hill being in the form of a truncated cone, was well suited to be a frontier station of the Franks in their wars with the Saxons, and also a refuge for the Christians during the Saxon invasions.

In this see Boniface placed Wizo, also called Witta or Wittana, all of which names signifying "white," have been Latinized into Albinus. He was probably of Irish origin and was one of the monks of Fritzlar to whom Boniface wrote from Rome the letter already quoted. He lived in the closest friendship with Lullus, Boniface s successor at Mayence; and when, A.D. 786, Lullus felt his end approaching, Wizo came to him, but his own death preceded that of his friend. Lullus lived only to carry him to Hersfeld, where both were buried near their old master S. Wigbert.

Magingoz, Abbot of Fritzlar, succeeding Wizo as bishop, the see was removed to Fritzlar and after his death the western portion of the diocese was added to the see of Mayence, and the eastern, which comprised the conquests of Pepin-le-Bref and Charlemagne, was formed into the new dioceses of Halberstadt and Paderborn. After the subjugation of the Saxons by Charlemagne, Buraburg lost its value as a frontier fortress, and by the fourteenth century the town had disappeared and the church dedicated to S. Bridget and S. Boniface alone remained, and was used by the neighboring villages till the Thirty Years War.

In the diocese of Erfurt Boniface placed Adelar or Adalgar, who was afterwards one of the companions of his martyrdom. This see was, however, of short duration, for Adelar had no successor and even in his lifetime, after Boniface became Archbishop of Mayence it was merged in the arch diocese.

The diocese of Wurzburg was in a more flourishing state than either Buraburg or Erfurt. Here S. Kilian had sowed the first seed of Christianity, and watered it with his blood. Here Duke Hethan had built a church in honor of our Blessed Lady, probably the oldest in Franconia. And here his daughter, S. Irmina, was still living at the head of a small community on the Marienberg. All around, too, were Christian neighbors, churches, and monasteries.

The first of the long line of bishops of Wurzburg, who afterwards took so prominent a place in Germany, was Burchard, an Englishman of noble birth, said to have been related to S. Boniface. He had been devoted to God s service from his childhood, and after living for a long time in France as a pilgrim, he was irresistibly drawn to Boniface, whose fame met him on every side. The attraction was mutual for when they met, Boniface, who seems to have already beheld him in a vision, said to those around him, "Rejoice, brethren, for God has sent us a comrade, to whom our Lord s flock collected in Wurzburg by S. Kilian, will be entrusted." Burchard went to Rome with S. Boniface, A.D. 738, and was presented to Pope S. Gregory III, who approved of the selection of him for the episcopal office. He was advanced in years when he became Bishop of Wurzburg, but he is said to have been much beloved by his flock, and to have been worthy of their love. When he entered his see he had neither cathedral nor episcopal residence. His only property was a hunting-lodge at Norlach on the Main, the gift of Charles Martel and his crozier was a simple staff of wood.

Strange was it for S. Irmina, after a long life of bereavement and isolation amid Pagan foes, to find herself suddenly transported to the centre of a Catholic bishopric. The increasing throng of people to Wurzburg, made her old asylum on the Marienberg too noisy an abode for her and her nuns and before long she proposed to Burchard to exchange her monastery for that at Karlburg, which tradition ascribed to the Frank princess, S. Gertrude, and which stood in a domain that Carloman, son of Charles Martel, had given to Burchard. Her offer was joyfully accepted, and for a time the small, old church of our Lady on the Marienberg, served Burchard for a cathedral. But the steep ascent and the scarcity of water making this position inconvenient, he built a large church and monastery, which were called S. Salvator's church and minister. In the year 854 this church being burnt, the present Neumunster was built almost on the same site.

Burchard s first care was to remove the relics of S. Kilian and his companions to a fitting place of honor. They were found under the floor of the stable where Duke Gotzbert's horses had been kept and a fragrant odor issued from the spot where they lay. They were carried in solemn procession to the church on the Marienberg; and when the new cathedral was built, they were translated to it and laid in the crypt which long bore S. Kilian s name.

Tradition ascribes to Burchard great skill as an architect, and associates his name with the foundation of several churches and monasteries. In his latter years he was entrusted with the delicate office of going to Home with Fulrad, Abbot of St. Denis, to obtain the Pope s sanction to the transfer of the French crown to the Carlovingian dynasty. After his return to Wurzburg age and infirmities compelled him to resign the see to Magingoz, a monk of Fritzlar. He then retired with six monks to a monastery which he had built at Homburg, where he died A.D. 751.

It is not known at what time or place Boniface consecrated these three bishops. But after their consecration he summoned them to meet him at Salzburg, an old royal castle on the Saal, where Neustadt now stands. Some have considered this meeting as the second council which Boniface held. But that it was not a council, is evident from Willibald s assertion that no council was held in Franconia till after Charles Martel s death, and from Boniface's letter to the Pope in the following year, in which he says that no council had been held for eighty years. At this meeting of bishops, three weeks before the feast of S. Martin, A.D. 741, Willibald was consecrated a bishop, but without a fixed see. Not only did the political circumstances of Eichstedt at this time unfit it to be the seat of a bishopric, but it was still only a wild forest, through which Willibald had recently cut his way axe in hand, and it contained no town, as the canons required, for a bishop s see. But so rapid was the development of these ecclesiastical foundations that only four years later, A.D. 745, when Carloman had completed the conquest of the district a town had arisen around Willibald s church, and Eichstedt was erected into a bishopric, with him for its first bishop. Thus was the Church of Central Germany placed under regular episcopal government.

CHAPTER XV.THE CHURCH IN AUSTRASIA AND NEUSTRIA

Boniface had already done more than it commonly falls to the lot even of saints to do. The conversion and organization of Germany might seem enough to fill not only one, but many lives. Yet God reserved for him a further work more difficult than the conversion of savages, namely, the reform of a corrupt race. Two hundred and fifty years had now elapsed since the submission of Clovis and his Franks to the faith of Christ and that period is almost enough to account for the decadence of most of the empires which have been established in the world. In addition, however, to the wear and tear of the mere lapse of time, it cannot have escaped the reader who has studied the conversion of the Franks, that there existed from the first seeds of corruption which were now bearing their baneful fruit. We have already seen terrible crimes side by side with heroic virtues. This is true to some extent of all human, even ecclesiastical history, but something more than the ordinary depravity of mankind is necessary to account for the fact, that the annals of the Merovingian kings are more like a Newgate calendar than the story of a royal dynasty. The fact is that the conversion of the Frank empire was never so thorough as that of Saxon England. This of course cannot be assumed without proof, yet there are numerous facts which show that even to the latest times of the empire heathen customs, and even heathen morals kept their ground. In a letter to Brunehaut S. Gregory moans over the fact, that many Franks frequented at once Christian churches and the altars of heathen gods. In the Italian wars of Theodebert I the Frank army offered human sacrifices, and Procopius bids us not be startled, "for" he says, "these men are barbarians though they are Christians, and keep much of their ancient creed; they make sacrifices of men, and other unholy rites for the purpose of augury." In the sixth century the peasants in the wilds of the Ardennes were converted from the worship of Diana only by the appearance among them of a pillar saint, S. Wulflaich, a remarkable phenomenon for Western Europe. In the same century S. Gall of Clermont burns a heathen grove near Cologne, and is pursued by the Pagan natives to the very court of the King, who with difficulty pacifies them. In 582 S. Radegunda also burnt a grove where heathen Franks still worshipped the old gods. Even down to the time of Pepin Heristal S. Plechelm found on Frank ground men who united the worship of Christ with the old gods of the North. The frequency of the canons of councils forbidding idolatry, is a proof of the same fact; and though, as we have seen, some Saxon synods show that Pagan usages still lingered in England, yet the tattooing of their persons and the custom of dis figuring their horses by cutting their tails and ears, which were forbidden to our Saxon ancestors, and treated as heathen enormities in the English legatine synods, are innocent compared with the heathen improprieties forbidden in the council of Chalons. That this state of things lasted down to the time of S. Boniface, is plain from his own complaint that he found priests who called themselves missionaries, and who in the morning offered the unbloody sacrifice of the Mass, and in the evening sacrificed bulls and goats to idols. This portentous fact took place it is true, in the semi-pagan lands beyond the proper boundary of the Frank empire but the priests came from elsewhere, and must have crossed the border from Austrasia.

It is only by such remnants of paganism that it is possible to account for the scandalous lives of the Merovingian kings. Only in such a heathen state of morals could such an event as has been recorded of S. Radegunda have taken place. The power of Christianity must have been enormous to have held its ground at all in such a state of things, much more to have produced such a pure lily as the saint out of a soil so corrupt. Their whole history is the story of the courageous fights of brave bishops with the unbridled passions of the Frank sovereigns. We know from Tacitus that though the Germans in general married but one wife, polygamy was the rule among the chiefs. In addition to heathen tradition came the miserable example of the

Romanized Gaul. Christian writers like Salvian mourn over the depravity of the Christians of their time. Not all the efforts of saintly bishops could root out the passion of their flocks for the obscene representations of the arena and the theatre, and Salvian describes the frenzy of the inhabitants of Treves, who, amidst the horrors of the barbarian invasions, consoled themselves for the burning of their city and the ruin of their fortunes by plunging madly into the enjoyments of a licentious stage. The Frank armies were thus in the very worst position for the acquisition of Christian virtue. The wild lusts of barbarian conquerors were brought out by the vicious civilization of the vanquished. The vast families of slaves kept by the rich Romans were hotbeds of depravity, and the households of the Frank victors were formed on this miserable model. The evil, by the end of the monarchy, had grown much greater, for the tendency of the age was to convert the small landed proprietors into slaves, so that the number of freemen was comparatively small. Thus every bad harvest increased the number of slaves, for the poor were compelled to sell themselves to the rich nobles from whom they had borrowed money. The nobility imitated the vices of the court. Long and bravely had the Church struggled with this enormous evil. The lives of the saints of this period are a sufficient proof of their courage. Yet it is a remarkable fact that under the early Merovingian kings the Church was never sufficiently settled to admit of the establishment of her regular discipline. The Irish monks, and especially S. Columban, attempted to introduce it; but the old bottles of the Frank race were too weak to bear the new wine. It may be that the Celtic harshness of the apostles made the restraint of discipline more unpalatable than it otherwise would have been. At all events, S. Columban, expelled from the Vosges, took refuge in Italy, and S. Gall found more patient hearers in the savage Allemanni round the Lake of Constance.

By the times that we have reached the clergy themselves were not in a position to enforce a severe discipline. Nothing can prove the slowness with which Christianity penetrated into the Franks more clearly than the length of time which it took to raise a native clergy. The old Roman bishops in Gaul were splendid men in a grand position; they stood forward as protectors of their vanquished countrymen, and their virtues awed their barbaric oppressors. By the common consent of both races the government of the cities was entrusted to them, and this temporal power was enhanced by the old possessions of the sees which were respected by the barbarians, while new lands were added by the munificence of the reigning monarchs. The statistics of councils prove that it was long before this old race of Roman ecclesiastics was replaced by a

Frank clergy, and when this time came the temporal prosperity of the Church proved a disadvantage to their virtue. Considered simply as nobles by the Merovingian kings, like the rest of the nobles they were looked upon as officials of the court. The Frank kings, though in theory protectors of the Church, ceased to respect her freedom and the bishoprics became too often the hereditary possessions of noble families ; as, for instance, the bishopric of Metz had fallen into the hands of the Ferreoli, the family to which S. Arnulf is said to have belonged. In fact during the period of Merovingian decay the corruption of the nation infected the clergy. The salt lost its savor, and only increased the ruin of the body politic. We even meet with portentous heresies which remind us of Mormonism, and which resemble far more a return to heathenism with a mixture of semi-Christian superstition than intellectual corruptions of Christianity. A lamentable state of things but by no means extraordinary. It never has been and never will be otherwise. Whenever the right relations between Church and State are disturbed, whenever the Church loses her independence, she ceases to be the guardian of the morals both of the clergy and people. The remedy for such a state of things can only come from a central authority, supreme over the clergy and independent of the State, that is, from Rome. It was to S. Boniface that Rome entrusted the cleansing of this Augean stable.

While Boniface was occupied, as we have seen, in Old Germany, death had made great changes on the thrones of Europe. On the 18th of June, A.D. 741, the Emperor Leo the Iconoclast died and was succeeded by his son Constantine Copronymus. This prince followed in his fathers steps and the rupture between Rome and the Eastern Empire was widened. On the 22nd of the following October Charles Martel died, and on the 18th of November, Pope S. Gregory III. S. Gregory s death made no difference to Boniface, for Rome s policy does not rest on human wisdom; and after an interval of only three days S. Peter s Chair was filled by Zachary, who inherited the zeal of his two predecessors for the conversion of Germany. It is significant that no confirmation of the election was asked from Ravenna. Even the last nominal bond between Rome and the Eastern Empire was snapped.

Charles Martel's death was a great gain to Boniface; for Charles was succeeded by his sons, Carloman and Pepin, both of whom were princes of sincere piety.

Carloman, who, as the elder, enjoyed a nominal supremacy, was Boniface s pupil. Educated at his father's court among rough soldiers and worthless clergy, he knew little about the Christian religion till he made the acquaintance of Boniface, through whose teaching and influence he became so penetrated with the fear and love of God, that his whole administration, whether of secular or ecclesiastical matters, was regulated with a view to God s service, and not according to mere worldly policy.

Immediately after his accession he summoned Boniface to his presence. The result of this interview is told in the following letter 8 to Pope Zachary, which also depicts the frightful state of the Church in the Eastern kingdom at that time.

After renewing his vows of obedience to S. Peter, and asking for the confirmation of the Holy See for the bishoprics at Wurzburg, Buraburg, and Erfurt, Boniface continues, "Be it known to you, Holy Father, that Carloman, Duke of the Franks, having summoned me to him, bade me assemble a synod in the part of the kingdom which he governs, and promised that he would correct and amend the ecclesiastical discipline, which has been neglected and trodden under foot for sixty or seventy years. Wherefore he wished to have the commands of the Apostolic See, in order that by the inspiration of God, he might obey them perfectly. It is said by old men among the Franks, that for eighty years there has been neither synod nor Archbishop, nor have the canons of the Church been enforced. Most of the bishoprics are held by laymen greedy of gain, or by grossly immoral and avaricious clergy. Should I find among the deacons some, who, though they have lived from their boyhood in sin and uncleanness have notwithstanding been raised to the diaconate; who though as deacons they have lived wicked lives, yet have neither been ashamed nor afraid to call themselves deacons and to read the Gospel; who then rising to the priesthood, and continuing in such sins and even adding to them, perform priestly functions, professing to intercede for the people, and to offer the Holy Sacrifice; and who finally, what is even worse, after rising with such a character through the different grades of Holy Orders, are consecrated and appointed bishops; if, I say, I should find such, I ask for a command from your authority regarding them, in order that sinners may be convicted and reproved by the Apostolic reply. There are also certain bishops, who, though they are not adulterers, are drunkards and unjust, or addicted to hunting: and who go to battle armed, and shed the blood of men, whether Pagans or Christians. Because I am the servant and legate of the Apostolic See, I wish my word and yours to be the same if it should happen that I refer these cases to your decision."

Boniface then proceeded to remind Zachary, that S. Gregory III in his presence, had given him leave to appoint a certain priest his successor but this being impracticable on account of a feud between this priest's family and that of Carloman, he asked leave to appoint another successor. He also said that a layman of rank asserted, that the late Pope had given him permission to marry his uncle s widow, who was also the wife of his cousin still living, whom she had left and who, moreover, had formerly vowed her chastity to God and taken the veil, but had thrown it off and married. This marriage was creating great scandal, and he could not believe that permission for it had been given; because in the Synod of London, in the Church of "Saxony beyond the sea in which he had been born and educated, such a union was declared to be incest. Further, great scandals and disputes had arisen, because certain foolish persons, Allemans, Bavarians, and Franks, insisted that many things which he and his priests forbade, were allowed in Rome, where they had seen Pagan feasts, with choruses singing Pagan hymns in the public streets, and women wearing magical amulets and phylacteries, and other Pagan superstitions. Wherefore he requested the Holy Father to prohibit these Pagan customs in Rome, both for the gain to his own soul and the profit of the Church. Finally, certain Frank bishops and priests who had been habitually immoral and to whom children had been born since they had been bishops or priests, said on their return from Rome, that the Pope had given them leave to officiate in the Church. But this he resisted, because the Apostolic See had never been known to give judgment contrary to the canons. Zachary in his answer, confirmed the erection of the sees of Wurzburg, Buraburg, and Erfurt, sanctioned the meeting of the council, forbade the ministrations of bishops, priests, and deacons who were living in sin, or had shed blood, or who having been married before their ordination, did not separate from their wives, and also the second marriage of clerics, who had not yet attained to the priesthood. Against such, and all other offenders against the canons, he ordered Boniface to proceed as the Church ordered, denying that the Holy See had ever granted any indulgence, as was pretended, to clergy living in sin. He also denied that his predecessor had ever given the alleged sanction to the incestuous marriage with an uncle s widow, who was also the wife of a cousin, and had once been a nun. As to the Pagan practices in Rome, of which Boniface complained, they were detested by him and all Christians and had been put down by himself and his predecessor. On one point alone did he oppose Boniface. For he would not give him leave to appoint a successor but directed that any one whom, at the hour of death he should publicly recommend as his successor, should come to Rome to be consecrated.

The mendacity of arrogant nobles and Church dignitaries who resisted Boniface's authority by the plea of pretended privileges from the Pope, and the ignorant error of the multitude who believed that whatever was done at Rome must be allowed by the Church, both alike show that the barbarians were conscious of the existence of that great spiritual force, which was to control them in S. Peter s name during the Middle Ages.

The council mentioned in the foregoing letters, was held on the 21st of April, A.D. 742 but the place of its meeting is not known. Some have supposed that it was at Worms and others at Frankfort but there is no historical ground for either conjecture. It was attended by Boniface, Burchard, Wizo, Willibald, Regenfried, Bishop of Cologne, Edda, Bishop of Strasburg, and Dadan, who is supposed to have been the coadjutor of Utrecht. It enacted seven canons, which confirmed the bishops in their sees and Boniface's authority over them as S. Peter s legate, ordered synods to be held every year, and provided for the enforcement of discipline, the punishment of unchaste clergy, monks, and nuns, and the restriction of the ministrations of bishops and priests to their respective dioceses and parishes, forbidding all unknown and wandering bishops and priests to officiate, and calling on the nobles to assist the bishops to put down idolatry and Pagan superstitions. It further forbade the clergy to dress as laymen, to carry arms or go to battle, to have women in their houses, and to hunt or keep hawks and falcons. It also ordered monks and nuns to live according to the rule of S. Benedict.

In obedience to these canons another council was held on the 1st of the following March 6, at Liptina or Liftina, a royal villa in the diocese of Cambray, near the spot where the Abbey of Laubium, or Lob, after wards stood. It was presided over by two legates extraordinary, George and John, who seem to have been sent to give it weight and to inquire into the errors of two heretics, Clement and Adalbert, at whose trial in Rome they afterwards assisted. It was attended by both clergy and laity, and its chief object was to give the authority of national laws to the canons of the former council, which had been purely ecclesiastical. Only four of its canons remain, which, besides confirm ing the enactments of the preceding synod, prohibit marriages within the forbidden degrees of kindred, and the giving up of Christian slaves to Pagans. There is also a very important canon regulating the terms on which Church lands held by military retainers in return for their service, might, on account of the impending wars, be kept temporarily by the present holders, but providing for their eventual reversion to the Church.

To the canons of this council is appended the form of abjuration required of converts from Paganism at their baptism. In answer to questions asked by the priest, the neophyte said, "I renounce the devil. I renounce all communion with the devil. I renounce all the works and words of the devil, Thunar, Woden, and Saxnot, and all the impure spirits that are with them. I love God the Father Almighty. I love Christ the Son of God. I love the Holy Ghost."

A curious list of thirty Pagan superstitions also was placed after this abjuration; and finally came two exhortations against unlawful marriages, and the observance of the Sabbath, as being a Judaizing practice opposed to our Lord s precepts in the Gospels.

Irregular marriages have always been a source of trouble to the Church, and they were more especially so at this time, when the Pagan custom of intermarrying within the family or tribe still prevailed, and the Christian restrictions were not familiar even to the clergy. Not only does this subject constantly recur in the canons of councils and Boniface's letters to successive Popes, but he himself had difficulties on certain points, as appears from his letters to his English friends.

After the restoration of synodal action in Austrasia, Boniface turned to Neustria, then generally called Gaul, which was governed by Pepin. Here a more difficult task awaited him. For this was the older portion of the kingdom, where lay for the most part the richest benefices, which Charles Martel had given to his military retainers. Here was Milo, the tonsured cleric, who had long wrongfully held the dioceses of Eheims and Treves. Here were the heretical bishops, Adalbert and Clement, and other wolves in sheep s clothing, and sacrilegious nobles, and immoral and blood-stained clergy, too numerous to name. It is easy to imagine what a stir Carloman s proceedings must have made among such as these. Pepin long felt that he was no match for this host of opponents, and he shrank from the contest. But at length, after two years he yielded to his brother s entreaties and fell heartily into Boni face's plans.

Many of the existing abuses in the Neustrian Church could be traced to the defective relations between bishops and metropolitans, the cessation of synodal action, and the heretical teaching of such men as Adalbert and Clement. During the late unsettled state of the country, bishops had often fallen under a different sovereign from him who claimed the allegiance of their metropolitan and in such cases, instead of seeking to place themselves under the authority of some superior within their own sub division of the kingdom, they had generally taken advantage of their isolated position to assert their independence. From this cause, and from not meeting in synods, the benefits of Catholic union were lost and the Church was not strong enough to check abuses, to support the weak and timid, and to resist the tyranny of princes and nobles.

To remedy this evil Carloman, Pepin, and Boniface wrote to the Pope in August, A.D.

743, asking him to extend Boniface's authority over Gaul as well as Ger many, and to increase the number of Metropolitans in Gaul by sending palls to Grimo, Archbishop of Rouen, Abel, Archbishop of Eheims, and Hartbert, Archbishop of Sens, who was the bearer of the letters.

The Pope accordingly sent the three palls, but before they reached Neustria Boniface wrote again, recalling the former request and asking for only one to be sent to Grimo of Rouen. It appears that a report had been spread by the party of opposition that the palls had been obtained simoniacally by the favored prelates, and in order to discredit the rumor Boniface wrote, no doubt with the concurrence of Carloman and Pepin and probably at their instigation, to suspend the transmission of two of them. In the absence of Boniface's letter it is impossible to say what he thought of the report but his conduct surprised the Pope and called forth a grave rebuke, though it did not disturb his relations with the Holy See.

On the 5th of November, A.D. 743, the Pope wrote, "We find in your letters what greatly disturbs us. For you tell us such things, as if we corrupted the canons and violated the traditions of the Fathers, and with our clergy fell into simoniacal heresy, which God forbid, demanding and accepting gifts from those to whom we sent palls. We exhort you, dearest brother, never henceforth write to us thus, because it is distressing and unjust to impute to us what we thoroughly detest. Far be it from us and our clergy that we should sell the gift which we have received from the Holy Spirit. The three palls which were asked of us at your suggestion, we gave without desiring any profit, and also the customary letters of confirmation and instruction, without receiving any thing for them. You ask us whether you have authority to preach in Bavaria, as our predecessor granted you. Far from curtailing what our predecessor gave you, we, by God s help, add to it. For we enjoin you, so long as God gives you life to preach in our stead, not only in Bavaria, but in all the provinces of Gaul, that whatever you find there contrary to the Christian religion or canonical rules, you may try to reform to the standard of righteousness."

On the 2nd of March, A.D. 744, a national synod, at which eleven Austrasian and twelve Neustrian bishops assisted, was held by Pepin at Soissons. It was summoned by Carloman s authority, but neither he nor Boniface was present probably because Soissons was in Pepin s territory, and the Neustrian nobles might not have brooked their personal interference. Ten canons of the same tenor as those of the two German councils were enacted, with the exceptions that the heretical Bishop Adelbert was condemned, and Abel and Ardobert, or Hartbert, were appointed arch bishops, Grimo being already Archbishop of Rouen. But in spite of the authority of the council and the good intentions of Pepin and the greater part of his bishops and their clergy, it was not in his power to do all that he and Boniface wished. Milo, the intruder into the sees of Rheims and Treves, was too powerful to be dislodged by force; he could not be induced to resign them voluntarily; and so long as he lived Abel could not exercise his functions as Metropolitan of Rheims. There arose also further difficulties in carrying out the arrangement. For in the year 751, seven years after the palls had been sent, Boniface complained to the Pope, that the matter was not yet completed, because the Neustrian bishops evaded or delayed the fulfillment of their promises of obedience.

Mention has been made of the heretics Adelbert and Clement. They were not connected together, and their heresies were totally different; but both had been ordained to the priesthood by unknown bishops, had taken on themselves the episcopal office, and had managed to gain many adherents. Adelbert was a Gaul of low origin, but he pretended to have been sanctified by God even before his birth. He showed the people a letter, which he said was from our Lord and had fallen from heaven into Jerusalem, where it had been found by the Archangel Michael, who, after passing it through the hands of several priests, had laid it on the tomb of S. Peter at Rome, "where the Keys of the Kingdom of Heaven are kept," where twelve fathers who were in the city fasted, watched, and prayed for three days and nights. He pretended to hold intercourse with S. Michael, and to heal the sick. He gave his hair and nails to his disciples as relics; and teaching them to despise the Catholic bishops, saints, and martyrs, he led them to assemble in oratories dedicated to himself, or at crosses erected in fields or at fountains, where they prayed "through the merits of S. Adelbert," and invoked six angels whom the Church has always held to be fallen spirits. And when people came to confess to him, he would say, "I know all your sins, for all secrets are revealed to me. It is unnecessary to confess; but all your sins are remitted. Go home in peace, and be absolved."

Clement, on the other hand, was an Irishman; being more learned than Adelbert, he set himself to refute the doctrines of the Church and taught his own views of Scripture. Though he had two sons born in sin after he called himself a bishop, he still claimed episcopal powers. He taught that a man might marry his brother's widow that our Lord, when He descended to hell, delivered all the imprisoned souls, bad as well as good and horrible doctrines concerning God s predestination.

Both these heretics had gathered round them a large band of followers, and Adelbert, through his mystical pretensions, had gained some influence over Carloman. Boniface at first tried privately to bring them to reason; but finding them obstinate, he summoned them before the councils of Liptina and Soissons, in both of which they were condemned. Depending on the strength of their party, they continued to defy him till they were again condemned, A.D. 745, by a council at which eight bishops were present, who referred the case to Rome. There it was carefully examined by the Pope at a synod in the Lateran, and they were finally condemned; after which they seem to have been imprisoned by Carloman, and no more was heard of them.

CHAPTER XVI.BONIFACE ARCHBISHOP OF MAYENCE AND UTRECHT

About this time several events occurred which greatly altered Boniface s position and added to his influence. Early in the year 744 S. Willibrord died. On receiving the news of his death, Boniface set out for Utrecht. As he approached the town, he was met by a procession of the monks whom Willibrord had collected in the Abbey of S. Martin's during the fifty years that he had held the see, and they led him to the church, where he joined with many tears and sighs in their prayers for their departed father.

Carloman was anxious that the see should be filled without delay, and Boniface met his wishes by keeping it in his own hands, as legate of the Apostolic See, and appointing as his coadjutors or chorepiscopi, Eoban, who afterwards shared his martyrdom, and Gregory, Adela s grandson, who had hitherto been his constant associate in all his labors. This arrangement was in accordance with the views of Pope Sergius, who fifty years before, in sending Willibrord to convert the Frisians, had made the see subject to the Roman chair as a bishopric in partibus infidelium and as the province was still in great part Pagan, it now naturally fell within Boniface s mission. He remained a considerable time at Utrecht arranging the affairs of the diocese, so as to facilitate the labors of his coadjutors when he should be called elsewhere.

Scarcely was this task completed when he was summoned to the court by the death of Regenfried, Archbishop of Cologne. Regenfried had held the see since the year 718; but notwithstanding the example of Willibrord and Boniface, he had made no attempt to convert the Pagans, and had even tried to hinder their work by claiming jurisdiction over both. But successive Popes rejected the pretensions of one who would neither sow the seed himself nor allow others to do so. Regenfried's death now opened the way for an arrangement, which gave a metropolitan to the new sees which Boniface had founded and a primate to Germany.

Under the Roman Empire the Church had adopted the organization of the State and placed her primates, metropolitans, and bishops in the towns already marked out for capitals by the civil power. Thus the Roman provinces of the first and second Belgium, and the first and second Germany, which included the left bank of the Rhine from Strasburg to the North Sea, had each its archbishop or metropolitan at Treves, Rheims, Mayence, and Cologne, each of whom again had several bishops under him, while the Archbishop of Treves held juris diction as Primate over the whole. But as this arrangement did not extend to the right bank of the Rhine, some alteration in the metropolitan provinces was necessary, in order to include the new Church that was springing up in Old Germany.

Boniface's first idea on Regenfried s death was to take Cologne for his own metropolitan see, and place the new German bishoprics under it. For Cologne was in a very central position between Friesland, to which his heart was always turning, and his own field of labor in Thuringia and Hesse; while it also stood like a fortress on the borders of Saxony, which was the ultimate object of his desires.

This plan met the hearty approval of the Pope. But the clergy of the diocese, who had long lived in indolent luxury, to say nothing of worse abuses, were filled with dread and horror at the thoughts of the strict discipline which Boniface would enforce, and opposed his appointment by every means in their power. However, before the arrangement could be carried out, it was upset by the unexpected vacancy of the Archbishopric of Mayence.

It may have been noticed that the name of the Archbishop of Mayence does not appear among those who attended Boniface s early councils. The see had been filled for many years by Gerold, a very immoral man and a homicide, who owed his position to his military prowess, and was, like Milo, too powerful to be forcibly degraded. In the year 743 the Saxons invaded Thuringia, when Gerold, as usual, following Carloman into the field, was mortally wounded by a shower of darts into which he had fearlessly rushed. He left a son, Gewilieb, "born in sin and brought up without restraint," who lived much at court, where he was very popular on account of his generous and affection at plunged in sorrow by his father s death and though he was a layman, Carloman, out of pity, gave him the bishopric, and he took priest s orders, intending in course of time to receive episcopal consecration.

The following year the Saxons broke again into Thuringia, and Carloman marched against them. Gewilieb accompanied him, panting to avenge his father s death. The two armies were encamped on the opposite banks of the Weser, when Gewilieb being told that he who had killed his father was in the enemy's host, sent to ask him to parley with him in the middle of the river. The Saxon, fearing no treachery, consented; but when they met Gewilieb plunged his sword into his enemy's heart, exclaiming, "There, take the steel with which I avenge my father!" This led to a general engagement in which Gewilieb took part. The Saxons were defeated with great slaughter, and Carloman s army returned home laden with spoils. But neither Carloman nor the nobles thought of reproaching the young bishop for "they did not deem it a crime to avenge his father, but said that he had only taken the just retaliation for his death."

Boniface, however, took another view of the case. Gewilieb's nomination to the see must always have been displeasing to him, though no doubt his objections were overruled by assurances that the young man was well disposed and would assume clerical habits with his clerical dignity. Gewilieb, however, had continued to indulge his love of field-sports, and was always to be seen surrounded by dogs and hawks, and now that he had committed homicide so publicly, there would be an end of all clerical reforms, if he were allowed to hold the metropolitan see. Boniface demanded his deposition, not only on the ground of the homicide, but also because he had himself seen him going about with dogs and hawks and Gewilieb was quite willing to resign the spiritual charge, for he had no inclination to perform the canonical penance, or to give up his sporting life. But he stipulated that as he had no patrimony, he should retain the domain of Spanheim and the Church of Caput Montis. Boniface would not consent, and wrote to the Pope, who answered, that should the pretended bishop come to him, "God's will would be done to him." Gewilieb was accordingly deposed by a synod, and though he at first threatened to appeal to Rome, yet after a time he retired quietly into private life. He managed, however, to retain the benefices for which he had stipulated; and on them he lived for fourteen years, practicing great hospitality, never assisting at any public assembly, and seldom appearing in church, even on Holy Thursday.

These proceedings occupied four years. But from their commencement all eyes were turned on Boniface as the fit occupant of the see of Mayence. The clergy of Cologne desired his appointment, since it would relieve them from his inconvenient zeal and strictness while the greater part of the clergy and laity of Mayence even at Mayence there was a small party of lukewarm and immoral priests who opposed him on the ground of his foreign birth. As for himself, "it was the less possible to accuse him of interested motives" for deposing Gewilieb, "because his removal to the see of Mayence was opposed to his own wishes and plans." He long strove to retain his favorite central position at Cologne; but the Pope overruled his wishes in a letter dated the 1st of May, A.D. 748.

Accordingly in that year Boniface became Archbishop of Mayence and Utrecht, and Agilolf was appointed to Cologne. The Pope made Mayence the primatial see of Germany with jurisdiction over Tongres, Cologne, Worms, Spire, and Utrecht, in addition to the four sees founded by Boniface, and Augsburg, Strasburg, Constance, and Coire, which were already subject to it. At a later period Cologne was formed into a separate metropolitan province, which included Tongres and Utrecht. But, on the other hand, the new bishoprics of Paderborn, Halberstadt, Hildesheim, and Verden, and later still Prague and Olmiitz, were given to Mayence.

Both before and after his elevation to the primacy, Boniface continued to hold councils in both Germany and France, and to attend the March or May-fields, at which the canons enacted by ecclesiastical synods, became national laws. He was so anxious to establish regular synodal action, that in the year 748 he requested the Pope to appoint a legate, who should be specially authorized to devote himself to this work, which his own many other avocations and the infirmities of age, prevented his carrying out so perfectly as he wished. The Pope, however, refused his request, but gave him leave to appoint suitable persons to assist him in his other duties. How many councils he held is not known. Seven at the very least have been reckoned but this number is evidently far too few. For as the three first councils ordered them to be held yearly, and the Pope was constantly urging the same, it may be reasonably concluded that

Boniface was careful to obey in a matter in which he so heartily concurred.

A general idea of the spirit and scope of Boniface's legislation, may be gathered from the letters of Popes S. Gregory II, S. Gregory III, and Zachary, in answer to his inquiries; from a capitulary addressed by Zachary to Pepin in consequence of an embassy sent by the latter to Rome, A.D. 747; from another capitulary published by Boniface at a council held about A.D. 745 and from a collection of his statutes made after his death.

In glancing over these documents three circumstances especially attract notice. First, one meets with the same laws and customs as those which, after a lapse of eleven hundred years, are still to be found in the Catholic Church. There are the same Holy Orders and ecclesiastical discipline, with restrictions as to the places where, and the priests by whom, Mass may be said the same Sacraments of Baptism, Confirmation, Penance, Holy Eucharist, Extreme Unction, and Viaticum; the observance of Lent, the Ember weeks, and the vigils of Easter and Pentecost as fasts, and of Sundays and eleven great festivals, among which are Our Lady's Nativity, Purification, and Assumption, as holidays of obligation. There are also the new fire and chrism, and the blessing of the font before Easter; the feet washing on Holy Thursday; the exclusion of laity from the chancel, and of secular men and women from sing ing choirs; and even the book marked with crosses at the places where the holy sign was to be made, which Pope Zachary gave Lullus for the guidance of the German Church.

In the second place, it is interesting in an historical point of view, to notice curious references to extinct Pagan superstitions, and statutes concerning parricide, fratricide, homicide, gross immorality, theft, arson, spoliation of the Church, right of way, and the treatment of slaves and foundlings, all telling of an age of barbaric violence, licentiousness, and cruelty.

But, above all, one is struck with the wide range of the subjects on which Boniface sought counsel of the Holy See and gave directions to his flock from the validity of Sacraments and the purity of clerical, monastic, and family morals, down to minute details of personal modesty, sanitary precaution, and both ordinary and Lenten food. Here it will be seen what a great revolution he was attempting, and how countless were the ties, running through every action of life, that had to be broken, before the lawless Pagan or nominal Christian could be brought under the yoke of Christian self-restraint. Nor had these ties been loosened, as in England, by removal from home associations and national sanctuaries but, on the contrary, Boniface had to tear them asunder where they were strongest, and most firmly bound round the very heart of the German nation. For so superhuman a task nought less than a supernatural power could suffice. As he knelt at S. Gregory s feet before the Apostle s tomb, he learnt what was the spiritual force through which he was to hope for success, and thus, ever turning to S. Peter s Chair, and working in S. Peter s name, seeking in simple faith solely the greater glory of God, he overcame the lawlessness of the barbarians by his docility, and conquered princes and nations through that extraordinary strength which is gained only by the perfect conquest of self.

In the course of Boniface s correspondence it appears how many heresies met him on every side. There was an Irish priest, called Samson, who affirmed that baptism with water in the name of the Blessed Trinity was unnecessary, and that the imposition of a bishop's hands sufficed to make a man a Christian and a Catholic. Others doubted whether baptism administered in the right form by a heretical or immoral priest was valid, or whether immersion in water by a holy man, without the invocation of the Blessed Trinity, was sufficient.

Again, two priests, Virgilius and Sidonius, wrote to Pope Zachary to complain, that Boniface was obliging them to rebaptize those who had been baptized by a priest who, mispronouncing Latin, was in the habit of saying, "Baptizo te in nominee Patria et Filia et Spiritus Sancti." The Pope was "disturbed and surprised" at this charge, which he could scarcely credit and as neither heresy nor error had been introduced, and there was only a mispronunciation of Latin through ignorance, he ordered Boniface peremptorily, "if it was as he had been informed," never to teach such a thing again, but to observe the traditions of the fathers. As Boniface's answer is lost, it is not possible to say whether the charge was well founded. But probably it was false; because the Pope says in a subsequent letter: "As to the priests, Sidonius above-mentioned and Virgilius, we acknowledge what your Holiness has written. We have indeed written to them, threatening them, as was fitting. You, brother, are to be believed rather than they. If it be the will of God, and life permit, we shall summon them, as is preferable, by apostolic letters to the Apostolic See. For thou didst teach them, and they did not accept thy teaching and what the wise man hath written is accomplished in them: He who teacheth a fool is like one that glueth a potsherd together. Sand and salt, and a mass of iron, is easier to bear than a man without sense that is both foolish and wicked. For he that wanteth understanding thinketh vain things and the foolish and erring man thinketh foolish things. Wherefore, brother, be not provoked to anger, but wherever thou findest such, patiently admonish, beseech, threaten them, that they may be turned from error to the way of truth. If they are converted, thou wilt have saved their souls but if they remain impenitent, thou wilt not lose the reward of thy ministry; and avoid them according to the Apostle's command."

There was another Virgil, who also gave Boniface trouble. In the paragraph immediately preceding the one just quoted, the Pope says, "You have informed us that that Virgil we know not if he is said to be a priest has been acting maliciously against you, because you put him to shame for erring against Catholic doctrine that he is trying to excite ill feeling between you and Odilo, Duke of Bavaria and that he says he had been absolved by us, in order to obtain the diocese of the deceased bishop, who is one of the four whom you consecrated. This is by no means true, and he has lied wickedly. As to the perverse and iniquitous doctrine, which he has uttered against God and his own soul, if it be made clear that he has said that there is another world and other men under the earth, he should be deprived of the sacerdotal dignity. We have therefore written to the duke, and sent letters summoning Virgil to appear before us, that after close examination, if he be found in error, he may be condemned by canonical authorities."

From the above passages in Pope Zachary's letter a charge has been framed against Boniface, that he was convicted of grave error regarding baptism by S. Virgil, Bishop of Salzburg, and that he persecuted this great Irish saint, because his knowledge was so far in advance of the age in which he lived, that he asserted the existence of the antipodes. The truth, however, is that this accusation is not sufficiently supported and in some points is even contradicted, by the facts of the case. For there is no reason for supposing that Boniface fell into this error, except the assertion of two of his opponents, whom the Pope, after hearing both parties, did not deem worthy of credence, but threatened and reproved in very strong terms, while he said that Boniface had taught them the way of truth. Moreover, the Virgil who accused Boniface of the error about baptism, is a different person from the Virgil who "lied wickedly" to obtain a diocese and held the doctrine about the other world beneath the earth, as is evident from the way in which the Pope distinguishes them in consecutive passages of the same letter. Further, there is not the least evidence whether the doctrine of the lying Virgil was connected with the antipodes, or with the opinion of certain Pagan philosophers, who affirmed the existence of a plurality of worlds. In default of evidence, one would incline to doubt whether it had any connexion with the antipodes, because as their existence had already been conjectured by S. Augustine, whose writings were much studied both at Rome and in England, such an opinion could not have been called "perverse and iniquitous" by the Pope. It is more likely that it was akin to the Pagan philosophy, and that by denying the descent of all men from Adam, it was in opposition to the Catholic doctrines of the fall and redemption of man. Finally, it is impossible that either of these Virgils could have been the great Irish Apostle of Carinthia, for his biographer says that after leaving Ireland, he lived for many years at Cressy in Neustria, till he was appointed Bishop of Salzburg by Pepin, A.D. 764, when he came to Bavaria; but being very reluctant to accept the dignity, he was not consecrated till two years later. No mention is made of his ever having seen S. Boniface, nor of his having gone to Rome, much less of his having been summoned thither to be tried for heresy, nor of his having intrigued and "wickedly" in order to obtain the other Bavarian bishopric which fell vacant nearly twenty years earlier.

CHAPTER XVII.DEVELOPMENT OF MONASTIC LIFE

The more perfect development of monastic life was one of the objects to which Boniface at this time directed his attention. For though his monasteries at Fritzlar, Ohrdruf, and many other places, were in a nourishing state, yet as the missionary work was the primary object of their foundation, it had not been possible to combine with it the contemplative life and the pursuit of learning, to the full extent that the Benedictine rule enjoined. While he was turning this subject in his thoughts, a circumstance occurred which opened the way to the attainment of his wishes.

Mention has already been made of Sturm, the noble Bavarian boy who was given by his parents to Boniface, and after traveling about with him for a time, was left at Fritzlar in charge of S. Wigbert. Here the beauty of his countenance, his sweet and recollected deportment, his rare wisdom and depth of thought, flowing from his unceasing meditation of Scripture, united to great humility, purity, charity, and affability, greatly endeared him to his brethren.

As soon as he was old enough, and apparently even before the usual age, he was ordained a priest at the unanimous desire of the community. For three years he preached with remarkable success, his miraculous gifts of healing the sick and driving out demons adding power to his words, and his loving spirit compelling even the most deadly enemies to be reconciled to each other.

At the end of that time the desire to lead a more austere life in solitude, came to him, and, after some consideration he mentioned it to Boniface, who joyfully accepted this indication of God's will.

Boniface accordingly chose two monks to be Sturm's companions, and giving them his blessing, he said to them, "Go into the wilderness called Buchonia, and look out for a suitable place for the servants of God to dwell in; for God is able to prepare a place in the desert for His servants." The three monks accordingly set forth, and entering the forest, they found themselves in a wild solitude where nothing but sky, and earth, and endless avenues of huge trees, was to be seen. For three days they traveled along till they came to the place since called Hersfeld. After carefully exploring all around this spot, they prayed God to bless it for their habitation, and building a hut, they settled themselves down to serve God by prayers, vigils, and fasts.

After some time Sturm left his companions and went to Boniface, whom he told about the place they had selected, describing its position, the soil, the streams and springs, the hills and valleys in the neighborhood, and all the other particulars. Boniface took careful note of all these details but he would not give any answer for some days, during which he infused spirit and courage into Sturm by frequent conferences with him on Holy Scripture. At length he said to him, "I fear the place which you have fixed on, is too near the Saxons. Go, therefore, and seek for a spot farther in the depths of the forest, where you may dwell in greater safety."

Far from being discouraged by this decision Sturm returned to his companions, whom he found in some anxiety on account of his long absence. But he soon revived their spirits by the messages he brought them from Boniface. They now built a rough boat, in which they went up the river Fulda, stopping wherever a stream running into it, showed the existence of springs, and carefully exploring all the hills and valleys up and down the banks for a suitable site. Thus they went on, till on the third day they came to the spot where the river Ludera falls into the Fulda and the village of Ludermund now stands. But notwithstanding all their searching they had seen only one place, since called Rohenbach, which seemed at all likely to suit them and even that, they thought, would not satisfy their bishop. Accordingly they returned to their little hermitage, where they resumed their round of prayers, vigils, and fasts, beseeching our Lord to show them an abode in the wilderness where they could serve Him in peace and security.

Meanwhile Boniface had not forgotten his hermits and wondering what had been the result of their search, he sent a messenger to bid Sturm come to him. Sturm, humbly thanking God that so holy a bishop should have remembered him, started the next day, and found Boniface at the Abbey of Fritzlar. Boniface received him very affectionately, and giving him his blessing, kissed him, and making him sit down beside him, begged of him for his sake somewhat to relax the severity of his fast. To which Sturm answered with due discretion, "I believe every thing to be holy which you shall order for me." Then the table was laid, and Sturm ate of the food which was set before him. As soon as he had finished and the dish was removed, Boniface took him to his private room, where he was in the habit of discussing spiritual matters with his monks, and began to question him as to his search. Then Sturm said, "We sailed up the river Fulda for several days, but we found no place that I should venture to recommend." But Boniface answered, "The place in that solitude is indeed prepared by God, which, when our Lord wills, He will show to His servants. Wherefore cease not your search, knowing and believing that without doubt you will find it there."

Once more Sturm returned to his companions, greatly encouraged by Boniface s prophetic words, and animated by a still greater desire for the contemplative life through the spiritual conferences they had had together. As soon as he was rested from his journey he mounted his ass, and taking with him a small supply of food, he set off alone in search of the wished for abode. Day after day, from dawn till nightfall he journeyed through the dark forest, cutting his way through close thickets of brushwood and brambles, meeting no sign of human creature, but coming frequently on the track of bears, wolves, and other wild animals, and seeing flocks of wild birds circling round his head, and breaking the solemn silence by their varied cries. And ever as he went along he recited psalms, or raised up his heart in prayer to God. When night closed in he cut down some of the young trees, and formed a fence round his ass to protect it from the wild beasts; and then, making the sign of the Cross on his forehead, he lay down and slept in peace.

Thus he proceeded till he came to the place by which traders were wont to pass from Thuringia to Mayence and at the spot at which the road crosses the Fulda he found a great multitude of Slaves bathing in the river, swimming and sporting in the stream, and amusing themselves by singing obscene songs and vile language. The sight of their naked bodies terrified the poor ass so that it began to tremble and its saintly rider was no less horrified at the disgusting smell, which his spiritual senses perceived to be emitted from their sinful souls. When they saw the monk s habit they began to hoot, as was the custom of the Pagans, and they were about to attack him but being restrained by God they contented themselves with asking whither he was bound and finding that he was only going into the depths of the forest, they let him pass unmolested.

After journeying on through the wildest solitudes, he came on the evening of the fourth day to the place, below the confluence of the Gysilaha, or Giesel, with the Fulda, where the town of Fulda now stands. As he was looking out for some high ground he passed farther on to Aihloha, i. e. the oak-grove, which lay on a path called Ortessueca, or Ortesweg, from its leading to the dwelling of Count Ortis or Orcis. As the sun was now set, he resolved to pass the night there, and began to make the usual fence for his ass. While he was thus employed he heard a noise, and being in doubt whether it proceeded from man or beast, he stood listening for a few seconds but being still unable to make up his mind and not liking to shout aloud, he struck a blow with his axe on the trunk of a tree. Hereupon a man came running up and saluted him. It turned out that he was coming from Wetterau, and was leading his master Count Ortis s horse. They spent the night amicably together on that spot, and as the man was very well acquainted with the forest, he told Sturm the names of the various parts of it and all about the streams and springs, and many other useful details.

The next morning the stranger went on his way and Sturm resumed his explorings. He did not like the place where he had spent the night, so he passed on to the river Grezibach or Grezbach. Then retracing his steps to a spot which he had already visited, and which was to be the site of the monastery, he was suddenly filled with such extraordinary interior joy, that he instantly arrived at the conclusion that this must be the place which our Lord had predestined for him. He spent the rest of the day examining the locality, and the more he saw of it the more charmed was he with its beauty and suitableness; and when evening drew on he blessed and marked the spot, and then turned his steps back to the hermitage rejoicing.

The next day he rejoined his companions, who had been praying incessantly for his success; and after telling them all about the place that he had found, he bade them prepare to remove thither, while he hastened to Seleheim, where he hoped to hear of Boniface. As Boniface was constantly moving about, Sturm had to follow him from place to place. But when after some days they met, and Sturm described his future forest home, Boniface exclaimed joyfully, "You have indeed found the very spot that we wished for." He kept Sturm with him for a few days, during which he spoke much to him about the contemplative life, and incited him to more fervent aspirations after communion with God. And at length he sent him back to the forest, while he himself went to the court to obtain possession of the land.

Sturm now took his companions from Hersfeld to Aihloha. But here a difficulty met them. For some ill-disposed persons had been stirred up to dispute with them the site which Sturm had first chosen and as the monks could not contest their claim, they moved on to another spot at no great distance called Chrylhari or Drylhar.

Meanwhile Boniface had sought an audience of Carloman and asked him to give him the place in the Buchonian forest on the banks of the Fulda, called Aihloha, telling him that he wished to build on it a monastery of quite a different character from any which had ever been erected to the east of the Ehine. Carloman willingly granted his request, and assembling all the principal persons of his court, with their consent he gave Boniface a deed of gift, making over to him a tract of land of four thousand paces each way. He then sent a messenger with Boniface to assemble the chief men of the district, called Grabfeld, within which Aihloha lay; and all of them with one accord made over to Sturm, who had repaired to the meeting, whatever rights they had to the place. This first charter is lost, but another drawn out by Boniface about three years later, A.D. 747, fully describing the property belonging to the abbey and signed by Carloman and Pepin, still exists. There is also extant a deed of Pope Zachary's, A.D. 751, granting to the abbey the privilege of being under the protection of the Apostolic See, and freeing it from all other jurisdiction.

Sturm with his companions and several other monks, who had joined the little community, took possession of their property on the 12th of January, A.D. 744. They now divided their time between prayer and manual labor, serving our Lord on the one hand day and night by fasts, vigils, psalms, and holy meditations, and on the other by hard work, felling the oaks and clearing the ground. At the end of two months Boniface made his first visit to the place, accompanied by a host of workmen. The site corresponded in every way to his wishes and expectations. Filled with joy and gratitude he set his workmen to clear the ground, and erect a church dedicated to our Lord by the name of S. Salvator, with cells for the monks. For one week the forest rung with the blows of hundreds of axes. Giant oaks and pines were felled huge piles of brushwood were heaped up; and a clear open space was laid bare. So vigorously did all work, that at the end of the week Boniface was able to leave his monks to carry on the building of their church and monastery without further help. Giving them his blessing he departed with his work men, and the forest returned to its primeval silence, broken only by the sweet chanting of the Divine office at the fixed hours of the day and night, and by the works of the monks during the hours of manual labor.

A year passed away in this calm and holy solitude; each day was like its predecessor and its successor and yet each day found the monks only more and more happy and devoted to this sweet, changeless round of holy contemplation. At the end of the year Boniface can again to visit them, and was much pleased with their progress. He took great pains to imbue all of them, and especially Sturm, who was their abbot, with the true spirit of S. Benedict, and to lead them on to the stricter observances to which he had been accustomed in England, and which he hoped to introduce through them into Germany. After a short stay he blessed them and departed. But he often revisited them and stayed with them as long as his other duties permitted. On these occasions he would take his part both in the choir and in their manual labors. Often he would shut himself up in a little cell, which he had built for himself on an adjoining hill, long called the Bischofsberg, where he would remain rapt in intimate communion with our Lord, or absorbed in the study of the deep mysteries of Holy Scripture.

At the end of four years the monks thought it would be well to send one of the brethren to study the Benedictine rule more perfectly at the fountain-head. Boniface approved of the plan, and appointed Sturm to carry it out. Accordingly Sturm, accompanied by two of his brethren, set out for Italy, where they spent a year, visiting Monte Cassino and the most celebrated monasteries at Rome and other places. At the end of that time they returned to Germany; and as soon as Sturm was recovered from a dangerous illness, which detained him four weeks at

Kissingen on the Main, he hastened to Boniface, who was now in Thuringia. Boniface was so pleased with Sturm s report of what he had heard and observed, that he said to him, "Go and teach the new community at Fulda, as much as you like of that monastic life which you have witnessed." He also at this time sent him to England to obtain further help for the promotion of monastic life among women, of which more will be said hereafter.

As soon as Sturm was again settled at Fulda, he set to work to train his brethren in the correct traditions of the Benedictine order, which he had learned in the Italian monasteries. He was always the first to practice what he imposed on others and his monks were animated by so fervent a spirit and by such a desire to follow the example of the saints that they responded generously to his teaching. The fame of their saintly discipline drew many novices to them, and numerous communities were established under the strict Benedictine rule.

One of the earliest of these was that of Heidenheim, founded by S. Winibald. On his arrival in Germany Boniface had set him over seven churches in Thuringia, in the charge of which he was assisted by the disciples who had followed him from England and Rome, and others who placed themselves under his rule. After some years he went into Bavaria, where he was well received by Duke Odilo, and preached for three years with great success.

He then went to Mayence, where Boniface was now Archbishop. His eloquence drew many, both men and women, noble and simple, to the love of God, some of whom he guided to the highest spiritual life while others he fed like children with the pure milk of God s Word. Honor and veneration met him on every side but rapt as he ever was in contemplation, living and conversing always with God, human praise and worldly honors had no power over him. He continued as humble as before, always calm and gentle, and the only thing which could disturb him was the obduracy of sinners. Strange indeed was it to see, how one so sweet and recollected would be stirred to indignation by the sight of sin, so that the severity of his reproofs would strike terror into the most obdurate hearts. For as sin is the only thing which God cannot tolerate in this beautiful world of His own creation, so Winibald, living ever in union with God, saw sin as God sees it, and recoiled from it as the thing most hateful to God.

But Mayence did not suit him. He feared for his monks the luxury of a capital, and especially the super abundance of Ehine wine. He therefore began to consider whether he should not serve God with more profit in some retired place, where he could devote himself to the contemplative life. With Boniface s permission he gave up the charge of his churches in

Thuringia and on the Rhine and by the advice of his brother Willibald, now Bishop of Eichstedt, he bought a piece of land in his diocese on which to build a monastery. It was a valley in the Salafeld, near the source of the Danube, buried between high mountains, covered with thick forests, well watered by springs and rushing streams, and so perfectly secluded that it was appropriately called Heidenheim, or the home in the wild. The neighboring proprietors added gifts of land in return for the monks, prayers, and thus a considerable domain gradually came into the hands of the community.

Winibald was forty-six years of age when, A.D. 750, he took possession of Heidenheim. His health had long been weak, and now his rheumatic infirmity was becoming so bad, that before very long it quite crippled him. Notwithstanding he joined his monks in their attack on the forest, helping them, axe in hand, to fell the oaks and pines, or carrying the uprooted thistles and brambles in his arms or on his back to the heap where they were to be burned. Thus a clearing was made, and a few temporary huts were erected. The church was their next care then came the monastery and when all was completed, he placed his monks under the rule of S. Benedict, and taught them to follow it perfectly, as he had himself been accustomed to do in the convent in Rome in which he had spent his youth.

Thus happily settled in his peaceful forest-home, Winibald did not forget the souls who were wander ing like sheep without a shepherd in the wilderness. Though Heidenheim stood in a perfect solitude, there was at no great distance a wild population, whose souls, during the long contest between Bavarians and Franks for the Nordgau, of which this district was a part, had not been cared for. Some were still Pagans; others, though nominally Christians, had married their near relatives, or were living in gross sin; and all were given to the practice of magic, divination, and various sorts of devilry. In spite of threats and violence, Winibald separated all who had formed unlawful marriages or immoral connexion, and day and night he strove to prevent all demoniacal practices. So great was the stir that he made, that the wild people around him often tried to kill him and plotted to burn his monastery. But he feared neither their threats nor their power, and went on calmly and boldly, scattering the seed of God's Word far and wide, and winning innumerable souls by the sweetness of love and the severity of zeal, by the wisdom of the serpent and the simplicity of the dove. Those whom he wounded by his zeal he healed by his gentleness and compassion and remembering the saying, "He will not be heard lovingly who does not love," he was as a brother to all who were in trouble, and by his loving piety led the docile in the ways of truth and peace.

Year by year Winibald advanced higher and higher in spiritual perfection. Tenderly and lovingly he ruled his monks as a father, supplying all the needs of both their bodies and their souls; and generously he extended his paternal care to all the poor and the serfs on his domain, to all their relatives, and all whom he fell in with. So constantly was he occupied with thoughts of God that he seldom or never ceased to praise Him in psalms, lections, or expositions of Scripture; and whether he ate, or drank, or whatever he did, the words of Holy Writ which were treasured up in his heart, ever welled forth on his lips.

Nor was it co-enobites alone who magnified God in this wild. Hermits also took their part in singing His praises. There was a monk, called Sola or Solus, who had been Boniface's pupil in England, and had followed him to Germany. Boniface ordained him priest, and employed him as a missionary but he had so decided a vocation for the eremitic life, that after some time Boniface allowed him to retire into solitude. He settled himself on the confines of Bavaria, on an almost inaccessible height in the Salafeld hemmed in by rocks and pines, and so sterile that nothing but rye would grow on it. In this retreat, since called Solenhus, or Solenhofen, he attained to the closest union with God. But crowds, attracted by his miraculous gifts, disturbed his solitude; and others with a like vocation to his, placed themselves on his barren rock. Winibald gave him a piece of land at Altheim, and Charlemagne liberally endowed the eremitic foundation, which was gradually formed round his cell. He was much attached to Willibald and Winibald, and also to Boniface, for love of whom he bequeathed his property at Altheim to the Abbey of Fulda. On his death at a very advanced age, A.D. 790, he was chosen to be one of the patron saints of the diocese of Eichstedt.

CHAPTER XVIII.ENGLISH NUNS

Boniface's work would indeed have been incomplete had he not extended his care to that sex, whom our Blessed Lady has raised to such honor, and whose ministrations the Church has always prized. More over, women exerted so much influence on German society that he could not afford to lose their aid.

His warm friendship for many English nuns has already been mentioned, and extracts from his correspondence with Eadburga, Abbess of Wimburn, have been given. In his public work he is seen to move along with a calm, heroic air, as if reft of all personal individuality, and animated only by that supernatural force of which he was the humble instrument. But his relations with these nuns have a peculiar interest, for in them appears that tender, sympathetic human nature, which gave him great influence over all who crossed his path.

Among Boniface s correspondents was another Eadburga, or Heaburg, surnamed Bugga, who was a relative of Ethelbert II, King of Kent, and therefore, no doubt a descendant of S. Ethelbert and S. Bertha. She is, moreover, supposed to have been the S. Eadburga who succeeded S. Mildreda as Abbess of Thanet. The first letter of this correspondence from Bugga, about A.D. 719, has been already given. Its tone is that of filial confidence, asking Boniface to write out portions of Scripture for her use, and expressing confidence in his prayers. The next is from her mother, Cangyth or Eangyth, conjointly with herself under the name of "Heaburg, surnamed Bugga," and both are styled abbesses. It is addressed to him as "the venerable priest Winfred," and must therefore have been written before A.D. 724. It is interesting to hear what were the trials of an abbess in the eighth century and to notice the confidence with which the old woman pours out her wail, feeling sure that she addresses one who will sympathize with her. "Dearest brother," she writes, "our brother in the spirit though not in the flesh, and exalted by so many spiritual graces, we wish to confide to you alone, with God for our sole witness, that these lines are bathed with our tears because we are weighed down with a load of accumulated misfortunes and the agitations of worldly matters. What afflicts us more than all exterior things, is the remembrance of our sins and the absence of all perfect good works and besides the care of our own souls, there is the far heavier charge of so many souls of both sexes and all ages, and of various characters and habits, which have been committed to us, and for whose actions, words, and even secret thoughts, hidden to men but open to God, we shall have to give account at Christ's judgment seat. To which must be added domestic difficulties, and the disputes which the enemy of all good sows among men, and especially in monasteries and religious communities. And because those in power suffer the most, we are in great straits on account of our poverty, our scarcity of temporal things, the narrow limits of our lands, and the accusations of those who envy us. There are also the exactions of the king and queen, the bishop and ealdorman, their officers and servants, all of which it would be too long to enumerate. Added to which there is the loss of a great many friends and relatives. We have neither son nor brother, father nor uncle, but one only daughter, who has no other relatives than a very aged mother and her sister, and a brother s son, who is very unhappy on our account and without any fault of his own, but because our king hates our family. We have no other relatives, for God has taken them in different ways. Some have died in their native land. Others left their home and trusting themselves to the waves, sought the threshold of the Apostles Peter and Paul and of the multitude of martyrs, virgins, and confessors, whose number and names God alone knows.

"From all these and many similar causes, which a whole day, even though it were a long summer s day, would suffice not to relate, we are weary of our life and almost tired of existence. Every one who is in adversity and mistrusts his own judgment, seeks a faithful friend, in whose advice he confides, and to whom he opens out all the secrets of his heart. We have long sought such a friend, and we trust that we have found in you him we wished and hoped for. Therefore we want you to know, brother Boniface, that we have long wished to go to Borne, the mistress of the world, there to obtain pardon for our sins, as so many of our relatives and others have done and are now doing. And I especially, who am the older and have committed most sins, desire this which wish of mine was known in times past to the Abbess Wala, and to my only daughter, who was then very young and did not share my feelings. But because we know that many persons blame this wish, and say that the canons order every one to remain in the place in which he was professed, and took his vows, in our uncertainty we both prostrate ourselves at your feet, and beseech you to support us with the help of your prayers that through you God may show us what will be best and most profitable for us, whether to remain in our native land, or to become exiles on pilgrimage. Farewell, spiritual brother, loved with a most faithful, warm, sincere, and pure love. May you prosper in the love of God. A friend has to be long sought, to be hardly found, and to be kept with difficulty. Pray for us that we may not be punished for our sins."

There are extant two letters 3 from Boniface, which might be taken as answers to this letter and the previous one from Bugga, because they refer to the same subjects. But they were evidently written some years later, when Boniface was a bishop, and Cangyth, whose name does not appear, was probably dead, and Bugga, wearied with her trials, had resigned the charge of her double monastery. The first of these letters to Bugga, expresses sympathy for the "tempests of manifold tribulations which God had allowed to come upon her in her old age." "I sighed," he writes, "in sorrow and sadness, considering that so many more and greater trials should have met you after you had cast aside the principal cares of your monasteries in order to lead a quiet and contemplative life. Now then, venerable sister, compassionating your tribulations and remembering your gifts and our ancient friendship, I send you this brotherly letter of exhortation and consolation." He then goes on to encourage her to be patient and even to rejoice in her tribulations, which will add in her old age to the beauty and loveliness, of her soul, which in her youth she vowed to Christ her Spouse so that when He comes, she may merit to go forth to meet Him with her lamp full of oil and brightly burning in her hand.

The other letter seems to have been written between A.D. 732 and 738, when the Saracens were ravaging France and threatening Rome. It is as follows:

"To the well -beloved lady and sister preferred in the love of Christ above all other women, the Abbess Bugga, Boniface, unworthy bishop in Christ, health."

"Be it known to you, dearest sister that I cannot presume either to forbid or to persuade you to under take the pilgrimage, about which you asked my advice in your letters. But I will say how it appears to me. If in order to obtain peace and communion with God, you have laid aside the cares that you formerly had about the monks and nuns and the monasteries, why should you wait with labor and wearying anxiety on the words and will of secular men? It seems to me that if, on account of seculars, you can in no way have freedom and a quiet mind in your own country, it would be better that you should gain the liberty of contemplation by a pilgrimage, if you wish and can make it. This is what our sister Wiethberga did; and she writes to me that she has found on the threshold of S. Peter the peaceful life that she had long sought. As to your wish, about which I had written to her, she says that you should wait till the rebellions, attacks and threats of the Saracens, which not long since occurred among the Romans, are put down, when she will send you letters of invitation. It therefore seems to me that it will be best to make your preparations for the journey, and to wait till you hear from her and then do what the goodness of our Lord shall order. As to the extracts which you asked for, you must pardon my sins. On account of my urgent labors and continued journeys I have not yet quite written what you asked but when they are finished I will take care to send them to you. Thanking you for your gift of vestments, I beseech Almighty God to give you an eternal reward with angels and archangels in the highest heaven. I entreat you, dearest sister, or rather sweetest mother and lady, to pray diligently for me, because for my sins I am worn out by many trials and agitated much more by mental tribulations and anxieties than by bodily labors. Be assured that our old friendship never fails. Farewell in Christ."

Bugga made the pilgrimage to Rome, where she met Boniface, A.D. 738, and consulted him about her affairs. She afterwards returned to England, where she probably led a more peaceful life than in former years, as she appears to have been on better terms with Ethelbert II, King of Kent, than with his predecessor. This may be inferred from the way in which Ethelbert mentions her in a letter, which he wrote to Boniface, asking- him to send him two falcons of a very fine kind, which were very rare in Kent. She died about A.D. 760, when Bregowin, Archbishop of Canterbury, wrote at her request to inform Lullus of her death, reminding him that S. Boniface had been her father and patron.

There is another letter 6 addressed to "Winfred, the holy abbot" by Egburga, the last of his disciples, of whom nothing more is known. It exhibits most beautifully how these English women retained the passion and force, and a certain dash of melancholy, which belonged to their barbarian nature, though softened and purified by grace and Christian education. It runs thus: "Ever since I have been united to you by the tie of affection, my soul has felt a savor of inexpressible sweetness. And though I am debarred from your bodily presence I never cease to encircle you with sisterly embraces. Formerly you were my dear brother, but now in the Lord of lords you are both my father and my brother. For since cruel death has taken away my brother, whom I loved above all, I prefer you in loving charity to all other men. Day and night I remember your lessons, and be assured, God is my witness, that I embrace you with extreme affection; and I am confident that you never forgot the friendship that you had for my brother. I am very inferior to him in knowledge and merit, but I am in no way behind him in affection for you. Though a long time has since then elapsed, the black cloud of grief has never left me but the longer I live the more I suffer; as it is written. The love of man brings sorrow, but the love of Christ illumines the heart."

"My heart has been wounded afresh by the loss of my Wechburg. She vanished suddenly from my sight, she with whom I had grown up, who had been nursed at the same breast, and had

had the same mother as myself, leaving, Jesus be my witness."

"I wished to die, if it had pleased God. But it was a more cruel separation than death that divided us she, indeed, happy, but I unhappy, who am left as a pledge in the service of the world. You know how I loved her, and now I hear that she is shut up in some prison in Rome. But the love of Christ which fills her heart is stronger and more powerful than bars and bolts, and perfect love casts out fear. She walks in the hard and narrow way, while I still lie in the depths bound by the law of the flesh. In the Day of Judgment she will sing joyfully with our Lord, I was in prison, and you visited me. You, too, in the resurrection will sit where the twelve Apostles will be seated on twelve thrones, and then you will rejoice as a glorious chief, for all the souls that you will have led through your labors to the tribunal of the Eternal King. But I still in this valley of tears, as is my due, weep for my sins, which have rendered me unworthy of such companions Therefore I, sinner that I am, prostrate at your feet, cry to you, blessed lord, from the bottom of my heart, and implore you to raise me up through your prayers, for you are my hope, and my tower of strength from visible and invisible foes. To console my immense grief, to soothe my sorrow, I beseech you to support my weakness, and to send me some solace, either by holy relics, or at least by some words written by your own hand, that through these I may always have you present to me."

Such was the ardent and devoted character of the abbesses and nuns to whom Boniface wrote after he became a bishop, inviting them to come and help their sisters in their old German home. They generously and joyfully responded to his call, and flocked to him in great numbers. But when and whence they came, where they settled, and how they toiled, is not known. Even the names of all except nine are lost, and of only two of these, S. Walburga and S. Lioba, have any particulars been preserved. But this obscurity is their greatest glory, since it unites them the more closely to the hidden life of their Immaculate prototype, the Virgin Mother of Nazareth.

Opinions are divided as to the time of their arrival in Germany. Some suppose that the greater number went over about A.D. 724; others, that they founded their principal convents shortly previous to A.D. 732 and others again, that very few had arrived before A.D. 748. That some had come before A.D. 738 is evident from the letter's which Boniface wrote from Rome to "all his brothers and sisters." But the unsettled state of the country, the frequent invasions of the Saxons, and the absence of either fixed bishop or civil ruler to afford them protection, render it probable that only a few went over before A.D. 748, when S. Walburga and S. Lioba are generally believed to have arrived.

It will be remembered that when S. Richard went on pilgrimage, he sent his wife and daughter to the Abbey of Wimburn. Here S. Walburga grew up under the care of S. Cuthburga, S. Coenburga, Eadburga, and Tetta, and in the society of her relative S. Lioba. She was taught the usual feminine works, especially a beautiful kind of embroidery in gold and silver, pearls and precious stones then known as English work. She also acquired such proficiency in Latin that in after years she wrote in that language the lives of her brothers, thus winning the honor of being the first English or German authoress. She spent twenty-seven years at Wimburn, during which time she must often have heard of her uncle Boniface s work in Germany, and she must have seen her brother Winibald when he was in England. No doubt, too, she heard about the nuns who first went abroad, some even whom she knew may have gone from Wimburn. But the thought of rejoining her nearest relatives in Germany never crossed her mind, till, in the year 748, Sturm came with a letter from Boniface to the Abbess Tetta, asking her to send Walburga, Lioba, and as many more of her nuns as would come, to help him with his work.

On hearing the invitation Walburga instantly retired to her cell to pray, when she came to the conclusion that the call was from God, and that she must not delay to obey it. Joyfully she hastened the preparations for her departure; and as the community at Wimburn numbered five hundred, and they were both rich and generous, she was soon ready to start with thirty companions.

The heroic band sailed with a fair wind and calm sea, but before long a storm arose, huge billows washed over the little vessel, and the sailors threw the cargo overboard to lighten her. But all was in vain, and death was each moment impending. Here upon Walburga, kneeling down on the deck, besought Him who rules the waves to calm the storm and to save them for the sake of His Son and her father S. Richard. Then rising bold in faith, she commanded the wind and the waves to be still, and they obeyed her. Soon after they came safely to the land, where the sailors proclaiming what they had beheld, Walburga was greeted wherever she passed with joy and veneration. But she meditated only on God s love and mercy, and rejoicing in Him alone she hastened on to Germany.

At Mayence she was received with great affection by Boniface and Willibald. But her heart yearned for her brother Winibald, whom alone of all her family she had long known and loved, and whose contemplative spirit was akin to her own. After a time Boniface sent her and her companions on to him in Thuringia, where he placed them in a convent attached to one of his churches, which was known even till the fourteenth century as the "Cocnobium S. Walpurgis."

But this was intended to be only their temporary home. For as soon as Winibald had finished his own monastery at Heidenheim, he and his monks set to work to build at a convenient distance a convent for Walburga. It was finished A.D. 752, when she and her nuns took possession of it. Both monks and nuns were governed by Winibald, under the regulations usual in double cloisters, and after his death the government of both monasteries devolved on Walburga. In this happy house of prayer in the wild, the saintly pair advanced from day to day in love to God and their neighbor, being especially remarkable for their spirit of compassion and generosity. The Abbey of Heidenheim was the refuge of all who were in want or in sorrow, and none who came there went away unconsoled. And when Winibald and Walburga saw that their lands were greatly increased, they gave the meadows on the adjoining hills to the poor who cultivated them, considering nothing as their own, but holding both themselves and all they possessed as the servants of God and of the poor.

Two incidents which occurred after Winibald's death attest Walburga s humility and sanctity. One evening, after vespers were over, she stayed alone to pray in the church of the monastery until it was late and the darkness closed in, when she arose from her prayers to return to her cell, and asked the sexton of the church, whose name was Goumerand, to light her to it. But the churlish monk refused. The abbess then meekly retired to her cell without a light, patiently taking the affront and the hour of the evening meal having passed, she remained without having supped. In the night the sisters were roused by a supernatural light streaming from Walburga s cell and illumining all the dormitory. Startled and terrified, they watched the strange sight which continued until the stroke of the bell for matins, when they gathered round Walburga and with wonder and fear told her what they had seen. Bursting into tears, she thanked God for the heavenly visitation which had been vouchsafed her, and ascribed it solely to the prayers and merits of her brother Winibald, through whom, she said, the contempt put on her had been turned to honor.

At another time, "late of an evening, while she yet mourned for her brother Winibald, she went out un attended and unobserved, and moved by a Divine impulse, she wandered to some distance to the house of a neighboring baron, whose daughter lay dying. There she stood at the door like a vagrant beggar, not venturing, through meekness, to pass within and present herself.

The baron was a huntsman of the forest, and his wolfhounds, hungry and fierce, gathered round the door of the hall about Walburga. Seeing her standing there, and in danger, as he supposed, of being torn down by the dogs, the rough huntsman asked angrily who she was, and what she wanted there. The abbess replied, that he need not fear the dogs would not touch Walburga; He who had brought her safe there would take her again safe home and from Him she was come to be a physician to his house, if he had faith to believe in Him, the great Physician. The baron, on hearing her name, started hastily from his seat, and asking why so noble a lady and a servant of God stood outside his door, he prayed her to enter and led her in with much respect. She said she was not come without a cause, and she would pass the night in his daughter's chamber. Thither she was led. The girl lay expiring, the death-chill was already upon her, and she was sobbing convulsively in the last struggle. The father groaned and burst into tears; the heart-broken mother hung over her child in agony; and the weeping servants prepared the grave. Walburga knelt and prayed, continuing all night in prayer and God restored the soul of the maiden, so that in the morning she arose in perfect health. The parents, full of gratitude and astonished at the miracle, tremblingly offered rich presents to Walburga, but she refused them, and returned on foot to the monastery. The more she received these signs of heavenly favor, the more she humiliated and dealt hardly with her self."

CHAPTER XIX.ENGLISH NUNS

Close as was Walburga s natural tie to Boniface, Lioba, who also was his relative, was still more closely united to him by spiritual affection. Both her parents, Tinne and Ebbe, were advanced in years and childless, when one night Ebbe dreamt that she gave birth to a church bell, which rang as she held it in her hand. On waking she consulted the aged slave who had nursed her as to the meaning of her dream and the old nurse told her that she would have a daughter, whom she must dedicate to our Lord to serve Him in holy virginity as long as she lived. In due time a daughter was born, and the happy parents, in their joy, gave freedom to the old slave who had foretold her birth. The child was baptized Truthgeba, but she was afterwards called Leobgytha, or Lioba, because she was greatly loved and as soon as she was old enough her parents gave her to God and the Abbey of Wimburn.

The abbey was then governed by Tetta, who had a great reputation for sanctity and the strict discipline she maintained in her double cloister. Great need had she for vigilance and prayer; for many of the five hundred nuns, to say nothing of the monks, whom she ruled, retained their passionate, barbarian nature, as will appear from the following incidents, which also attest her sanctity.

There was in the community a nun who, being austere in her own life, was often elected to fill various high offices. But being indiscreet in her government of others, she came to be hated by almost all her sisters, and especially by the younger nuns who suffered most from her undue severity. The painful consciousness of the odium which she had excited only made her gloomy and morose and becoming more and more severe and repulsive, even on her death-bed no gentle feeling softened her heart. Thus she died and was buried, and over her last resting-place a mound of earth was raised. But so bitter was the hatred of the younger nuns towards her that they rushed to her grave and cursing her cruelty to them, jumped on the mound above her with expressions of insult and rejoicing till the earth had sunk down six inches under their feet. When Tetta came to the spot and saw what had happened, she was struck with horror at the conduct of her nuns, and still more at the thought of the sufferings of this poor soul in Purgatory, of which she considered the sinking of the grave to be a sign. Assembling the community, she reproved the offenders for their barbarity and unchristian feeling; and when their hearts were touched she induced them to join in a tri-duo of fasting and prayer for the departed soul. At the end of three days solemn litanies were chanted while Tetta lay prostrate before the altar. As she wept and prayed the earth on the grave was seen to rise gradually, till as she got up from her knees the hollow was found to be quite filled, which all looked on as a token that her saintly prayers had been heard.

It happened one night that the sister who had charge of the church, on rising to summon the community to prayer, could not find her bunch of keys, some of which were of silver and others of brass or iron, according to the diversity of the treasures which they guarded. After long fruitless search she went to the abbess, and with tears confessed her fault. But Tetta, perceiving that the loss was only a device of the devil to shut her nuns out of the church, calmly bade them go to another chapel, where they chanted the nocturns with due solemnity. When the Office was ended they all knelt in prayer before the closed door of their church and suddenly a young wolf ran past and was seen to fall down dead, and in its mouth was found the lost keys. Then Tetta, opening the door of the church, went in at the head of her nuns, and they all sang joyful praises to .Him who had mercifully heard His children who placed their trust in Him.

Under the care of this holy abbess Lioba grew up. From her earliest years she took no pleasure in childish plays or foolish stories but inflamed with the love of Jesus, her only delight was to read or hear God's word and meditate on it. She was very temperate in eating and drinking, despising all delicacies, taking cheerfully what was given her, and wishing for nought else. She was never idle, and whenever she was not praying, she was busy either reading or working but she preferred reading to work, and even when she was at work her thoughts were occupied with the words of Scripture that she had read or heard. She was always remarked on account of her humble and affectionate disposition, loving her sisters tenderly, obeying them all, trying to imitate the peculiar virtues of each, but, above all, striving to acquire charity, without which she knew that all other virtues were nought.

After many years it came to pass, that one night she saw in a dream a purple thread come out of her mouth. She put up her hand to remove it, but as she tried to do so, a still longer thread appeared, and the more she drew out, the more still seemed to remain within. Soon her hand was full, and she began to wind it into a ball but it ever grew longer and longer, and seemed to be endless, till at last, heated and wearied, she awoke. She felt sure that this must be a vision, and that it had some hidden meaning, but she had no idea what it was.

There was in the convent a nun of mature age who was believed to have the gift of prophecy. Not liking to consult this nun herself, she told her dream to one of the young girls under her care, and bade her go and ask the old nun about it, as if it had been her own. The girl did as she was bid but as soon as the nun heard the dream, she exclaimed indignantly, "It is indeed a true vision, and portends good. But why do you tell a lie about it?" Such things do not befit you but the chosen of God and beloved referring to the name Lioba. "They have been shown to her to whose holiness and wisdom they are suitable. The thread which came out of her mouth is the doctrine of wisdom, proceeding from her heart through the ministry of her voice. That it filled her hand signifies that she will do by her works whatsoever her mouth teaches. The ball which she made by winding, and which through its roundness rolled easily, expresses the mystery of God's word, which rolls along through the teaching of preachers, now going down to the depths through the active life, then mounting to the heights through contemplation, now humbling itself through compassion for a neighbor, and again rising through love to God. By these signs God shows that your mistress will profit many but it will be in a far distant place and among other nations, to whom she will have to go."

Boniface and his work were now the great objects of interest to the religious communities in England, and at Wimburn, where he was personally known and had many relatives and friends, his prosperous course caused much joy. Attached to him by the strong tie of blood and still stronger bond of spiritual communion, Lioba wrote him the following letter in Latin.

"To the most Reverend Lord Boniface, most dear in Christ, and united by the bonds of the highest dignities and of near relationship, Leobgytha, the last of the servants under the light yoke of Christ, health and eternal salvation."

"I entreat your clemency to deign to remember the friendship which bound you long ago in the west country to my father, Tinne. He died eight years ago. Refuse not to pray to God for his soul. I also commend to you my mother, Ebbe, who is, as you well know, united to you by the ties of blood. She still lives, but she is in difficulties, and is oppressed by her infirmities. I am the only child of both my parents. Would that, although unworthy, I might have you as a brother for there is no man among my kindred in whom I have trust and hope as in you. I send the accompanying little gift not that it is worthy of your acceptance, but in order that you may remember my littleness, and instead of consigning me to oblivion on account of the distance between us, a true affection may on the contrary link us together for eternity. Beloved brother, I earnestly beseech that your prayers may shield me from the poisonous darts of the hidden enemy. I beg you also to correct the rusticity of this letter, and not to refuse to send me, as a model, some words of friendship, for which I eagerly long. The under-written verses I have tried to compose according to the rules of the poetic art, not with bold confidence, but wishing to exercise my poor talent, and desiring your help. This art I learnt from my mistress Eadburga, who incessantly turns the Holy Scriptures into rhyme. Farewell. May you live long and happily, interceding for me." Then follow four lines of Latin verse.

The graceful gentleness and sweetness of this letter excite regret that it is the only one of Lioba s now extant. Boniface's answer, too, is lost and all further particulars of the correspondence are unknown.

At length, in the year 748, Sturm arrived at Wimburn with a forenamed letter from Boniface to Tetta, asking her to send him as a solace in his pilgrimage and a help in his mission, Lioba, the fame of whose sanctity was in every mouth. Tetta was reluctant to part with the most cherished one of her community but she could not resist what appeared to be God's will, and she granted Boniface s request. Though Lioba and Walburga went to Germany about the same time, they seem to have gone separately, each at the head of the party of nuns who were to form their respective communities.

Boniface received Lioba with love and veneration, for he foresaw how great a work she was to do by her example and teaching. He placed her with a large community at Bischofsheim on the Tauber; and he gave her authority over his other convents of women, in order that she might train all the nuns of Germany to the correct observance of the Benedictine rule. She succeeded so well with her task that her nuns at Bischofsheim were soon qualified to instruct others, and most of the convents in Germany sent for one of them to govern them.

Lioba is described as being a woman of heroic courage, who allowed no mere human consideration to interfere with any work that she had undertaken, but carried it through resolutely and perfectly in the sight of God and man. She was careful to impose nothing on others that she did not herself practice. Her countenance was angelic; her demeanor, in variably humble, courteous, and kind her conversation, cheerful; her intellect, clear; her judgment, excellent and her charity, unbounded. Though a look of joy ever beamed on her face she was never seen to laugh; nor was an angry word ever known to cross her lips. She ate hardly enough to satisfy the necessities of nature, and always drank out of a small glass, which her nuns in their peculiar Latin used to call, "Dilectae parvus," or "the little one of the beloved." But though herself so abstemious, she practiced hospitality in the true spirit of S. Benedict, washing the feet of strangers with her own hands, and feeding them generously while she herself was fasting. She was so fond of reading that whenever she was not working or praying she had a book in her hand.

She was careful that the community should take during the summer the mid-day sleep, which the rule orders, herself setting them the example and saying, "Want of sleep makes want of intellect, especially for reading." But both on these occasions and at night she would frequently make some one read to her while she slept, the younger nuns taking this office in turns, so as to avoid fatigue. But even in her sleep she would correct any mistake that they made, or if they ceased reading, which they often did purposely to try her, she would bid them go on. Thus was she able to say with the spouse in the Canticle, "I sleep, and my heart watch."

She was held in such veneration that her prayers were believed to have miraculous power. On one occasion, while she was reading the Scriptures with her pupils, a part of the outbuildings which were thatched with straw took fire, and the flames spread so rapidly that not only the whole abbey, but its in mates and the cattle, were in imminent danger. The affrighted nuns gathered round her and besought her to quench the fire by her prayers. But turning with humility from the suggestion, yet not the less strong in faith, she took some salt which S. Boniface had blest and of which she always kept a supply for holy water, and bade them throw it into the river and then draw the water to cast on the flames. They obeyed and scarcely did the water touch the fire than its fury was checked and it was suddenly extinguished, as if by rain from heaven.

On another occasion a violent hurricane with thunder, and lightning, and torrents of rain set in. The community and all the neighbors assembled in the church, and as the storm increased every moment the trembling crowd awaited in awe the judgments of God. At length, when it seemed as if the raging elements must overthrow the whole building, the people unable any longer to endure the suspense, rushed to the spot where Lioba knelt, and one of the nuns, called Thecla exclaimed, "O beloved, beloved, in thee is the hope of these people! Towards thee the vows of all turn. Rise, then, and invoke for us thy blessed Lady, the Mother of God, that by her intercession we may be delivered from this tempest." At these words Lioba rose from prayer, as if called to combat with the powers of the air. Throwing off her cloak she boldly opened the church-door, and standing on its threshold she made the sign of the Cross and invoked the Blessed Trinity. Then, stretching out her arms to heaven, she thrice called aloud to Jesus, beseeching Him of His mercy and through the intercession of His Virgin Mother, to come quickly to the succour of His people. Instantly the power of God appeared the thunder ceased, the wind was stilled, the dark clouds dispersed, the sky became serene, and the sun shone forth brightly.

Again; a very holy nun, called Willeswind, being very ill, her parents who lived close by, took her home to nurse her. She soon became worse, and as she was expiring her parents sent for the abbess to commend her departing soul. When Lioba arrived, passing through the crowd of weeping neighbors she went up to the bed, and bidding them remove the winding sheet which already covered Willeswind, who, they thought, was dead, she laid her hand on her and said, "Weep not, for her soul is still in her." She sent with haste to the abbey for a small spoon that she was in the habit of using, and with it she put a drop of milk into Willeswind's mouth. As soon as the milk touched the dying woman s throat, she opened her eyes, and began to speak. She now rallied so rapidly that the next day she was able to take strengthening food, and before the end of a week she walked to the abbey, whence she had been carried in a litter. She lived many years, surviving Lioba, and continuing to serve God in perfect health even till the reign of Louis le Debonnaire.

But the power of Lioba s faith and prayers shone forth most conspicuously under the following distressing circumstances. The abbey was built on the banks of the Tauber, so that the stream ran through the centre of the building, and thus the nuns were supplied with water and could grind their corn in their own mill without leaving their enclosure. One day a woman, going to draw water, found in the stream the body of a new-born babe. It is impossible to describe the horror and indignation that stirred the whole neighborhood at the double crime of unchastity and infanticide, to say nothing of the pollution of their stream, by the very women who had hitherto pretended, with hateful hypocrisy as it now appeared, to superior purity and sanctity. One of the nuns, called Agatha, having lately gone, with the permission of her superior, to her parents on important business, the crime was naturally imputed to her and she was the object of universal execration.

In this terrible conjuncture Lioba sent at once for Agatha, and when, on her arrival, she protested her innocence, the abbess summoned the whole community to the church to join in devotions for the clearing of their reputation. First they recited the whole Psalter, all standing with their arms extended in the form of a cross and then Lioba bade them make the circuit of the monastery at tierce, text, and none, chanting litanies in solemn procession, with the Cross borne be fore them. This they did at tierce and sext and at none they all assembled in the church and prepared to begin the processional chant. Then Lioba, going up to the Cross which stood at the altar, and stretching out her arms to heaven, cried with tears and sighs, "Lord Jesus Christ, King of virgins, lover of purity, unconquerable God, show Thy power, and deliver us from this infamy, for the reproach of those who revile Thee has fallen upon us." Scarcely had she spoken when a wretched woman, a cripple, who had long been daily fed and clothed by the nuns, crying out as if she were possessed by the devil and tortured in the flames of hell, confessed that the crime was hers. The nuns wept for joy, while the surrounding crowd proclaimed with one voice, the power of Christ our Savior and the virtue of Lioba, His virgin spouse. But though the unhappy sinner had thus been compelled to clear the nuns, no true contrition touched her heart, and she continued till her death in the wicked course on which she had entered.

But while Lioba was universally loved and revered, her humility and obedience led her to take no step, even in trifling matters of which she was the best judge, without asking permission of her spiritual superior, as appears in the following letter to her from Boniface.

"To Leobgytha, the venerable servant of Christ, eternally united to Him by sincere charity, Boniface, servant of the servants of God, the desirable salvation in Christ."

"Our brother and fellow priest, for that, tells us that you asked his mediation to obtain our consent to have for some time a certain girl who is skilful in work. Be assured that we are constantly favorably disposed, and consent to whatever your charity, after due consultation, shall consider best for the increase of your eternal reward. Farewell in Christ."

Thecla, whose name has already been mentioned, was a relative of Lioba's, and is supposed to have accompanied her from Wimburn. She remained with her at Bischofsheim for a long time, and at length she became abbess of the convents of Kissingen on the Main and Ochsenfurt. Her name does not appear on the list of abbesses of Kissingen but it is generally thought that she is designated as Heilga, or the Saint, who succeeded S. Hadeloga, the foundress of the Abbey of Kissingen. She is supposed to have been sister to Magingoz, the second Bishop of Wurzburg, who, in a letter to Lullus, then Archbishop of Mayence, mentions the death of his sister, who was an abbess in his diocese, and requests Lullus's advice because he fears that one of the daughters of his brother, who are nuns in the same convent, may be chosen as her successor, and he thinks them unfitted for the office by their youth and their character.

Among Boniface s letters is one addressed by him to Lioba, Thecla, and Cynehild, as the heads of separate religious communities. Cynehild was aunt to Lullus, and both she and her daughter Berathgit were learned in the liberal sciences, and were placed at the head of schools in Thuringia, but in what convent is not known. After Cynehik's death Berathgit probably returned to England, for there are extant three letters from her to her brother, a priest, describing most piteously the misery of her position alone among strangers in a foreign land, and beseeching him with heart-breaking earnestness, to come without delay and carry her back to her home and her kindred in England. These letters have the same impassioned character as those of Cangyth and Egburga.

Besides the above, Chunitrud is mentioned as having gone to Bavaria, and Nana and Eoliba as two of the nuns from whom the materials for S. Lioba's biography were collected; but nothing more is known about them.

CHAPTER XX.LOSS OF FERVOR IN ENGLAND

While Boniface was thus engaged in Germany the Church of his own native land was passing through a very difficult phase of its existence. There comes to Churches as to individuals a time when their first fervor is over. Even the Church of Laodicea had lost its first love, and therefore it is not wonderful if after nearly a century and a half of existence, time began to tell upon England. This decline often coincides with the transition from a missionary to a settled state of things. In fact the introduction of strict canonical law is generally meant to meet it. It is to be accurately distinguished from the decay of a Church, such as that into which the Eastern Churches fell even before the first triumph of heresy. As long as the great swing of missionary impulse lasts, the zeal of converts and the impetus of success carry people and priest over many trials. When, however, the wandering apostle has got to be turned into the parish-priest, and the preaching monk to exchange the excitement of seeking lost sheep in forest and fen, and over hill and dale, for the quiet regularity of his cloister, then comes the real difficulty. There is often even something of a conflict between the old spirit and the new, for the inevitable entrance of hierarchical discipline, while it directs and strengthens, also restrains exertion. To this, perhaps, owing in some respects the transient misunderstanding between Theodore the founder of ecclesiastical law in England and a Saint like Wilfrid, who converted the last pagan in his country. It would require some time before Theodore could quite comprehend the untiring, never-resting spirit which carried the deprived bishop through the thickets of Andred's weald among the savages of Sussex, and enabled him to rescue by his influence the remnant of the Isle of Wight from the brutal Ceadwalla. More than all, however, we must remember that the increasing property of a settled Church was a snare to its possessors and a temptation to the laity. To this we must ascribe much of the moral misery which both Bede and Boniface describe. That riches had begun to introduce grave sin even into the cloister is evident. The greatest disorder, however, was introduced by laymen, who established themselves on the property of the Church and exempted themselves from military service to the State, while they set at defiance the laws of morality. A monastic system, however, which at one and the same time produced the Venerable Bede at home and S. Boniface abroad, could hardly be said to be in a state of decay.

As for the condition of the laity, questions of comparative morals are always difficult yet the very letter which contains the complaints of Bede, bears witness to their general purity.

"Innumerable boys and girls" he says, "youths and maidens, old men and women, all leading most innocent and chaste lives" are fit to receive the Holy Communion every Sunday. It is to be observed also that the chief disorders were in Northumbria, and were owing to the dreadfully disturbed state of that kingdom, the nobles of which on account of their treachery to their kings, are described by Charlemagne as worse than Pagans. Even there the time assigned to the beginning of corruption by Alcuin, is the death of king Elfwald, a very much later date than the life of S. Boniface. The English Church had still vitality enough to produce in the next century a martyr king like S. Edmund and a great Christian like Alfred, and to convert the savage Danes. A Church thus capable of reforming itself, cannot be in a state of decay. Nevertheless great disorders were creeping in, and the heart of S. Boniface in the midst of his labors in Germany, turned with affectionate anxiety to England. To under stand the condition of the country we must turn to the pages of his great contemporary, the Venerable Bede.

There is extant a letter written by Bede, about A.D. 734, to his friend Egbert, Archbishop of York, which shows what were the causes of this early loss of fervor, and throws light on the religious practices of the day in England and elsewhere. He complains of the size of his friend s diocese, which renders it impossible for him to visit every village and corner of it annually, and he says that he even knows many villages in Northumbria which pay tithes regularly, and yet no bishop has ever gone to them, to baptize and preach to the people. He therefore urges Egbert to increase the number of bishops sees to twelve, as S. Gregory originally intended; and to send priests to reside in each village, who were to teach and instruct each individual to repeat the Creed and the Lord s Prayer in his own tongue, and to understand them. For S. Ambrose gives the admonition, that all the faithful should repeat the Creed every morning early, and thus fortify themselves as by a spiritual antidote, against the poison which the malignant cunning of the devil may, either by night or by day, cast out against them. But the Lord s Prayer should be very frequently repeated, as indeed was the general custom, with earnestness and on bended knees.

Further he recommends to the archbishop's "most anxious care" all others who lived in the world, that they might be provided with competent teachers, who would instruct them as to what they ought to know, what virtues to cultivate, what sins to avoid, with what devotions to worship God, with what frequent diligence to fortify themselves with the sign of our Lord s cross, and how salutary it is for Christians of all classes to receive daily "our Lord's Body and Blood." "This" he adds, "you well know is done by Christ's Church throughout Italy, Gaul,

Africa, Greece, and the East or at least on every Sunday and all the birthdays of the Apostles and Martyrs, as you yourself have seen in the Holy Roman and Apostolic Church Whereas, through the neglect of our teachers, almost all the laity of our province, even those who seem to be the most religious among them, communicate only on Christmas Day, Epiphany, and Easter."

As to the endowment of the bishoprics, since, through the profuse generosity of past monarchs, there re mained no vacant lands which could be bestowed on them, Bede proposes that the great council of the nation be held, when, with the consent of the bishops and the king, they should be provided from the property of some monastery, the monks of which should have the privilege of electing the bishop, who would also be their abbot and govern both the diocese and the abbey. Besides, there were innumerable places which were called monasteries, but did not follow the monastic life, and were of no profit either to God or man, being exempted from military service for the defense of the State, and yet practicing no monastic virtue. These monasteries belonged to lay men, who, under pretence of founding a house for God s service and by dint of presents to the king and bishop, had secured for themselves certain lands, on which they lived with their wives and children in luxury, or even license, surrounded by pseudo-monks who had been expelled from regular monasteries for their vices, or preferred a loose, vagrant life to monastic discipline, sometimes compelling one of their serfs to receive the tonsure and govern the community in obedience to themselves and at others keeping the rule in their own hands, and pretending to direct from their own luxurious family home the interior discipline of an ascetic community. So general was this abuse, that there was scarcely a great noble, ealdorman, or court official, who was not both an abbot and a governor of a province or servant of the kings and sometimes even while living as laymen they took the tonsure, in order to keep the government of the monks more completely in their own hands. They even obtained similar privileges for their consorts and these ladies, while still living as wives and mothers, pretended to guide as abbesses the virgin spouses of Christ. To apply the property of such establishments to the endowment of bishoprics, far from being a usurpation, would, he said, be a meritorious act.

The erection of twelve bishoprics in Northumbria was beyond Egbert s power. But he set to work so vigorously to reform abuses, composing a Pontifical and enacting canons of discipline, that his long archiepiscopate, from A.D. 732 to A.D. 766, forms an era in the history of his Church. His zeal was rewarded by the Pope with the pallium, which none of his predecessors since S. Paulinus had possessed. But though he was fervently aided by two successive kings of Northumbria, his relative Ceolwulf, who became a monk of Lindisfarne, A.D. 737, and his own brother Eadbert, who also received S. Peter s tonsure A.D. 758, yet he seems to have been unable to do more than retard the advance of that flood of vice and worldliness, which after some time laid waste the fairest province of Christendom.

Reports of the state of the English Church reached Boniface, and in the year 745, having occasion to write to Cuthbert, Archbishop of Canterbury, to thank him for a present that he had sent him, he seized the opportunity to give him some advice. After telling him about the synods which he had lately held and descanting on the responsibilities of the episcopal office, he continues: "Let us place our trust in Him, who laid the burden on us. What we cannot bear of ourselves, let us bear through Him who is omnipotent. Let us die, if it be God s will, for the holy laws of our fathers, that we may attain to the eternal inheritance with them I will not conceal from you, that all God's servants here who are noted for their knowledge of Scripture and fear of God, are grieved because the piety, morality and modesty of your Church are spoken of scornfully. It would be some mitigation of the disgrace, if your synod and your kings would forbid women and veiled nuns to make such frequent journeys to Rome and back; in which the greater number perish, and few remain pure. For there are few cities in Lombardy, France, or Gaul, in which profligate and abandoned women of the English race are not to be found which is a shame to the whole Church. Also laymen, whether king or governor, or persons invested with secular power by the earls and nobles, who by violence take monasteries away from the bishop, or the abbot or abbess, and pretend to rule in the place of the abbot, and to have monks under them, and to possess the property which was bought with Christ s blood, such men the old fathers call robbers, sacrilegious, murderers of the poor, wolves and devils entering into Christ's fold, accursed and condemned at Christ's judgment-seat Such, if they will not accept correction from the Church, are heathens and publicans, who, whether living or dead, have no communion with the Church. To such, who are to be found both here and with you, we sound the trumpet of God, lest we should be condemned. Endeavor by all means to prohibit superfluous and hateful worship of dress; because those ornaments, dresses covered with broad stripes and images of serpents, precede the coming of Antichrist, by whose cunning and through whose ministers, they were sent, in order to introduce gross immorality and luxury into cloisters."

The love of dress was one of the national failings of the English. S. Cuthbert had found it difficult to persuade the monks of Lindisfarne to wear the same habit as himself. S. Aldhelm, too, complained that the dress of nuns often resembled that which they had worn in the world, with the becoming addition of a veil tied with ribbons to the head, crossing over the chest, and falling behind down to the feet. But this was at that time only a childish foible, so to say, lingering in the midst of great virtues and it would not be worth noticing, were it not that the love of gaudy and rich dress afterwards became one of the prominent causes of the decay of religious life in England.

In the year 747 Pope Zachary wrote to Cuthbert, no doubt at Boniface's instigation, ordering him to oppose the authority of the canons to the corrupt practices of the times. Cuthbert called a council at Clovesho, where thirty-two canons were passed for the reform of the clergy and monks, the greater regularity and uniformity of public worship, and the general encouragement of piety and devotion. The clergy and monks were forbidden to eat and drink to excess, to seek for delicate viands, or to make their cells the resort of gleemen, harpers, and buffoons and they were ordered to spend their time in prayer, study, and silence. The nuns were enjoined to give more attention to study and prayer, and less to the weaving and embroidering of many-colored dresses which encouraged pride and vanity; and to close their cells against lay society, superfluous visits, and private feasting. Both monks and nuns were also forbidden to wear secular dresses.

There was another matter in England, which also called forth Boniface s zeal. This was the reclaiming of Ethelbald, King of the Mercians, from a life of sin. Ethelbald was grandson to a brother of the old King Penda, and being thus collaterally connected with the reigning family, he became an object of jealous suspicion to the king, Ceolred, son of S. Ethelred, and was obliged to lead a fugitive life. In his wanderings his most secure asylum was the cell of Guthlac, a saintly hermit, who lived in the ruins of an ancient sepulchral barrow in the heart of the fens and forests of Lincolnshire. Guthlac had a strange history, characteristic of the times. He, too, belonged to the royal race of Mercia, being descended from Icles, the fifth progenitor of Penda, and from the age of fifteen he lived as a bandit chief, pillaging towns and castles, collecting heaps of treasure, and admired and dreaded for his deeds of barbaric heroism. When he was twenty-four years of age, A.D. 697, it happened that one night he encamped in a forest with his robber band, and lying awake under the greenwood his thoughts turned on the crimes, excesses, and miserable deaths of his ancestors, whom he had hitherto emulated, and then on his own inevitable death and the nothingness of earthly wealth. Suddenly he felt his heart inflamed with strange, unknown aspirations after heavenly joys, and at the first peep of dawn he awoke his companions and bade them seek another chief, for he had just vowed himself to Christ's service. In vain did they weep, and groan, and entreat him not to forsake them deaf alike to their grief and their love he tore himself from their embraces, and taking with him only a short, broad sword, such as was used by rude peasants, he set out for the Abbey of Repton, which was a double monastery under the rule of Eadburga, grand-daughter of Anna and Heresuid, king and queen of East Anglia. Here he remained two years, at the end of which time he retired to the marsh-lands of Croyland, where he spent the remaining fifteen years of his life as a hermit.

His life at Croyland was marked by the same interior combats, the same familiarity with the lower animals, and the same throng of venerating crowds, as that of other hermit saints. To one who expressed surprise at seeing the swallows perch on his knees, his head and his chest, and allow him to help them to build their nests, he replied, "Do you not know that he who unites himself to God, sees in return all created beings unite themselves to him? Wild beasts and birds, as well as angels, associate with him who denies him self the society of man." So great was the veneration with which he was regarded far and near, that Beccelinus, the monk who used to come every three weeks to renew his tonsure, was once tempted to cut his throat with his razor, for the sake of the profit that would accrue to the place from the concourse of kings and princes who would come to venerate the abode and relics of so great a saint.

With Guthlac the fugitive Ethelbald found sympathy and peace but after a time he would go forth on some wild adventure, which he hoped would retrieve his fortunes. At length one day on his return from one of these perilous excursions, Guthlac said to him, "My son, I know all your troubles; wherefore I have prayed much to God for you, and He has given you dominion over your nation. Your sword will conquer your enemies and put them to flight. But you must wait. For you will obtain the kingdom, not by rapine and violence, but from God, when He has overthrown the sinner who now reigns and who will pass away as a shadow. From this time Ethelbald placed his trust in God alone, and giving up all his wild projects, remained quietly with the saint in his hermitage. Before very long S. Guthlac fell ill, and after a week of great suffering, during which he rose each day to say Mass, he died A.D. 714. This was a great trial to Ethelbert s faith and patience, and at first he was inconsolable. But one night, as he wept and prayed, S. Guthlac appeared to him surrounded with glory," and said, "Grieve not, for the days of your misery will soon pass away." In two years from this time Ceolred, who led a most licentious and sacrilegious life, went raving mad at a great feast that he was giving to his court and perished miserably. Ethelbald was then called by the unanimous voice of the nation to the throne, on which he sat for forty years.

Ethelbald s first act after his accession was to erect a noble monument to his friend. Piles of oak and earth were brought in boats from a distance, and sunk in the swamps of Croyland on the spot where stood the rude hut in which S. Guthlac and he used to pray; and on them he erected an immense abbey, richly endowed, and peopled by monks from our Lady s Abbey at Evesham. There was a large stone church, in which S. Guthlac's body was laid in a splendid shrine, and in later times a bell, said to be the largest and sweetest in England, which bore S. Guthlac's name till it perished with his abbey and his memory in the ruin of religion in the sixteenth century.

But while Ethelbald thus consecrated to his friend a perishing monument of stone, he unhappily neglected to enshrine his memory in the undying tablet of his own heart. Forgetting the lessons of piety and purity which the saint had taught him, he abandoned himself to a life of licentiousness, not even shrinking from violating God s sanctuaries and carrying off the virgin spouses of Christ.

Such were the circumstances which called forth Boniface s zeal. Strengthening his own Apostolic authority by that of eight bishops, all Englishmen, assembled in synod, he wrote Ethelbald a letter in their joint names, which he sent first to Egbert, Archbishop of York for any corrections that he might think desirable, and then to Herefrith, a priest renowned for his sanctity, who feared no man and was said to have some influence with Ethelbald. In his letter to Herefrith, "he declares, that their only motive for writing is pure friendship, and because, having been born and educated in England and now living abroad by the command of the Apostolic See, they rejoice at all good reports of their nation, and grieve over their sins and the reproaches cast on them for their immorality by both Pagans and Christians."

This letter to Ethelbald is remarkable for the wise gentleness, as well as the boldness of its tone. Boniface begins by praising Ethelbald s good and just government, and his many works of charity and then he goes on to speak of a report that had reached him, that Ethelbald had never taken a wife in lawful matrimony. He suggests that if he refrained from doing so through the love and fear of God and in a spirit of mortification, this was not only allowable but praiseworthy. But if, as many said, but which God forbid, Ethelbald s motive was to have the more liberty for licentiousness, he grieved greatly, for this was a sin in God's sight and a blot on his fame before men. Moreover, he was told what was even worse, that some of the partners of his guilt were nuns and virgins consecrated to God, which was, without doubt, a twofold sin. How would the servant who sinned against his lord's wife be punished? How much more lie who insulted the spouse of Christ, the Creator of heaven and earth! Even the Greeks and Romans considered it a blasphemy to touch the conse crated virgins. And among the Pagan Saxons, who had only the light of nature, so great was their horror of impurity, that in some tribes the woman who sinned thus was forced to hang herself, and the accomplice of her guilt was hanged over her burning pyre; and in others the women collected round her, and drove her from village to village, whipping her with rods, and cutting her with their knives, till she fell down dead or dying; while among the Wends, who were the most barbarous of men, so great was their zeal for the inviolability of the marriage tie that the women refused to survive their husbands, and it was deemed praiseworthy for a woman to kill herself, so as to be burnt on the same pyre as her husband. Boniface then proceeds to press on Ethelbald the higher Christian motives for purity and finally he sets before him the awful fate of his predecessor, Ceolred, and of Osred, the King of Northumbria, both of whom having committed the same sacrilegious crimes as himself, had perished miserably, Ceolred going raving mad in the midst of a banquet, and Osred dying ignominiously in his youth.

This letter told happily on Ethelbald. The following year Boniface wrote again to him, thanking him for the kindness with which he had received his former messenger, and begging him to listen attentively to what the bearer of this letter was commissioned by him to say to him. Subsequently Ethelbald s name appears as having taken part in the Council of Clovesho and also in a decree dated A.D. 749, by which he freed the monasteries and churches in Mercia from all tribute and service, except building bridges and the defense of strongholds.

CHAPTER XXI. THE CARLOVINGIAN DYNASTY

The only thing now wanting to Boniface's work was a strong and permanent civil government, under the protection of which the Catholic unity that he had established, might be consolidated. Several events which occurred at this time combined to bring about this most desirable result.

In the year 747, Boniface s pupil and friend, Carloman, resigned his share in the government to his brother Pepin and set out for Rome, where he proposed to end his days as a monk. This circumstance proclaims the advent of a new era in France, when Christ s service was deemed the highest honor to which prince or noble could aspire, and the tonsure was no longer a mark of reproach, as it had been considered by the Merovingians.

On his way to Italy Carloman stopped at the Abbey of S. Grail, which he recommended to Pepin s charity, as has already been told. At Rome he received the tonsure from Pope Zachary, and then built for himself a monastery in honor of S. Silvester on Mount Soracte, where this Pope had hid himself during the Diocletian persecution. But he found that the frequent visits of Frank pilgrims disturbed his devotions; and therefore, after some time by the Pope's advice he retired secretly to Monte Cassino, attended by only a single confidential friend.

At the gate of the abbey he was received by S. Petronax, when, concealing his rank he prostrated himself at the abbot s feet, and told him in answer to his inquiries, that he was a Frank who was guilty of homicide and many other great crimes, and that fearing to lose the heavenly country, he had voluntarily left his earthly home in order to pass his remaining days in penance in the abbey. He and his companion were accordingly admitted as novices, and at the end of a year they made their profession.

At Monte Cassino Carloman was distinguished by his fervor and humility. It happened one day, that taking his turn in the kitchen, he did his work so badly that the cook gave him a blow; whereupon he only answered, "God and Carloman forgive you." Before long he got another blow and made the same reply. But when the cook was about to strike him a third time, his faithful follower, unable any longer to endure such violence to his prince, seized a fagot and attacked the cook. The abbot called the Frank to account for his insubordination, and the latter in self-defense be strayed Carloman's secret. The abbot gratified Carloman s humility by employing him in the lowest offices, such as tilling the garden and tending the sheep and geese. One day, having failed in saving one of his geese from a wolf, he exclaimed, Behold, Lord to whom thou didst entrust a kingdom! How could I have governed and defended my people, when I cannot even keep these poor creatures safely?

Carloman was not the only royal monk at this time at Monte Cassino. Luitprand, King of the Lombards, was succeeded, A.D. 744, by his nephew Hildebrand, who made himself so odious to his subjects that they deposed him, and chose Eatchis, Duke of Friuli, to be their king. Eatchis having laid siege to Perugia, A.D. 749, Pope Zachary, attended by the principal clergy and nobles of Rome, went to his camp to remonstrate, and induced him to retire. But the Pope s words sank so deep into Eatchis heart, that a few days after he resigned the Lombard crown, went to Rome, where he received the tonsure and monk s habit from Pope Zachary, and then retired to the Abbey of Monte Cassino, in which he spent the rest of his life. His wife Tasia and his daughter Eatruda, who had accompanied him, rebuilt and richly endowed the Abbey of Plombariola, which is supposed to have been the abode of S. Scholastica, and here, surrounded by a community of nuns, they ended their days. Three centuries later there was to be seen at Monte Cassino a vine, which Eatchis is said to have planted, and which bore his name.

Before quitting France Carloman had committed his son, Drogo, to Pepin's care. Pepin accordingly gave some share in the government both to him and to his own step brother, Grifo. But these young men would not be satisfied without such a partition of the empire as would have endangered the safety of the whole. They fled to the Saxons, whence Grifo went to Bavaria and for several years the border provinces were a prey to Pagan invaders. How terrible were these incursions of Pagan hosts, appears from two letters which Boniface wrote at this time. In one addressed to Grifo, he adjures him in the most solemn and touching terms, by the thought of Christ s judgment, and the memory of his father and mother, who had commended him to his care, to defend the priests, monks, and nuns in Thuringia from the cruelty of the Pagans. In the other, written A.D. 752, to Pope Stephen II on his elevation to the Papal Chair, he tells him that the Pagans had pillaged and burnt above thirty parish churches and abbeys.

Pepin seems to have treated these young men with great forbearance. For even after this outbreak, he gave Grifo the town of Mans and twelve countships in Neustria, and allowed Drogo to have a certain degree of authority in Austrasia. But it appears from a letter to an abbot, without date or the writer s name, which is found among Boniface s correspondence, that there existed a party feeling in connexion with the latter, which must have tended to civil disunion for the writer inquires eagerly of his friend in Friesland, whether Boniface had attended Pepin s national assembly or that of Drogo.

The empire which Charles Martel bequeathed to his sons, was composed of the most heterogeneous materials, descendants of the old Latin and Celtic races, intermixed with their German conquerors, split into in numerable subdivisions of tribe and family, and kept apart by hereditary feuds, differences of language and national customs, and the barbaric pride of isolation and independence. Moreover, this discordant mass had not been welded together like the Roman Empire by long centuries of gradual conquest, but had been, so to say, thrown loosely in a heap as the war spoils of a single hero, without even the halo of a kingly title to inspire veneration, loyalty, and love. Charles Martel's remarkable military talents, and the unanimity which existed between Carloman and Pepin, concealed for a time the weakness of their position, as the self-constituted representatives of an imbecile king, with no claim to allegiance except sheer physical force. But the revolt of Drogo and Grifo brought out all its defects, and made it evident, that at any moment an accident might replunge Europe into the chaos of anarchy and barbarism. Pepin, therefore, resolved to take advantage of the season of peace to found a monarchy which would be based on the national custom of popular election, and would have also a sacred character and be held together by the spiritual bonds of a common religion.

Accordingly, about the year 751 he sent his Arch chaplain, Fulrad, Abbot of S. Denis, and Burchard, Bishop of Wurzburg, to Rome, to ask the Pope whether the state of the government in France was good. Zachary answered, that "It would be better for the preservation of order, that he who had the royal power should be called king, and not he who had it not." And "he sent to the Frank nation to say, by the authority of the Apostle S. Peter, that Pepin, who exercised the royal authority, ought also to have the royal."

The following year, A.D. 752, the question was submitted to the national assembly of the Franks. For among all the Teutonic nations the right to the throne rested on popular election, and not on hereditary succession and primogeniture; and though for two hundred and fifty years the Franks had elected their kings from the Merovingian family, yet this arose out of accidental circumstances, and not from any real right, as appears from the earlier history of the nation. In this assembly, "by the advice and with the consent of all the nation, and with the authority of the Apostolic See, Pepin, by the election of all the Franks, the consecration of the bishops, and the submission of the princes, was raised to the throne with Queen Bertrade, according to the old customs." And being thus "elected king according to the custom of the Franks," he was "anointed by the hand of Arch bishop Boniface, and raised to the throne of the Franks in the city of Soissons." He was the first king of the Franks who received the sacred unction, his predecessors having been only crowned but not anointed and thus a sacred character was given to the kingly office. The Jewish rite of anointing kings had not been adopted by the Christian emperors. It was first used by the British princes, when, on the withdrawal of the Roman legions, they assumed the sceptre of their forefathers. It was afterwards introduced into Ireland by S. Columba, who anointed Aidan, King of the Northern Scots, according to the directions contained in the book which an angel was said to have brought to him from heaven. The German form of coronation resembles that in the Pontifical of Egbert, Archbishop of York, which is the most ancient extant, and doubt less Boniface used it on this occasion.

The deposed Merovingian king, Childeric III, retired to the Abbey of Sithieu at S. Omer, where he received the tonsure and ended his days as a monk. His wife, Gisilda, found an asylum in the Abbey of Kochelsee in Bavaria, and became a nun under the Abbess Gailswinde.

It is disappointing not to find in the contemporary biographies nor in the letters of Boniface and Zachary, any mention of Boniface s share in this change of dynasty. The only possible allusion to it is in a letter from Boniface to the Pope, A.D. 751, of which Lullus was the bearer, and in which it is said, that there are certain secret matters intended only for his Holiness's ear, which Lullus will mention and consult him about viva vote. The Pope in his answer, dated November A.D. 751, observes the same caution, and refers Boni face to Lullus for a verbal answer to his verbal communication. But since we are expressly told that Pepin not only asked Boniface s advice in all important matters, but "obeyed his precepts in the Lord," there can be no doubt that Boniface took a leading part in this important event, which was so completely in accordance with his own principles of action and calculated to be so beneficial to both the Church and the nation.

Pepin soon proved himself worthy of the new title that had been conferred on him. In the first year of his reign he expelled the Saracens from his kingdom and carried his victorious arms as far as Barcelona. In the following year he marched against the Saxons, who had again broken across the frontier, and were burning churches and massacring Christians. He destroyed several of their fortresses, and granted them peace only on condition that the Christian missionaries should have full liberty to preach and baptize in Saxony.

Before the close of the same year he entered on that course of action in defense of the Pope, which finally extinguished the pretensions of the Byzantine court to either territory or influence in Italy, and led eventually to the revival of the Western Empire in his own family. Astolphus, who had succeeded his brother Ratchis on the throne of the Lombards, at an early period of his reign conquered Istria, Ravenna, and the whole of the Exarchate; the Exarch Eutychius fled to Naples and thence to Greece; and thus the last remnant of the Western Empire passed out of the hands of the Emperors of the East. Elated by this success, Astolphus, on the accession of Pope Stephen II A.D. 752, prepared to take possession of Rome and its dependent territory, and threatened to put all the inhabitants to the sword if they made the least resistance. In vain did the Pope try to recall him to a sense of justice or mercy. In vain did he sue for aid from the Emperor of the East. Constantino Copronymus was so engrossed with his sacrilegious war against images, that far from helping the Pope, he made no attempt to recover his own Italian territory by arms, but satisfied himself with sending ambassadors to Rome to solicit the Pope's mediation with Astolphus for its restoration. In this extremity, after much fruitless negotiation with Astolphus and many prayers and processions, in which all the inhabitants of Rome bathed in tears, took part, Stephen wrote to Pepin, beseeching his protection, and begging him to send ambassadors to Rome to take him to his presence. Pepin at once granted the Pope s requests and sent S. Chrodegang, Bishop of Metz, to bring him to his court.

Accordingly on the 14th of October, A.D. 753, Pope Stephen set out from Rome in company with S. Chrodegang and followed by a crowd of the inhabitants of Rome and the towns on his route, weeping, and trying to prevent his proceeding, so fearful were they of the risk that he ran of ill treatment from Astolphus. But offering himself as a victim for the safety of his flock and placing his trust in God, he advanced boldly, and Astolphus, hearing whither he was bound, did not dare to touch him. He had expected to meet Pepin at the celebrated Abbey of S. Maurice at Agaune in the Valais but Pepin being called away by the war with the Saxons, first sent Fulrad, his Archchaplain, and afterwards his eldest son Charles, then a boy of twelve years of age and since known as Charlemagne, to escort the Pope to Pontyon in Champagne. When the latter approached the town, Pepin went out a league to meet him, and on beholding him dismounted from his horse, prostrated himself with his wife, children, and nobles before Christ s Vicar, and then walking by his horse, led him in solemn procession to the palace of Pontyon on the Feast of the Epiphany, A.D. 754.

Astolphus was greatly alarmed at the step which the Pope had taken, and desired the Abbot of Monte Cassino to send Carloman to negotiate with Pepin on his behalf. Neither of them daring to refuse Carloman went to France, but within a short time, some say a few days, and others a few months after his arrival, he fell ill and died in the Abbey of Vienne. Pepin, who loved him tenderly, placed his body in a coffin of gold and sent it to Monte Cassino, where his ashes still lie under the High Altar in an onyx urn with an inscription dated A.D. 1628.

Pope Stephen was present at a national assembly which Pepin held at Quercy surprise, in April, A.D. 754, and decided several points concerning baptism, confirmation, marriage, and the validity of priests orders, which were submitted to him. In this assembly an expedition to Italy on the Pope s behalf, was resolved on, and Pepin, in his own name and those of his sons, Charles and Carloman, made a donation to the Roman Church of the towns of the Exarchate and other imperial territory, which the Lombards had seized, and which he hoped to take from them.

About three months later, on the 28th of July, at the Abbey of S. Denis, the Pope crowned Pepin, his sons Charles and Carloman, and his queen Bertrade, constituted Pepin and his sons protectors of the Catholic Church under the title of Patricians of Rome, and in S. Peter's name forbade the Franks under pain of excommunication, ever to choose their king out of another family.

After three attempts at negotiation, which Astolphus answered only by threats, Pepin set out for Italy, signally defeated the Lombards in the passes of the Alps, where they had fallen suddenly on him with far superior numbers, and laid siege to Astolphus in Pavia. By the Pope s mediation further bloodshed was prevented and a treaty was concluded, by which Astolphus bound himself to give up Ravenna and twenty other towns to the Roman Church. The Pope tried to persuade Pepin to remain in Italy till the terms of the peace should be executed, but Pepin had no doubt of Astolphus s good faith, and took only the precaution to carry Lombard hostages with him to France.

Scarcely had he departed when the Pope's fore bodings were verified. Astolphus, far from giving up a single town or inch of territory, began to ill-treat the Romans, and on the first day of the year 755 laid siege to Rome. His troops ravaged all the surrounding country with fire and sword burnt the churches, houses, and farms, carried off the cattle, cut down the vines, destroyed the growing harvests, pillaged the altars, and sacrilegiously consumed the consecrated Hosts. They also cruelly beat the monks, outraged and killed the nuns, massacred or carried into captivity great numbers of peasants, and even tore young infants from their mother s arms and cut their throats. Astolphus meanwhile sent repeated messages to the Romans, saying, "Open the Salarian Gate to me and give up to me your Pope. Otherwise I will level your walls and put you all to the sword and we shall see who will deliver you out of my hand."

Surrounded by these horrors, and threatened with worse outrages than even the Pagans had ever inflicted on the City, the Pope wrote the most pressing letters to Pepin and his sons as Patricians of Rome, adjuring them to remember the great honor that God had conferred on them in placing His Church under their protection, and to hasten to the rescue of S. Peter. In one of these letters written on the fifty-fifth day of the siege, he says, "Haste then, my beloved, I conjure you in the name of the true and living God, and of blessed Peter, the Prince of the Apostles, hasten to succour us, lest we perish, and all the nations of the earth say, Where is the confidence with which the Romans relied, after God, on the kings and nation of the Franks?"

But as the danger daily became greater and greater, he wrote finally in the name of S. Peter, conjointly with himself and the Catholic Apostolic Roman Church, saying, "I, Peter, called by Jesus Christ to be an Apostle, to whom He committed the care of His sheep and the keys of the kingdom of heaven, I have chosen you to be my adopted sons, and depending on your love for me I exhort and beseech you with the most pressing entreaties, as if I were myself before you, to deliver my town of Rome, my people, and the church where my body rests, from the outrages of the Lombards. The Mother of God, Ever Virgin, all the choirs of angels, and the holy martyrs and confessors, entreat and command you, as I do, to have compassion on Rome. The nation of the Franks has shown more love to me, the Apostle Peter, than all the nations of the earth; wherefore I have called upon you through my Vicar, to deliver the Church which our Lord has confided to me. If you obey quickly, be assured that you will have a great reward in this life and without doubt eternal glory. Otherwise, know by the authority of the Holy Trinity and the grace of my apostleship, that you will be deprived of the kingdom of God and eternal life."

At the expiration of three months Rome was relieved by the appearance of Pepin in Lombardy. He invested Pavia and pressed the siege so vigorously that Astolphus begged for mercy, and promised to fulfill the terms of the preceding year s treaty, and to add Commacchio to the towns that he would restore.

Ambassadors from the Emperor Constantino waited on Pepin to solicit the restoration of Ravenna and the other towns in the Exarchate to their master. But Pepin answered, that he had exposed his life in so many battles solely for the love of S. Peter and the pardon of his own sins, and no earthly consideration should ever induce him to defraud the Apostle of the smallest part of what he had once vowed to him.

Pepin was obliged to return to his own dominions, but he left Fulrad behind him in Italy to receive over the stipulated towns. Accordingly Fulrad, accompanied by deputies from Astolphus, repaired to Ravenna and all the towns in the Emilia and Pentapolis, and after receiving their keys he proceeded, attended by the principal citizens, to Rome, where he laid the keys on S. Peter s tomb, together with a deed of gift by which Pepin made over these towns to S. Peter, to the Roman Church, and to all successive Popes forever.

CHAPTER XXII. THE MARTYRDOM

Boniface was now above seventy years of age, and his increasing infirmities warned him that his time on earth would be short. He therefore began to make preparations for his departure. He had already appointed Lullus his coadjutor, in virtue of the Pope's permission; and now he wished to recommend him to Pepin as his successor, and to secure the royal protection for all his sons. He therefore wrote, A.D. 752, to Fulrad, Abbot of S. Denis and Archchaplain to Pepin, saying, "I and my friends perceive that these infirmities of mine must soon end my life. Wherefore, I beseech his Majesty for the love of Christ, the Son of God, to deign to tell me in my lifetime what provision he will be pleased to make hereafter for my disciples. For almost all are foreigners, some of them priests who minister in the churches and to the people in many various places, others monks in our monasteries who teach little children to read, and others again old men who have long lived with me and helped me in my 1 Ep. 82 Wurdt. 140 Serar. Ep. 90 Wurdt. 92 Serar work. I am very anxious for all of them, that after my death they be not dispersed like sheep without a shepherd, and that the people near the Pagan frontier lose not the law of Christ. Wherefore, I earnestly entreat in God s name, that if it be His will and pleasing to you, Lullus my son and coadjutor may be appointed the teacher and doctor of the priests and the people and I trust in God that the priests and monks will have an experienced master and doctor, and the people a faithful preacher and pastor. I ask this more especially because my priests lead a life of poverty near the Pagan frontier. They can get bread to eat, but they cannot get clothes, unless some one helps them as I have done, so as to enable them to remain there to minister to the people." This letter was well received by Pepin, to whom Boniface wrote soon after to thank him for having granted his petitions.

In the following year, A.D. 753, death removed Milo, the tonsured cleric, who for nearly forty years had usurped the archdioceses of Treves and Rheims; and thus Boniface was at last able to complete his ecclesiastical arrangements, by making Weomad Archbishop of Treves, and Tilpin Archbishop of Eheims. In this year, too, Hildegar, Archbishop of Cologne, was killed in an irruption of the Saxons, and Hildebert was appointed in his stead. Hildegar had claimed jurisdiction over Utrecht but Boniface having referred the matter to the Pope, who confirmed the independence of Utrecht, Pepin in the May-field of this year, held at Virrneria, now Verberie, a royal villa on the Oise in the diocese of Soissons, confirmed all the donations of his family to the Church of Utrecht, and made them over to Boniface, as Archbishop of Utrecht and Mayence.

The favor being now granted to Boniface to foresee his approaching end he spent this last year of his life in a final visitation of his diocese. He went into Friesland and made many converts in remote places which were still Pagan. He founded an abbey and consecrated the Church of S. Martin, at Aschaffenburg in Franconia. He went also into Bavaria, where, besides visiting all his churches and abbeys, he consecrated a monastery in the diocese of Freisingen, built by Alto, an Irish hermit, and since known as Altomunster. He wished women to be excluded from the church, but Alto begged that it might be a parish church open to all since men would often be called away by various duties, while the women would always remain at home to pray both for them and themselves. To this Boniface consented, but he made the monastery a close cloister and specially excluded women from a well within the enclosure.

Boniface also paid a visit to S. Pirminian at the Abbey of Hornbach, on the confines of the dioceses of Treves and Metz. "It is easy to imagine," the monk biographer says, "what happiness and exultation overflowed the hearts of both these saints from the outpouring of the Holy Spirit, how they mutually received and imparted grace, how each taught while he learnt from the other, how each gave forth and drank in Christ, and how the longer they talked, the more closely they were knit together in the love of Christ." Mutually refreshed and strengthened, the saints parted. But Pirminian gained such fervor from this communion with Boniface, that from this time he entered on a new spiritual life so that all the virtues he had hitherto practiced, seemed poor and worthless. Especially he withdrew himself as much as possible from active work, and devoted himself day and night to prayer and loving contemplation. In token of friendship Boniface entrusted certain parishes of his diocese to the monks of Hornbach. At the end of his correspondence is a letter from Dodo, Abbot of Hornbach, to Lullus, renewing the ties of friendship and communion and another from Amalardus to Riculfus, Lullus's successor complaining of some ill-disposed persons and begging that the above parishes be not taken away from the abbey.

On his return to Mayence, Boniface held a council, at which, in the presence of the bishops, abbots, and nobles, with Pepin s consent and by the Pope's authority, he consecrated Lullus to act as bishop for him and then taking him by the hand, he presented him to the assembly and bade them obey him as a father and help him whenever he should want their aid.

Afterwards he made the round of all the churches in Thuringia and the Rhine provinces, and presented Lullus to the clergy and laity in the neighborhood of each.

He then sent for Lioba, and solemnly exhorted her never to quit the land of her pilgrimage nor to allow bodily weakness, or advancing age, or the difficulties and labors of a life of virtue, to make her lukewarm in completing the good works that she had undertaken. He commended her to the care of Lullus and the elder monks of Fulda, bidding them treat her with honor and reverence, and place her body when she died, beside his in the church at Fulda, that as they had in life served Christ in union of work and devotion, so they might together await the Resurrection Day. Finally, he gave her his cowl, repeating his pressing exhortations never to leave the land of her pilgrimage.

He also earnestly commended to Lullus the flock that he was about to commit to his charge, and bade him be ever most zealous in preaching, and most diligent in recalling them from error. He further directed him to finish all the churches that ho had begun, and especially that of Fulda, because the monks were very poor and depended on their manual labor for subsistence. When all his last arrangements had thus been made, he said finally to Lullus, "I wish to accomplish this long desired journey, and I cannot draw back from it. For the hour of my departure draws nigh and my will is to go wherever God s grace leads me that when I am released from the prison of my body, I may attain to the prize of the eternal reward. And wherever I may die, carry my aged body to the church at Fulda, and bury it there. Now, my son, provide carefully all that we shall need for this journey and the winding sheet, in which my decrepit body is to be wrapped, place in the box with my books." These words pierced Lullus s heart with such anguish that he burst into tears and all who were present, wept. But they did not presume to suggest or do ought but what so holy and loving a father directed.

A few days later Boniface embarked on the Rhine, and sailed down the river to Utrecht, where he re mained a considerable time, preaching and baptizing, and putting all things in order. He appointed his old pupil, Gregory, now Abbot of S. Martin's, to govern the diocese of Utrecht, which he feared might fall into disorder after his death. Bishop Eoban, who had hitherto been his coadjutor at Utrecht, he now chose to be the support of his feebleness and old age in his last journey. His other companions were Adalgar, who had formerly been Bishop of Erfurt, Wintrung and Walther, priests, Scorbalt, Halumert, and Bosa, deacons, Vaccar, Gundwaccar, Williher, and Adolf, monks, all of whom being united to him in spirit and will, and in his missionary labors, merited to have a share in his martyr's crown and eternal reward. Besides these there were several servants and other attendants.

Embarking once more on the Rhine with these chosen companions, he passed on to the Yssel, and thence into the Zuider Zee, then called Aelmere or Almere, and landed on its eastern shore at the place where the town of Kampten now stands. This country was intersected by innumerable rivers, streams, and arms of the sea, on the banks of which, thus divided into separate districts, dwelt various tribes distinguished by different names, but all belonging to the Frisian nation. The navigation of these waters was often dangerous, especially when their surface was agitated by storms, and the waves of the ocean were driven upon the shores and up the creeks. But Boniface passed through them in perfect safety.

In his little ship he sailed through the country, penetrating into every nook and corner, stopping at every village or cluster of huts, and wherever souls were to be found, scattering the Divine seed far and near, dispelling the darkness of error, and shedding all around him the heavenly light of faith. Wherever he passed all hearts were stirred; crowds flocked to hear him and so great was the grace that hung on his lips, that thousands of men, women, and children were converted. Some of these had formerly been baptized, and had since relapsed into idolatry but the greater part were Pagans, whom lie and Eoban baptized. In suitable places he built churches, or repaired those which had become ruined. Thus he proceeded till on the 4th of June, A.D. 754, he arrived at a place called Docking, or Dockum, on the river Bordne, now Bordau, which was the boundary between East and West Friesland. Here he proposed to administer the Sacrament of Confirmation, and he had appointed the converts and others who had not yet been confirmed, to meet him here on the following day. He and his companions therefore landed, and pitched their tents, awaiting the arrival of the candidates for Confirmation from all parts of the province.

But while the Gospel was thus resounding through Friesland, some Pagan zealots, enraged at its triumph, loudly proclaimed that they would rather die than forsake the religion of their fathers, and that they would avenge their gods by sacrificing the Christian missionaries to them. When Boniface arrived at Dockinga he was told that a band of Pagans who had made a vow to kill him and his companions, was encamped in the neighborhood. But nothing moved, he said to the others, "Brethren, be strong for the faith of Christ, and united in hope ; and fear not those who can kill the body, but cannot hurt the soul." And they all with one accord answered, "Father, S. Willibrord taught us, that if we received the faith of Christ, we must be ready to lay down our lives for Him, because He died on the cross to redeem us by His own blood." Thus exhorting each other, and praising and blessing God, they prepared themselves for martyrdom.

For some time past Boniface, knowing by Divine revelation that the hour of his death was close at hand, had been more diligent than ever in preparing himself as well as his clergy and lay attendants, to resist the assaults of their enemies. That last night of his life on earth he spent in prayer and praise, and it was noticed that a bright celestial light shone round the tent in which he prayed. The next morning Eoban with all the clergy and monks, came to him, and exhorted him not to desist from preaching, but to announce God's word only the more boldly, the more furiously the heathen raged. Filled with joy at the strength of their faith and love, he went out of the tent to preach to the people of the village till the candidates for Confirmation should arrive.

As Boniface stood at the door of the tent, he held a book of the Gospels in his hand. His hair was white as snow, his tall, majestic form was bent by age, and his countenance beamed with the fullness of grace and virtue. While he preached with more than usual fervor and eloquence and the listening crowd hung with riveted attention on his words, a hum of distant voices floated on the air. It might be his neophytes, singing joyful hymns as they came along, and he paused not in his discourse. But soon the Pagan war-cry rose upon the breeze, rapidly drawing nearer and nearer for instead of friends there came enemies, instead of devout worshippers, fierce, blood-thirsty executioners, fully armed with swords and spears, uttering loud cries and clashing their arms together. Now all was tumult and confusion, and the servants and converts who had joined the party, seized their arms, and hastily girding them on, prepared to defend the camp. But Boniface, who had gone into the tent to obtain spiritual aid by praying before the relics which he always carried with him, soon hastened out at the head of his clergy to stop the intended combat. "My children," cried he to the young men, "fight not, and make not war on our enemies for the Holy Scriptures teach us, not only not to return evil for evil, but rather to render good for evil. Now the long wished for day has dawned, now the time is come, when we are invited from the labors and toils of this world to the joys of eternal blessedness. Why then would you deprive us of such gain and glory? Rather be strong in the Lord, and allow us to receive with joy the gifts of Divine grace that are offered to us. Hope only in the Lord, and He will deliver us from all dangers." With these and similar words he restrained the ardor of his followers. Then turning to the clergy he said affectionately to them, "My dearest brethren, if any thought of God's love, if any admonition of mine lives in your memory, show it in this hour, recollecting our Lord's words, Fear not them who kill the body, but cannot kill the soul. Rejoice in our Lord, and fix the anchor of your hope in Him, that He may bestow on you the reward of eternal blessedness, and grant you to sit in heaven among the choirs of angels. Lose not in this short hour the fruits of your long life of combat and victory but accept with firmness and constancy this sudden peril of death which threatens us, for the love of Him who suffered for us, that you may reign with Him in joy to all eternity." While S. Boniface was thus animating his children with the hope of the Martyr's crown, the furious multitude of Pagans rushed upon them.

Hildebrand, whose office it was to serve the bishop s table, and who was only half dressed was the first who was killed. The next was his brother Habmunt, the deacon, who was struck down as he came out of his tent. Then all the others one after another were dispatched; last of all came the turn of Boniface. As he fell, he raised his hands to heaven, and the fatal blow almost cut in two the book of the Gospels which ho still held in his hand. Thus what he had most loved in life, was his sole defense in death.

When the massacre was completed, the Pagans trampled the bleeding bodies of the martyrs under their feet with shouts of triumph and insult. Then entering the camp, they carried off all that was in it, and among the rest the chests which contained the books and reliquaries, but which they supposed to be filled with gold and silver. After this they pillaged the ships, and finding in them only the stock of provisions, they broke open the cases of wine, and sat down to feast, eating and drinking and making merry according to their national custom after a bloody combat. The wine to which they were unaccustomed, quickly mounted to their brains, and in their excitement they began to quarrel about the division of the supposed treasures of gold and silver in the chests; angry words soon led to blows a general fight began and by a just retribution the same swords which had so recently shed the blood of God s saints, pierced their own hearts. After most of the party had thus perished by the hands of their friends, the survivors broke open the chests which had been the cause of the quarrel, when to their inexpressible disgust, they found, instead of gold and silver, only books and relics. These they flung scornfully into the adjoining fields and marshes and then disappointed and dispirited, they returned to their homes.

Scarcely had three days elapsed when the just punishment of their crime overtook them. When the news of the massacre spread through the country, the Christians assembled in great force, and marched upon the Pagan tribe, who had been guilty of it. After a brief resistance the Pagans took to flight, and all perished miserably, leaving their wives and children, their slaves and all their possessions in the hands of the Christians. The Pagans in the neighborhood, terrified at the fate of the murderers, now embraced the faith in great numbers and thus once more the blood of the martyrs was the seed of the Church.

No words can describe the universal grief and horror, when the news of the martyrdom spread through Germany and Gaul. The clergy of Utrecht hastened to Dockinga and collected all the relics of the martyrs, except S. Eoban s head which they could not find. S. Boniface, the twelve whose names have been mentioned, and thirteen others, who probably had formed the original party and were known to them, they carried to Utrecht, where they buried them with great reverence and solemnity. The rest of the martyrs, numbering twenty-seven, they interred on the spot where they fell. Pepin built in their honor a church on the top of a high mound of earth, so as to escape the frequent inundations; and a miraculous spring, which burst forth from the mound, attested the sanctity of these martyrs, whose names unknown to us, are written in the

Book of Life.

As soon as Lullus heard of S. Boniface s death, he sent a large party of influential persons to Utrecht to claim his body, in order that he might bury it according to the saint's directions. At first the citizens of Utrecht prepared to resist the removal by force; but finding that they were greatly out-numbered by Lullus s deputation, they pretended that the king had ordered them not to part with the saint's body. The others, however, knew that this was not true, and they insisted on having it. Thus the contest was running high, when suddenly the bell of the church, untouched by human hand, began to toll in a mysterious way, whereupon the awe-struck citizens consented to allow the saint's orders to be obeyed. The bodies of S. Boniface, S. Eoban, and S. Adalgar, were accordingly placed in a ship, which, wafted by breezes from heaven without the aid of an oar, bore them up the Rhine to Mayence, where they were received with mingled reverence and sorrow, all weeping for the loss of their beloved father and friend.

And now a fresh contest arose. The clergy and laity of Mayence, supported by Pepin, insisted that it was the universal custom to bury a bishop in his own cathedral; and Lullus, being now by no means so zealous about obeying the saint as he had been when the body was at Utrecht, was inclined to yield to the popular wish. But Sturm and his monks loudly protested, appealing not only to the saint s last directions, but to his having chosen the very spot at Fulda where he was to be laid. While matters stood thus, S. Boniface appeared one night to a deacon, called Otpert, and said to him, "Why dost thou delay to carry me to my place in Fulda? Rise quickly, and hasten to bear me to the place in the wild which God has prepared for me. The deacon rose at once, and told the vision to Sturm and all the principal persons in the place. At first Lullus gave no credit to the tale. But when Otpert took a solemn oath, with his hand on the relics of the saints, that he had indeed seen the vision, no further opposition was made, and those who had hitherto been most eager in resisting the translation, were now most zealous in forwarding it."

The relics were conveyed by water from Mayence to Hochheim, and thence by land to Fulda. A vast con course of people of all classes chanting psalms and litanies, accompanied them; and at all the places at which the procession stopped for the night, churches were afterwards built. Thus was S. Boniface conveyed to Fulda, where with extraordinary funereal solemnity, amid the tears and sighs of his monks and clergy, he was laid in the spot which he had chosen for himself. The companions of his martyrdom, S. Eoban and Adalgar, were placed in the same grave, whence a few years later they were removed to Erfurt by Lullus.

CHAPTER XXIII.AFTER S. BONIFACE'S DEATH

S. Boniface's work was so firmly based and so closely knit together in Catholic unity that his death did not affect its prosperity. S. Gregory, Abbot of S. Martin's at Utrecht, took charge of the diocese but being only a priest, he sent Adelbert, one of his English monks, to be consecrated bishop by the Archbishop of York, in order that he might exercise the necessary episcopal functions as his coadjutor.

Lullus continued at Mayence though for some reason, now unknown, he did not receive the pall till the pontificate of Adrian, who became Pope A.D. 772, Lullus was a man of both talent and sanctity. He enjoyed the favor of Pepin and Charlemagne and was employed by the latter to make up a difference between himself and Offa, King of the Mercians. But what most redounds to his credit is that he possessed the love and confidence of his fellow disciples, who were now called on to obey him as their superior. The only exception was in the case of Sturm and the monks of Fulda.

It is hard to understand how the quarrel between these two saints arose. On the one hand, Eigil, a monk of Fulda, says hat Lullus envied Sturm, who was greatly beloved and on the other, an anonymous writer, says that Sturm, though a holy man, had a violent temper and received Lullus's gifts ungraciously. It is very conceivable that Lullus, in carrying out S. Boniface's last directions, may have thought himself entitled to interfere with the affairs of the abbey in a degree which was inconsistent with the Benedictine rule and this Sturm would naturally resist. At length three of the monks of Fulda, out of private pique, accused Sturm of treason and Lullus sent them on to Pepin, who banished Sturm to the Abbey of Jumieges.

Lullus now appointed one of his own priests, called Marcus, who obeyed him in all things to be Abbot of Fulda. The monks regarded Marcus as an intruder, and since he had not been trained to the strict Benedictine rule, his habits and theirs were dissimilar. Disputes arose and at last the monks turned him out of the abbey, refused to allow another abbot to be forced on them by Lullus, and prepared to go in a body to Pepin to petition for Sturm's return.

Lullus then gave them leave to elect one of themselves to be abbot and they chose Prezzoldus, who had been educated from childhood by Sturm but they stipulated that he would daily pray and consult with them how, by God's grace and S. Boniface's help, the should obtain Sturm's return. And as Sturm was universally beloved and the case involved the independence of all the Benedictine abbeys, there was not a single church or abbey in Germany in which prayers were not offered on hid behalf.

Meanwhile, Sturm remained at the Abbey of Jumieges, where his great saintliness won universal love and veneration. At length at the end of two years Pepin removed him to the court; on arriving there he was lodged in the royal chapel awaiting the king's orders. After several days it happened that early one morning Pepin came to the chapel to pray, as was his custom, before he went out to hunt. All the clergy, except Sturm, had gone to bed after singing matins and lands but he still remained watching and praying and when he heard the king coming he opened the door for him and carried lights before him to the place where he was accustomed to pray. Pepin knelt at the altar for some time and then rising, said graciously to Sturm, "God has brought us together, but I forget what it was of which your monks accused you and I know not why I was angry with you." Sturm humbly answered, "Though I am not free from sin, yet I never committed aught against you." Sturm humbly answered, "Though I am not free from sin, yet I never committed aught against you, O king." And the king replied, "If you have ever thought or done anything at any time against me, may God forgive it you, as I from my heart forgive it. Henceforth be in my favor and friendship so long as I live." Then drawing a thread out of his cloak, he threw it on the ground, saying, "There! I throw that thread on the ground as a sign of my perfect forgiveness." Thus peace and friendship were confirmed between the king and Sturm after which the king went away to hunt.

As soon as it became known that Sturm was reinstated in the king's favor, the monks of Fulda petitioned earnestly for his return. Pepin granted their request and not only restored Sturm to his dignity as abbot but freed him totally from Lullus's jurisdiction. After his return Sturm set to work with redoubled zeal to promote the discipline and welfare of the community. With this view he turned the river Fulda from its course and brought it close to the abbey, thus adding to the beauty of the domain and enabling the monks to erect mills and carry on all necessary works within their own precints, as their rule enjoined. He also repaired all the buildings and adorned the church and more especially the tomb of S. Boniface. But above all he encouraged those literary labors, for which the community soon became famous. Both Pepin and Charlemagne made large donations to the abbey and Charlemagne, who was warmly attached to Sturm, employed him to negotiate a treaty with Tassilo, Duke of Bavaria. He also took him with him in his wars with the Saxons, to preach to the Pagans whom he conquered. Sturm died A.D. 779.

As for Lullus, when he found that the monks of Fulda did not wish for his gifts or his advice, he turned his generosity elsewhere and built the Abbey of Hersfeld on the spot which Sturm had first chosen, and which was now no longer exposed to the Saxons. Here he and his friend S. Wizo were afterwards buried beside their master, S. Wigbert.

S. Lioba happily preserved the friendship of both Lullus and the monks of Fulda, the latter of whom granted her the extraordinary privilege of admission to their church. It was her habit to leave her attendants at a cell in the neighborhood, while, accompanied by one elderly man alone, she went into the church to pray. Afterwards she would take her collation with the monks, and return before night to the cell where she had left her nuns.

When she was advanced in years she inspected all the monasteries under her rule and having placed everything in order, she left Bischofsheim by Lullus's advice, but for what reason is not said. She now took up her abode at Schonersheim, four miles south of Mayence where "she served God day and night by prayers and fasts." Hence she was summoned to Aix-la-Chapelle by Charlemagne's queen, Hildegard, who was tenderly attached to her. Hildegard wished her to stay with her for some days but she refused and kissing her friend's mouth, eyes and forehead and embracing her with her usual warmth of affection, she said on parting, "Farewell forever, my beloved lady and sister; farewell, precious portion of my soul! Christ our Creator and Redeemer grant that we may behold each other without shame in the Day of Judgment; for we shall never see each other again in this world."

Lioba then returned to Schonersheim, where a few days after she was taken ill and having received the last Sacraments from Sorabert, an English priest, who always remained with her and served her with love and reverence she expired on the 28th of September, about A.D. 772. Her body was taken to Fulda, as S. Boniface had directed but the monks, fearing to open his grave, laid her on the north side of the altar which Boniface had erected in honor of our Lord and His twelve Apostles. Eigil, the fourth Abbot of Fulda, translated her to the east porch near the altar of S. Ignatius the Martyr; and Rabanus Maurus mentions an altar erected to her honor.

Of the subsequent history of the Abbey of Bischofsheim scarcely any thing is known. Its name appears only once, in a rather doubtful deed of gift from the Abbess Einhard to the Abbey of Fulda in Charlemagne s reign and then every trace of it is lost, till in the year 1636 it comes again to light in a deed, by which Archbishop Anselm Casimir gave the "hospital and cloister" of S, Lioba at Bischofsheim to the Franciscans, who dedicated the high altar of their church to her. In this church, now attached to a college, may still be seen over the high altar, a picture of the finding of the infant in the river, in which S. Lioba appears in the Benedictine habit. Also over the door there is a statue of her in wood, with her crosier in one hand and a book with a bell on it in the other, in allusion to her mother s vision before her birth.

At the Abbey of Heidenheim the holy and happy monotony of the cloister remained unbroken, till in the year 757, Winibald fell dangerously ill at the abbey of Fulda, whither he had gone to pray at S. Boniface's tomb. At the end of three weeks he rallied, and went on to visit Bishop Magingoz at Wurzburg but he was detained by illness on the way; and after spending three days at Wurzburg, he returned to Heidenheim.

From this time he seldom went out, and only on a few occasions got so far as the farms in the immediate neighborhood of the abbey. Notwithstanding, he conceived a great desire to go and end his days at the tomb of S. Benedict, and wrote to the abbot and monks of Monte Cassino, entreating them, since he was already their brother, to admit him to their community. They joyfully granted his request, and promising him a share in their prayers, pressed him to come to them. He therefore sent for his brother and some other holy friends whom he was in the habit of consulting, and told them his plans and wishes. But they unanimously dissuaded him from deserting the children whom he had gained for God, and advised him to remain in his wild forest home till our Lord should call him to receive the prize of glory in the heavenly kingdom. He accordingly bowed to their opinion, and gave up his own wishes.

When his infirmities became so great that he could not go to the church, he had an altar placed in a corner of his cell, at which he said Mass daily and he also continued his usual prayers, vigils, fasts, and other austerities to the last. At length, about three years from the beginning of his illness, he told his monks on what day he should die, and gave them directions how to lay him out in his vestments. On the day that he had mentioned, being Saturday, the 18th of December, as Willibald, Walburga, and his monks stood round his bed, he bade them all farewell. Then lifting his eyes to heaven he said, "Into Thy hands, O Lord, I commend my spirit," and sitting as he was, raised up in his bed, he expired. The monks washed and vested his body, as he had directed and the next day they placed him in a new stone coffin, which he had long kept ready in his cell, and buried him in the church.

After Winibald s death Walburga governed the double monastery, and Willibald often came to support and advise her. About fourteen years later Willibald began to rebuild the church on a very grand scale and at the end of two years, the crypt at the east end which was to contain Winibald s body, being finished, the 23rd of September, A.D. 776, was appointed for his translation. But when they opened the stone coffin, greatly amazed were they to find that time and death had left no trace on the saintly abbot, who lay with a calm and holy look as if he had just fallen asleep. Willibald and Walburga were the first to kiss him, and his friends and disciples then did the same after which they lifted him up, and the clergy, monks, and crowds of people pressing eagerly to touch him, they carried him to the crypt and laid him in the new stone tomb that had been prepared for him.

Not long after this Walburga was taken ill, and after receiving the last Sacraments she expired on the 25th of February, A.D. 777. Willibald buried her close to S. Winibald, to show that she was his sister no less in sanctity than by blood; and many miracles were wrought both at her tomb and that of S. Winibald. Willibald was of a more active spirit than either his brother or sister, but he was not their inferior in sanctity. He was S. Boniface s chancellor and prolocutor at the synods which he held, and Boniface highly valued his judgment and discretion. He went to Eichstedt with only three companions but soon hundreds of monks and nuns were to be seen under his rule; and before his death the wilderness had been converted into a fertile region, over which villages and towns, and numerous churches and monasteries, were scattered. He survived till A.D. 786, thus being able to assist at several of Charlemagne's most important councils, and to hand on S. Boniface's discipline and teaching to a new generation.

Nearly a century after S. Walburga s death, the monastery of Heidenheim had fallen into a ruinous state, and repairs were begun by Otkar, sixth Bishop of Eichstedt. The workmen having desecrated! Walburga s grave, she appeared one night to Otgar, and said to him, "Why dost thou treat with dishonor the house of God in which my body awaits the Last Judgment? For my tomb is trodden under foot by those who pass by. Be assured that thou shalt have a sign that thou hast not dealt well with me nor with the house of God. Early the next morning a monk called Renifred, arrived in haste from Heidenheim with the news that the north wall of the church, which was to have been roofed in the next day, had fallen down with a crash during the night.

Awe-struck at the speedy fulfillment of S. Walburga s threat, Otgar lost no time in repairing the church, after which he translated S. Walburga s relics with solemn pomp to the Cathedral of Eichstedt."

In the year 893 Bishop Erchanbold, Otkar's successor, opened S. Walburga's coffin to take out a portion of the relics which he had promised to Liubula, Abbess of Monheim, and the body was found to be immersed in a holy dew or oil, which neither dust nor other impurity would touch or soil, as is attested by Wolfhard, who was present. From that time to this day the oil has continued to flow from the tomb, falling drop by drop into a silver vessel placed to receive it, and at fixed periods it is put into small phials and distributed far and near for the anointing and cure of the sick. Even in England there now are persons of high position and undoubted veracity, who can attest their own cure or that of their relations and friends through the holy oil from S. Walburga s tomb. This privilege S. Walburga shares with S. Agnes of Tuscany, S. Nicholas of Mira, S. Elizabeth of Hesse, S. Lawrence, and other saints who were distinguished by the virtues of compassion and mercy. For as oil is used to give light, to feed, and to heal wounds, so does saintly mercy enlighten the blind, feed the hungry in body and spirit, and comfort the sick and broken-hearted. Thus is S. Walburga s fame, as a beautiful and fruitful olive tree, diffused throughout the whole Church.

Nor was it S. Boniface s abbeys and churches alone that prospered after his death. The missionary work which was even closer to his heart, far from being checked by his removal, was carried on with unabated fervor by a new generation of English monks, who year by year advanced the Christian outposts, and at last penetrated to Old Saxony.

One of the most distinguished of these missionaries was S. Lebuin, or Liafwin. Moved by a Divine command twice repeated, to go and preach to the Franks and Saxons on the banks of the Yssel, he left his English home, and presenting himself to S. Gregory at Utrecht, asked for a guide to conduct him to his appointed field of labor. Gregory gave him for his companion, Marcellinus, also of English birth, who had lived from boyhood under the rule of S. Willibrord. Marcellinus led him to the Yssel which then divided the Frank and Saxon territories; and here he made many converts and built several churches. But after some time, A.D. 772, hearing that the Saxons were holding a national assembly on the Weser, he suddenly presented himself before them, clad in the priestly vestments with a crucifix in his hand, and announced himself as the ambassador of the One true God. He set before them the folly of the idol worship in which he had found them engaged, invited them to believe in Him who had sent him to them and who alone could deliver them from all evil here and hereafter, and threatened them, should they reject the faith, with defeat and captivity at the hands of the powerful king, who was even then preparing to invade and ravage their country. Infuriated at his bold words the Saxons cuts takes from the adjoining grove, and were about to kill him, when Buto, one of their chiefs whose heart God s grace had touched, cried out to them, "Listen, all who have any sense! The Normans, Slaves, and Frisians have often sent us ambassadors, and we have given them an honorable reception. Why then should we treat so shamefully the ambassador of the great God? Truly the woes which he has announced to us will fall on us." Calmed by this remonstrance the Pagans allowed Lebuin to depart in peace. He then returned to Deventor, and after rebuilding the church which had been burnt in his absence, he died and was buried there the following year.

Another zealous missionary was S. Willehad, a Northumbrian noble, united by blood to S. Boniface and by friendship to Alcuin. He first went to Dockum, where he was received with great honor and remained for a considerable time, inciting the Christians to lead more holy lives, instructing their children, and converting many Pagans to the faith. He afterwards crossed the river Lawers into Groningen and the more southerly district of Drent, where for some years he not only preached boldly, but encouraged his converts at the risk of his life, to pull down the idol temples. On one occasion the Pagans took him captive, and cast lots to see if they should kill him; but as, through God's Providence, the death lot never fell on him, they did not dare to strike him, but let him depart in peace. At another time they rushed upon him and wounded him with their staves, and one of them struck him across the neck with a sword, intending to cut off his head. But though the blow partly severed the strap from which his reliquary hung, yet he himself was unhurt; whereupon the Pagans, awestruck at his marvelous escape, feared to molest him further.

After the conclusion of the first Saxon war, A.D. 778, Charlemagne sent him to preach to the conquered tribes on the banks of the Weser, where he made many converts among both Saxons and Frisians, built several churches, and appointed priests to minister in them. But the following year, on the fresh outbreak of the Saxons under Witikind, this district was overrun with fire and sword, his churches were burnt, his priests were massacred, and he himself hardly escaped by sea to Friesland.

Heartbroken at the desolation which had fallen on his flourishing vineyard, he journeyed to Rome, where with many prayers and tears he poured out his grief at the tomb of S. Peter. Consoled and encouraged by Pope Adrian, he retraced his steps to Friesland and collecting round him some of his fugitive disciples, he spent two years in solitude at Epternach after which, by Charlemagne's order, he returned, A.D. 785, to his old district on the Weser, where he lost no time in rebuild ing his churches and collecting the survivors of his flock. On the final pacification of this western portion of Saxony, then known as Westphalia, Charlemagne had him consecrated bishop A.D. 787. He fixed his see at Bremen, where he built a cathedral dedicated to S. Peter, round which the town of the same name has sprung up, and here a few mouths later he was buried.

Another laborer in the same field was S. Luidger, born of Frisian nobles, who had long enjoyed the friend ship of S. Willibrord and S. Boniface. As soon as he could walk or speak, he would collect scraps of leather and bark, sew them together in the form of books, and pretending to write on them with a twig and any liquid that he could find, he would give them to his nurse to treasure up for him. If any one asked him what he had been doing all day, he would answer that he had been reading, writing, or composing books. And if he was asked further who had taught him to do so, he would reply, "God has taught me."

At an early age he was given at his own request to S. Gregory at Utrecht. Here he saw S. Boniface, as he was on his way to martyrdom, took note of his snow-white hair, majestic form bent with age, and countenance beaming with grace, heard his parting words, and received his last blessing. After S. Boniface's death he accompanied Adelbert to England, received deacon s orders from the Archbishop of York, and studied for above four years under Alcuin. Thus his early promise of piety and love of learning were so happily developed, that on his return to the Abbey of S. Martin at Utrecht, he shone pre-eminent above his brethren even in that community of future saints, martyrs, and great missionary bishops. After S. Gregory's death he was raised to the priesthood, and was placed in charge of the district round Dockum, where he preached with great success for several years, till the invasion of the Saxons, A.D. 782, uprooted the Christian colonies in Friesland as far as the Zuider Zee. He then went to Rome to consult the Pope about the foundation of a monastery in honor of our Lord, S. Mary the Mother of God, and the Apostles S. Peter and S. Paul, on his paternal estate near the mouth of the Rhine. By the Pope s advice he proceeded to the Abbey of Monte Cassino, where he remained for above two years. Gladly would he have stayed even longer, but his name had become known through Alcuin to

Charlemagne, who, always trusting more to his priests and monks than his soldiers for the subjugation of the Pagans, summoned him home, A.D. 785, and gave over to him the north and west part of Friesland. Here he toiled for sixteen years, made many converts among both Frisians and Danes, and established the faith in Fositesland, or Heligoland, where S. Willibrord had been so nearly martyred. At length, A.D. 801, Charlemagne removed him to the district then called Suthergowe, where, after being raised to the episcopal dignity, he founded the see of Mimigernefort, since called Munster. He died A.D. 809.

CHAPTER XXIV.CHARLEMAGNE

It was, however, on Charlemagne that S. Boniface's mantle may be said to have fallen, for it was he who completed and confirmed Boniface s twofold work. The mission of both emanated from Rome, and while "Boniface appears as the living word of the Apostolic See, Charlemagne is the armed hand to protect that word."

In order to show this it will be necessary to recount some facts which took place after Boniface's death. We must remember that he was the actual contemporary and the friend of Pepin, and that his life reached into that of Pepin s greater son, whom we know under the name of Charlemagne. The future emperor, however, was only Prince Karl, a boy of thirteen when Boniface died. They therefore belonged to different generations. Nevertheless there is no anachronism in representing the Saint as a fellow-worker with the Emperor. It is quite true that the Saint could have had but little influence on the personal character of Charles. It might have been better for the man whom with all his faults we can conscientiously call great, if Boniface in stead of Alcuin had stood by his side. We must never forget that Charles was not a S. Louis. The old Adam was by no means dead in the strong will, which could at once beat down the Saxons and tenaciously fix itself upon the minutest details of the administration of his vast dominions. Although the licentious character of Eginhard himself may throw some doubt on the stories which reach us through his testimony, yet after all allowances made for the possibility of successive morganatic marriages, it appears likely that for a time after the death of his last empress, the private life of Charlemagne was disedifying to his subjects. That he repented and led a holy life long before he died, and that his death was most saintly, is certain. Whether at times the remembrance of the old Saint, whom he had seen in his father s palace, came across the Emperor to rebuke him during the time when his strong pleasure loving nature betrayed him into sin, we cannot tell. What is certain is that the work of Boniface made the work of Charlemagne possible. The unity of Germany in the Christian faith and its firm ecclesiastical organization were necessary conditions to the existence of the empire. The notion of a Christendom united under one great monarch, who was to be the defender of the faith and the personification of justice, was, it must be owned, a grand ideal. It turned out to be a dream but that for centuries the dream had a partial fulfillment, was owing to the deep foundations laid by Boni face. We must, therefore, devote a few pages to the remarkable man who built upon them, and who, if not always perfect, was certainly a hero.

Charlemagne was fitted by nature to be a hero. His gigantic stature, robust frame, and commanding mien, his countenance beaming with beauty and joy, his flowing eloquence and powerful intellect, his imperturbable equanimity and greatness of soul, his military genius and his world-wide fame, all combined to recall the ideal hero of the poet's dream.

These dazzling characteristics were grafted on the Teutonic nature, and thus fear and admiration were merged in love. Though he stood pre-eminent above all through his innate superiority, yet far from being betrayed into pride by his own greatness, he yearned only for sympathy with all around him, and ever labored indefatigably to raise them to his own level. He lived in the midst of his court like the father of a family, surrounded by his wife and children, always genial, sociable, and easy of access, hunting or studying with his bishops and nobles, instructing them by quaint lectures or practical jokes, examining, rewarding, or punishing the children in his schools, and even break ing through his personal habits and seasons of privacy at the call of the Count of his palace, in order to give judgment in the petty squabbles of his courtiers and household. His affections were warm and tender. Unable to tear himself from his wife and daughters, he took them with him on horseback in his constant journeys from end to end of his vast empire. Easily susceptible of friendship, he was true and constant to those to whom he had once given his love or favor. When William, Duke of Aquitaine, distinguished above all his other nobles as a soldier and scholar, asked his leave to become a monk, he remained for a time pale and speechless from emotion, and then throwing himself into his friend s arms with passionate grief, he declared that had William preferred the friendship of any earthly king to his, he would have raised the whole universe to prevent his quitting him but as he wished to become the soldier of the King of angels, he could not oppose him. He wept long and bitterly for the death of his children and friends and when basking in his old age in the full sunshine of his power and glory, he shed tears at the sight of the Northmen's ships in the Mediterranean Sea, foreseeing the misery they would inflict on future generations of his subjects, whom he loved as his own children.

S. Boniface s influence and Pope Stephen's unction early impressed a Christian character on this heroic spirit. By habitual temperance and devout participation in the daily offices of the Church, he at least strove to subdue his passionate nature. His alms were generously bestowed on the Church and the poor within his own dominions, and profusely scattered among the Christians in Carthage, Egypt, Syria, and Jerusalem; while his great influence with the Mahometan princes was exerted to soften the lot of the faithful under their rule. Even his foes shared his Christian charity. For when he had conquered the Duke of Beneventum, considerate of the welfare of the vanquished nation and forgetting the obstinacy of the contest, he declined to accept both of the Duke's sons who were offered him as hostages and retaining only the younger, restored the elder to his father.

The conscientiousness with which he took on himself the burden of governing his vast empire, appears in the numerous councils which he held, and the capitularies which he issued. The national customs of the Germans and their daily routine of life having been closely linked with Paganism, had been totally upset by their recent conversion to Christianity and society in the other parts of his empire had been scarcely less disorganized by a century of war and anarchy. To remedy these evils and place the whole being of his subjects on a Christian basis, was the great object of his legislation. How thoroughly the performed his task may be seen in his capitularies, which are unparalleled alike for their grandness of design and minuteness of detail, and embrace every conceivable subject, from the inculcation of the truths necessary to salvation and the encouragement of learning and education, down to the planting of fruit trees, roses, lilies, vegetables, and medicinal herbs. This remarkable code of laws renewed and regulated the religious and national life of France and Germany during the Middle Ages, and thus gave a

Christian character to modern society.

Charlemagne's capitularies regarding the education of his subjects will be hereafter noticed. He was not, however, satisfied with issuing legislative enactments, but took this matter under his own superintendence and devoted to it much time, thought, and money. He founded monasteries and schools wherever they did not already exist, and established schools in all the cathedrals. Wherever he passed in his constant journeys he himself examined into the state of the schools and the discipline of the clergy and monks, especially inquiring whether sermons were regularly preached to the people in a suitable style by competent persons and to the places beyond his own reach he sent official visitors, who acted as his deputies. His principal advisers in this great work were Alcuin and S. Benedict of Anagni, the latter of whom in the next reign reformed all the monasteries in France in conformity with the Benedictine rule.

But Charlemagne s sympathetic nature yearned for a still more personal part in the work that he had so much at heart. His court and camp were like schools to the half-civilized Franks and wild Germans who gathered round his victorious banner: and in both they were trained to Christian practice and the observance of the Church s annual round of fasts and penance, solemn processions, daily Mass, and joyous festal ceremonials.

He watched over the due performance of the religious offices, the style of the sermons, the pronunciation of Latin, the Roman chant, in his chapel, and the progress of the children in his palace school. He seized every opportunity to give his courtiers lectures or practical lessons as to their conduct in their several stations. He gathered round him the most distinguished scholars from all countries. A reputation for learning as the surest passport to his favor. He himself, with all his sons, daughters, and other relatives, and all his courtiers, both clergy and laity, became the pupils of Alcuin; and so enthusiastic was he in his new studies, that he gave himself and all his fellow- scholars biblical, patristic, or classical names. He was called David, Alcuin was Flaccus, his cousin Adalhard was Augustine, his son-in-law Angilbert was Homer, and so on with the rest. One day in the ardor of his zeal for knowledge, he exclaimed, "Oh! that I had twelve such wise and learned clerics as Jerome and Augustine!" "What!" answered Alcuin, "the Creator of heaven and earth has had only two men of such merit, and you want to have a dozen!"

His range of study was very wide, considering how much of his time was necessarily given to war, legislation, and the business of his vast empire. He studied rhetoric, dialectics, astronomy, and theology with Alcuin. He took great pleasure in the writings of the Fathers, especially S. Augustine's City of God. He spoke Latin as fluently as he did German, and he knew enough of Greek to understand the Byzantine ambassadors. He was so fond of his native tongue that he began to compose a German grammar, and made a collection of the old German poetry, writing out several of the songs with his own hand. So ardent was his desire to be able to write well, that he always had his tablets within reach, so as to turn every leisure moment to profit; though, from having begun late in life, he never attained to great proficiency.

Out of two hundred and thirty-two letters by Alcuin still extant, thirty are addressed to Charlemagne. They treat of astronomy, grammar, various religious and theological questions, and matters connected with his legislative capitularies and in one congratulating him on his great victory over the Huns, Alcuin exhorts him to treat them with clemency, and gives him advice how to facilitate their conversion.

The same Christian spirit characterized Charlemagne's military career. The Eastern Empire had already fallen into its long-protracted last agony, and offered an easy conquest to his genius and prowess. But he turned away from the glittering prize, and preferred the far harder task of combating Saracens, Lombards, Saxons, Slaves, and Huns, in fulfillment of the twofold task of strengthening the Church s authority and extending her frontiers, which he had set himself on his accession. Insensible to military glory and personal ambition, he devoted his sword with Teutonic fidelity and the Crusader's zeal to the service of Christ and His Church, nor ever unsheathed it for any lower cause. Nay, even when, A.D. 802, in the course of his wars with the Huns and Slaves, he had conquered several provinces which had formerly belonged to the Eastern Empire, he retained only Istria, Pannonia, and part of Dalmatia, which were necessary for the security of his own frontier, and gave up the maritime towns of Dalmatia and the isles along its coast to the Emperor Nicephorus. By this act of forbearance and magnanimity he vanquished the jealous pride of Nicephorus, who had taken umbrage at his recent assumption of the imperial title.

Charlemagne twice brought relief to the Christians in Spain who were groaning under the Saracen yoke. In the year 778 several Saracen emirs, disgusted by the tyranny of the Caliph Abderraman, came to Paderborn to offer him fealty and at their invitation he led his army in person across the Pyrenees, made himself master of Catalonia and Aragon, established the friendly emirs in the conquered provinces as his vassals and freed the Christians from tribute to the Mahometans. It was on his return from this expedition that his rear-guard was cut off in the pass of Roncesvalles in the Pyrenees, and the celebrated Roland is said to have perished. Twenty years later, A.D. 799, he sent an army into Spain under his son Louis, Duke of Aquitaine, to repress the incursions of the Saracens, who had taken advantage of his wars in Germany to cross the Pyrenees, ravage Septimania and Languedoc and burn Narbonne. Louis was very successful in this expedition, and after besieging Barcelona for two years, entered it in triumph.

But the wars which added most to Charlemagne's fame and have had the most important results were those which he undertook in defense of the Pope and against the Saxons.

Didier, who had succeeded Astolphus on the throne of the Lombards, A.D. 756, left no means untried during the pontificates of S. Paul I and Stephen III, to recover the territory which Pepin had conquered from his predecessor, and establish his authority over Rome and the Pope. Sometimes he seized the towns that he coveted and ravaged the Roman territory at others he fomented dissensions and gave his countenance to anti-popes then he tried to persuade the Emperor Constantino to send an army to recover Ravenna and the Exarchate, well knowing that it would afterwards be easy for him to wrest them from the Greeks again he strove to detach Charlemagne and his brother Carloman from the Papal interest by offering them his two daughters in marriage and finally, on Carloman's death and Charlemagne's succession to his share of the Frank empire, A.D. 771, he set up Carloman's sons in opposition to Charlemagne, and sought to induce the Pope to crown and anoint them.

But having failed in all these projects, at length on the accession of Pope Adrian, A.D. 772, he threw off all disguise, seized several towns of the Exarchate, ravaged the Papal territory with the atrocious cruelty characteristic of his nation, blockaded Ravenna, and refused the inhabitants any terms unless the Pope himself would come and treat with him. But as Adrian did not dare to trust himself in Didier s hands, the latter sent him a message that he was coming to besiege Rome and would force the Romans to obey him; and meanwhile he made Paul Afiarte, one of the Pope's envoys, promise that he would bring the Holy Father to him, even should it be necessary to drag him to his presence by a cord tied round his feet. As Didier was approaching with a large army, Adrian built up several of the gates of Rome and made preparations for defense, while at the same time he sent messengers to entreat Charlemagne to come to his aid.

Charlemagne was now engaged in his war with the Saxons but he took advantage of the first opportunity to make peace with them, and hastened with a large army to Mont Cenis. There he found all the mountain passes in the hands of Didier, and he was meditating a retreat when an unaccountable panic seized the Lombards, who fled, leaving their tents and baggage behind them. The Franks pursued, killed great numbers of them, and laid siege to Pavia in which Didier was shut up.

The siege of Pavia had lasted six months, when Easter being come, Charlemagne resolved to celebrate the festival at the tombs of the Apostles in Rome. Accordingly, leaving his army to continue the siege, he set out for Rome, where he arrived on Holy Saturday, which that year, A.D. 774, fell on the 2nd of April. The Roman clergy and principal citizens went out to meet him with all the honors usually rendered to the Exarch or Patrician; children carrying branches of olive and palm, greeted him with joyful acclamations while the Pope awaited him at the great door of S. Peter's, which was then outside the walls of Rome. On reaching the steps which led up to S. Peter's, Charlemagne knelt down and kissed each step reverently as he went up them, till on the upper step the Pope raised and embraced him, and led him to the Apostle's tomb. After finishing his devotions in S. Peter's he wished to fulfill the vows of his pilgrimage in the various churches in Rome. But he would not enter the city till he had asked and obtained the Pope's leave to do so. On the following Wednesday he confirmed his father's donation to the Holy See, and added to it several other towns, placing the deed of gift first on the altar of S. Peter's, and afterwards on the Apostle's tomb.

After thus satisfying his devotion he returned to Pavia, which soon opened its gates to him, and Didier became his prisoner. The whole of Lombardy being now in his hands, he placed the iron crown of the Lombards on his own head, and thus effectually secured peace to the Pope. Didier went with him to Franco and eventually became a monk of Corby. S. Syngrius, who was a monk at S. Pons and afterwards Bishop of Nice, is supposed to have been one of Carloman's sons.

Subsequently, in the year 781, Charlemagne went again to Rome from motives of devotion. In the year 787 having gone to Italy to oppose Adalgisus, son of Didier, who with the aid of Constantino Porphyrogenitus had attacked his Italian dominions, he paid a third visit to the city. After completely subduing the Lombards and taking from them their remaining possessions in Italy, he made a further gift to the Church of several towns in Tuscany and the Duchy of Beneventum. Adalgisus retired to Constantinople, where he lived to an advanced age; and thus was finally extinguished the power of the Lombards, who for two centuries and a half had been such terrible enemies to the Roman Church.

For twenty-five years Rome enjoyed peace. The seventh General Council met at Nicaea A.D. 787, and at the request of the Empress Irene and her son Constantino Porphyrogenitus, the legates of Pope Adrian presided. Charlemagne maintained the most affectionate relations with Adrian and his successor S. Leo III, the latter of whom paid him a friendly visit in France.

But in the year 799, after Adrian s death, unexpected troubles arose. Some of Adrian s relatives deeming themselves aggrieved by S. Leo s election to the Papal throne, conspired against him, attacked him on the feast of S. Mark, April 25th, in the streets of Rome carried him off to the monastery of S. Stephen, where at the foot of the altar they tore out his eyes, covered him with wounds, and threw him half-dead into a dungeon. Before long a band of Romans came to his rescue, and took him to Charlemagne's envoy Virondus, Abbot of Stavelo, who was then at S. Peter's. Thence he was conveyed the next day to Spoleto by Vinigisus, the duke of that town, when to the joy and amazement of all present, he was found to be miraculously cured.

Charlemagne was greatly distressed at this outrage to the Pope, and sent an embassy to offer his condolence, and consult with him on the best means of repairing the wrong done him and punishing the culprits. Whereupon S. Leo, whose only earthly hope was in Charlemagne, at once set out to seek a personal interview with him. Charlemagne sent his eldest son Pepin, at the head of the army of a hundred thousand men with which he had just conquered the Huns, to meet the Pope and conduct him to Paderborn, where he received him with extraordinary honors.

After some little time Charlemagne sent the Pope back to Italy under the escort of the Archbishops of Cologne and Strasburg and several other prelates, while he himself made preparations to follow. On his journey through Italy S. Leo was received every where with veneration as if he had been S. Peter himself. The whole population of Rome came out to meet him and conducted him in triumph to S. Peter's on the 29th of November, A.D. 799.

The following year Charlemagne entered Rome on the 24th of November. A week later he held in the Church of S. Peter's a council, at which all the Roman and Frank clergy and nobles were present and he and the Pope conjointly presided. After his opening speech he proposed to inquire into the accusations which S. Leo's enemies had brought against him, charging him with the most atrocious crimes. But all the arch bishops, bishops, and abbots, both Romans and Franks, exclaimed unanimously, "We dare not judge the Apostolic See, which is the head of all God s Churches; for we all are judged by this Chair and Christ s Vicar, but this Chair is judged by no one. This is the ancient custom. But however the Sovereign Pontiff may judge himself, we will obey canonically." S. Leo answered, "I walk in the footsteps of my predecessors, and am ready to clear myself from the calumnies with which it has been sought to blacken my name." Accordingly, the next day in the Church of S. Peter's and in the presence of Charlemagne and all the prelates and nobles, he took a solemn oath, with the Book of the Gospels in his hand, that he had not committed any of the crimes which were laid to his charge; adding, "I take this oath without being obliged by any law to do so, and without intending to impose a similar custom or law on my successors, but solely in order to remove more certainly all unjust suspicions." Then the king, and all the clergy and laity who were present, intoned the Te Deum and recited litanies as an act of thanksgiving.

The following Christmas Pope S. Leo said the midnight Mass in S. Peter's, and Charlemagne was present. After the Mass was over Charlemagne went to pray at S. Peter's tomb and as he knelt, S. Leo placed the imperial crown on his head, and anointed him and his son Pepin with the holy oils, while the Roman people thrice proclaimed, "Life and victory to Charles, Augustus, crowned by the hand of God, great and pacific Emperor of the Romans." Thus was revived the Empire of the West. Thus, too, was completely fulfilled S. Remits promise to Clovis and the Franks that if they would keep God's law faithfully, they should inherit the power of the Roman Empire, exalt the Church, restrain the incursions of other nations, and reign gloriously. The new emperor offered in the principal churches of Rome tables, crowns, vases, patens, chalices, and other articles of gold and silver set with precious stones, all of extraordinary magnificence, which his army had found in the camp of the Huns and which had been carried off by the Huns, Goths, Vandals, and other barbarians from Rome and all the richest towns in the old Roman Empire.

But while Charlemagne was thus the patron and protector of the Church he did not pretend to govern her. His first capitulary opens with the declaration that he makes the following enactments as the "defender of Holy Church and the helper in all things of the Apostolic See, and in consequence of the exhortations of all the faithful, and especially by the advice of the bishops and priests." It is true that at times he was tempted by political considerations to meddle with matters which were beyond his power. Thus out of jealousy of the Eastern Empire, he attempted to op pose the Council of Frankfort to that of Nicaea, and to dictate to the Pope on the subject of the introduction of the Procession of the Holy Ghost into the Liturgy. He, however, generally consulted the bishops of his empire and the Papal legates and referred difficult questions to the

Pope's decision, and invariably bowed to his authority. So careful was he of the Pope's temporal independence that though the restoration of Rome's ancient glory was the object of his most ardent desires, and his proudest titles were those of Patrician and Emperor of the Romans, yet during his long reign of well nigh fifty years he made only four visits to the City, and then merely as a pilgrim to fulfill his vows. It has been seen, that even when he had just rescued Adrian from Didier, he would not enter Rome till he had obtained the Pope's permission to do so. And when S. Leo placed the imperial crown on his head, he accepted it only in obedience to Christ's Vicar, and told his attendants on his return from S. Peter's, that had he foreseen the Pope's intention he would not have gone to the church, although it was a great feast.

Charlemagne's other task of extending the limits of Christendom, was performed in a crusader's After devout consideration and consultation with clergy how he could win the Saxons to Christ, I opened his mind to his subjects at the May-field at Worms, A.D. 772, and then, accompanied by a band missionaries, he marched at the head of a large into Saxony.

This celebrated war with the Saxons may be due into three periods. During the first period, which extended from A.D. 772 to A.D. 777, Charlemagne repeatedly conquered the whole of Saxony, and after receive oaths of allegiance from the vanquished tribes, them in the hands of the clergy and monks with freedom to accept or reject their teaching, sooner would he be called away to some distant part his empire, than the Saxons would break out in open rebellion with the usual ravaging incursions into Frank territory, and their conquest had to be recommenced. At length in the year 777, when peace thus been several times made and broken, Charlemagne held a May-field at Paderborn, at which, surround his nobles and prelates, he gave audience to the emirs from Spain, who came, as has been told his aid against the Caliph Abderraman, and themselves as his vassals. The Saxon chiefs who also were present, were so overawed by the magnificence and military pomp displayed by Charlemagne on this occasion, that all of them, except Witikind, voluntarily took the most solemn oaths of allegiance, and asked for baptism in such countless multitudes, that all Christendom thrilled with joy at the news of the wonderful conversion.

Scarcely, however, had a year elapsed when the second period of the Saxon war, from A.D. 778 to A.D. 785, began. A report that Charlemagne had been killed at Roncesvalles having reached Germany, Witikind, who alone had not taken the oath of allegiance, broke into the Frank territory at the head of a large band of Frisians and Danes, and was joined enthusiastically by his own countrymen. Again began the former round of cruel ravages, bloody Saxon defeats, feigned submissions, and hypocritical baptisms, to be followed only by fresh outbreaks, when the same hopeless round would recommence. The resistance of the Saxons was much more obstinate than before, for Witikind was a leader of more than ordinary prowess, and he had trained his countrymen as well as his Frisian and Danish allies into disciplined soldiers, so as to unite the impetuosity of the barbarian with the cool steadiness of his more civilized foe.

At length, A.D. 782, Charlemagne held a conference with the rebels at Verdun on the Aller, when the Saxon nobles laid the blame of the revolt on Witikind, and gave up four thousand five hundred Saxons whom they accused of being his accomplices. Charlemagne s patience was exhausted by ten years of treachery and bloodshed, and he fell into the error which has left the sole stain on his fame. He caused the four thousand five hundred culprits to be tried by a tribunal of their own chiefs according to their national laws, and when they were found guilty as traitors, he beheaded them all in one day as those laws directed. Cruel and unjustifiable as was this punishment, it ought to be remarked that it was not a massacre of prisoners in cold blood, but rather a barbaric exaggeration of justice.

All Saxony rose in order to avenge the blood shed at Verdun, and for three years war without quarter was carried on by both Saxons and Franks, till after a bloody victory at Detmuhl, A.D. 785, when Charlemagne offered peace to the exhausted Saxons. Then, to the great amazement of all, Witikind asked for baptism, and his example was followed by crowds of Saxons and Frisians. Popular tradition relates, that on Easter Day when Mass was being said in Charlemagne's tent, Witikind, having from curiosity disguised himself as a beggar and mingled with the crowd that awaited the king's alms, beheld at the Elevation and Communion our Lord in the Host under the form of a beautiful child; and the fierce chief whom no defeat could bend, was vanquished by this vision of Divine love. After his baptism Witikind proved himself worthy of the extraordinary favor that had been granted him, and was no less distinguished by his piety than he had formerly been by his military deeds. In order that he might be able to hear Mass frequently and to send missionaries to his fellow-countrymen, he founded the see of Minden, and obtained Erembert from Charlemagne to be its first bishop.

At this time Charlemagne held a council at Paderborn at which he issued a capitulary, which punished with death all who refused baptism, burnt or desecrated churches, offered human sacrifices, practiced cannibalism, and other Pagan customs, or were guilty of sacrilege and contempt of Christian practices. Both Pope Adrian and Alcuin remonstrated against the severity of this enactment, for the Church has always protested against the use of force to spread Christianity, and in the treatment of lapsed Christians has made a broad distinction between persons who had been fully instructed in the faith and had enjoyed the means of grace, and ignorant, unconverted barbarians like the Saxons. Their efforts on behalf of these poor people seem to have been successful, for the Capitulary of A.D. 797, was framed in a less severe spirit.

The third period of the Saxon war from A.D. 793 to A.D. 804 was limited to the tribes in the neighborhood of the Weser and Elbe. After five years of bloody warfare, broken from time to time by feigned submissions, peace was obtained by the compulsory emigration of one third of the population of this region into Gaul and the more settled parts of Germany.

Charlemagne took advantage of this season of peace to conquer the Huns or Avars, whose settlement at no great distance from his frontier was a constant danger to his empire. It will be remembered that only a few years before they had been accustomed to make incursions and levy tribute as far as Thuringia. He accordingly now sent against them an army of a hundred thousand men under the command of his eldest son Pepin, who, after encountering a fierce resistance, captured and destroyed their central fortified village, in which were accumulated the richest spoils of the ancient world, and killed so many of the nation that their power was totally crushed. The capture of this stronghold of the Huns effected a great financial revolution in Gaul and Germany for gold and silver had for centuries been very scarce, but now they became abundant in consequence of the great mass of treasures brought anew into circulation. Charlemagne also strengthened his eastern frontier by conquering the Bohemians and the Slaves in Istria, Dalmatia, and Pannonia from the Drave to the north of the Elbe, where he came in contact with the Northmen or Danes. He is said to have intended to found a northern metropolis at Hamburg for the conversion of the Northmen and the diffusion of Christianity in the north. But this plan was carried out only by his successor.

In the year 802 the Saxons to the north of tho Elbe having again revolted, Charlemagne removed them into France, and gave their lands to the tribes who then inhabited Mecklenburg and had been faithful to him. After above thirty years of warfare a final peace with the Saxons was signed at Selz A.D. 804. The Saxons acknowledged the power of both the Franks and the Church, and in consideration of their paying tithe to the latter they were released from all tribute. The possession of the territory was secured by the erection of castles and forts in strong positions, and churches and monasteries all over the country. Then the Gospel of peace bound up the wounds that the sword had made, and S. Boniface s life-long wish was at length accomplished his kindred in Old Saxony were won to the faith, and Germany was a Christian Empire, closely bound to the Apostolic See by the ties of faith and love.

CHAPTER XXV. LEARNING AND EDUCATION

From the interior of the Benedictine abbeys, which Boniface had founded or remodeled there burst forth an educational movement which, for energy and important results, will stand comparison with the glorious Renaissance period or the nineteenth century, while its spirit throws both alike into the shade. Its character may be traced in detail in the canons of Boniface's councils and the capitularies of Pepin and Charlemagne. Its fruits may be culled through the whole early Middle Ages, from A.D. 750 to A.D. 1150, during which period the seed which Boniface had sown, was gradually developing itself and coming to maturity. But its most glorious and enduring trophy is the existing German language.

That Boniface distinctly contemplated education, is plain from his recommending to Pepin his "monks employed in their different cloisters in the education of youth" before his last journey. Above all ho began the great work of Christianizing and forming the German language. It is distinctly said of him, that while Columban could not preach in German, Boniface could address the Hessians in their own tongue. It is remarkable that Fulda l was distinguished above all other monasteries in the study and the teaching of German; and a monk of Fulda completed the German grammar begun by Charlemagne. It was, moreover, to Baugulf, Abbot of Fulda, that the emperor addressed the famous ordinance of 787, requiring the erection of schools in monasteries and episcopal sees.

The spring and abiding spirit of this educational movement was the supernatural love of God and of souls. Its seat was the field of Boniface s labors and its centre was the Abbey of Fulda. In the province of Mayence the most celebrated schools were at Fulda, S. Gall, Hersfeld, Fritzlar, and Ellwangen; Lauresham and Weissenburg in Alsace; Hirsau, S. Peter, and S. Blaise in the Black Forest and Reichenau, Einsiedeln, Weingarten, and Weissenau in Allemania. In the province of Salzburg there were celebrated schools at Tegernsee, S. Emmeran s in Ratisbon, Monsee, Obernaltach, Benedictbeuern, Wessobrun, Freisingen, Prufling, Weihanstephan, and many other places.

At first, monks, secular clergy, and laity were all educated together but from the year 817, in obedience to the Council of Aix-la-Chapelle, every abbey had its outer and inner schools. The preservation of strict discipline was, however, the sole object of this separation for the education in the cathedral and outer conventual schools, which were attended by the secular clergy and laity, was the same as in the inner or monks schools.

The general education consisted, as in England and elsewhere, of the Trivium and Quadrivium, the former of which included grammar, rhetoric, and dialectics, and the latter, arithmetic, geometry, astronomy, and music to which were added the writing of deeds and letters, the Roman chant, and the calculation of the calendar.

Latin was the ordinary language of many monasteries, insomuch that the monks of S. Gall used to boast that no one in their abbey, except the boys in the lower forms, habitually spoke German. Greek, and occasionally Hebrew and Arabic were studied, but only by a few among the learned, and never with a view to correcting or elucidating the authorized text of Holy Scripture as found in the Vulgate. Much time and care too were given to German, as will here after be more fully explained.

That the old classics, as a sound foundation for future progress, were not neglected, is evident from the pains taken to collect every relic of antiquity, as well as from the fact, that all the classics now extant have been handed down to modern times through MSS. of this period. But it may be inferred from the few glosses of them that exist, that they were not in common use. Nor were they read with what is considered a true classical spirit, as a means of forming the taste and with due appreciation of the best models. For the German scholars had caught the spirit of their English masters, as expressed in S. Aldhelm s letter already given, and they prized learning chiefly as a means to promote the glory of God and the salvation of souls. Thus Notker Balbulus, a learned monk of S. Gall, who died A.D. 912, and whose genius shone forth especially in music and poetry, did not hesitate to write to one of his pupils, "But if you seek poetry also, you do not need the fables of the ancients, for you have among Christian authors the writings of the prudentissimus Prudentius. In fact the great merit of this age was not taste or philology, but religious zeal, practical common sense, and wonderful ardor and industry in the pursuit of learning under the greatest disadvantages."

The history of this century is that of the continued and courageous struggle of the Church with general and enormous ignorance. We are ever meeting with the most startling contrasts.

While it is quite true that Charlemagne knew Latin and a little Greek, it is also true that he could not write at all till late in life and that then his performances were about on a par with those of an adult learning to write at a night school. We meet with proofs that more laymen than we should have supposed, knew something of the classics while we have equal proofs of general darkness. We know that Boniface's successor and disciple, Gregory of Utrecht, set up in his newly-converted see a school where noble youths from Saxony, Friesland, Bavaria, and Suabia were to be found, and where we have reason to think that Boniface s own Latin grammar was taught. On the other hand, we meet with canons of German Councils in the time of Charlemagne, which prove that the laity of the empire required the threat of corporal punishment to induce them so much as to learn by heart the Lord s Prayer and the Creed in German. The same contrast is observable in the different ways of looking at the classics common at the time. There was a sort of double feeling in men's minds. They instinctively felt that the treasures of antiquity ought to be preserved on the other hand they had some qualms of conscience in studying pagan lore. To the German of the time of Charlemagne Venus was a demon, such as those who appeared in legends of the Black Forest to Christian warriors in seductive forms to lead them astray. Virgil was a wizard, beneficent it is true, but still a wizard. There was much pedantry in Charlemagne s Academy and with all his learning, Rabanus Maurus wrote verses for which a modern schoolboy would be whipped. The real taste for antiquity was wanting. In fact Boniface and his contemporaries had something infinitely better than classical lore. They hewed their way bravely through a jungle of ignorance, and their battle with it was a part of their fight with the world, the flesh, and the devil. They created the magnificent tongue in which Tauler and Henry Suso wrote. If they failed to understand the beauty of Grecian art they had souls keenly alive to Christian loveliness. This want of appreciative classical taste did not arise from any deficiency of poetic feeling, for it was in poetry alone that this age was creative; and to it is the Church indebted for many of those beautiful hymns, which are one of her most precious treasures.

Of the five MSS. of old High German alliterated poetry which alone are now extant, two, on Christian subjects, were written respectively at S. Emmeran's and Wessobrun in the ninth century, and the other three are the celebrated Hildebrautslied written at Fulda in the eighth or ninth century, and two fragments of a poem on the old German gods, written in the tenth century and found in the cathedral library of Merseburg. And when rhymed poetry took the place of alliterated, the earliest specimen is the "Liber Evangeliorum Domini," by Otfried, a monk of

Weissenburg and pupil of Rabanus Maurus at Fulda, in the ninth century. There is also a poem on the woman of Samaria, two hymns in honor of S. Peter and S. George, and the Ludwigslied, celebrating a victory of Louis III over the Normans, all of the ninth century.

But the prince of German poets at this time was Notker Balbulus, who has been already mentioned. Born of noble parents at Elk in the canton of Zurich, he was given as a child to the Abbey of S. Gall. He lived only for prayer and study, and was remarkable for the extent of his learning and his critical appreciation of the authors that he read while at the same time all that he saw or heard inspired musical ideas, which his devout spirit turned into religious strains or Christian poetry. Thus, a beautiful air was suggested to him by the creaking of a mill-wheel as it turned slowly on its axle; and one of his finest hymns was composed as he looked down the ravine of the Martistobel at some workmen who were building a bridge, and saw the danger they were in of falling down the precipice.

But though the scholars of this age cannot lay claim to originality, except as poets, yet they were not wanting in genius. For by a supernatural intuition they grasped the idea of their own position and perceiving that they stood on the wreck of the old civilized world, while around them floated hurricane clouds of barbarism ever threatening to burst over them in blood and ruin, they resisted all temptations to advance for mere selfish gratification into unknown regions of that world of learning which so greatly charmed them, and contented themselves with collecting and preserving the relics of antiquity scattered in ruins around them and diffusing as widely as possible the treasures they had heaped up, so as to clear the stormy atmosphere that lowered over them.

At the head of this noble phalanx stands Alcuin, who came from "Saxony beyond the sea." He was born at York A.D. 735, and spent his youth in the monastery built at the mouth of the Humber by S. Willibrord s father, of which he rose to be abbot. In the year 782 he went to France, where at Charlemagne's court, and afterwards at the Abbey of S. Martin at Tours, he trained a crowd of distinguished scholars and gave a marvelous impulse to learning.

Scarcely inferior to him was Kabanus Maurus, born at Mayence, A.D. 776, and educated at Fulda. He went to Tours, A.D. 800, to learn Alcuin's method, and after spending a year there he returned to Fulda, where for above twenty years he was master of the school, till he became abbot A.D. 822, and Archbishop of Mayence A.D. 847. He used to say, "He who would attain to the summit of wisdom must have reached the summit of love, for no one can know perfectly who does not love perfectly." His whole life breathed this spirit of love. For though the pursuit of learning, in which he displayed remarkable activity and perseverance, was his greatest delight, yet, for love of the poor ignorant barbarians around him he denied him self the full enjoyment of this pure pleasure, in order to devote himself to the culture of the German language and the glossing of MSS, as the means of imparting the fruits of his own studies to them.

There was also his pupil, Walafridus Strabo, Abbot of Reichenau from A.D. 842 to A.D. 847 and Kero and Winitharius, monks of S. Gall and contemporaries of S. Boniface and three other monks of S. Gall, all called Notker, besides Notker Balbulus; and Hermannus Contractus, a monk of Eeichenau (+1054), who was the most learned man of the early Middle Ages. Besides these, there was a host of distinguished scholars too numerous to name, and a crowd of nameless priests and monks celebrated in their own day in the schools, which were then the great field of intellectual labor but whose memory has perished because they were not authors.

A general idea as to which were the books in most common use, may be gathered from the comparative number of glossed MSS of each made in Germany at this time, and still extant. Far above all others stand the MSS of the Bible, of which forty with running Latin and German commentaries, now remain, besides a far greater number of exegetical works and a heap of alphabetical glossaries, all of which have for their special object the elucidation of the text of Holy Writ. Thus is proved at once the ardent love and deep reverence for the Divine fountain of truth which inspired these monkish scholars, and the purity of that living stream with which they watered and fertilized those dark German forests. After this supernatural love of Holy Scripture, though far below it, came the national poetic spirit, and thus the next most numerous MSS. are the poems of Prudentius, of which twenty one MSS are extant; and also glossed MSS of S. Ambrose's hymns, and the poems of Avitus, Juvencus, Prosper, Sedulius, and other Christian writers from the fourth to the sixth century. Then came seventeen MSS of S. Gregory's Pastorals, which was the handbook of the clergy sixteen of the Canons of the Church, which was the universal guide on all questions of theology and discipline; and, finally, a vast number of the writings of the Fathers, especially S. Gregory's Dialogues and Homilies, S. Augustine, S. Jerome, S. Isidore "De Officiis," the Venerable Bede, and S. Aldhelm "Do Virginitate," which last was highly prized in all the monasteries.

But it was to the education of the clergy and monks as guides to salvation, and not as instructors in learning, that S. Boniface and Charlemagne especially directed their attention. The legislation of this period is most interesting for its earnestness and completeness and for the enlightened spirit which is displayed in recognizing the wants of the age and duly providing for them.

Besides the general education already described, which it will be perceived was a high one for the time, the examination of all classes of the clergy and monks in the duties of their respective offices was repeatedly enjoined, and the points on which inquiry was to be made were clearly laid down.

Thus, no priest was to be ordained till it was proved that he held the Catholic faith, knew and understood the Lord's Prayer and the Creeds, and could explain them to others; that he was well versed in the Penitential, the Canons of the Church, and the Roman ritual for the various Masses and ceremony and the administration of the Sacraments; that could catechize, give instructions for confession, and explain the Gospels and Homilies from which he was to preach on Sundays and festivals; and that he was familiar with S. Gregory s Pastorals and S. Isidore "De Officiis" Abbots and monks were to be as to their knowledge and observance of the Benedictine rule and canons and the inferior clergy as to their performance of the duties of their respective states. Above all inquiry was to be made as to their general and demeanor, whether they were chaste, modest, permeable, obedient to their bishops and other super and whether they lived in charity with each other a set a good example to all around them. Bishops were to award praise or penance according to the deserts of those whom they examined. Ignorant priests were not to be tolerated and if after due admonition they did not improve, they were to be removed from their office and forfeit their income. For it was said, "he who knows not the law of God cannot announce it to others."

Much stress, too, was laid upon preaching, and directions were given as to the subjects to be selected and the way in which they were to be treated. Every bishop was required to have a collection of Homilies, with suitable exhortations which his flock could comprehend, from which he was to preach to them in the vernacular on Sundays and festivals and if he were ill and unable himself to preach, some one else was to take his place, so that no Sunday or festival should pass without the word of God being announced in such a way as people could understand.

There are extant fifteen Latin sermons by S. Boniface, some of which appear to have been addressed to clerical, and others to lay auditors. They are remarkable for the full and yet simple form in which each dogma of the faith and each moral precept is stated, with touching appeals to the higher affections and hence, though there is not the least attempt to work on the feelings or imagination, they have singular force and may even now be used profitably as subjects for meditation. Their style suggests the idea that they were compendiums of longer discourses, either in Latin translated into the vernacular for his barbarian converts when his eloquence under the excitement of the occasion, would have supplied the impassioned to not in which they are now deficient.

S. Boniface is said to have written also treatises on various subjects. But the two, "On the Unity of the Catholic Faith and On Faith, Doctrine and Religion are supposed to be contained in statutes of his councils; that -Against Heretics his accusation of Clement and Adalbert;" that Church in his letter to Archbishop Cuthbert that. On his Labors in Germany in his letters Bishop Daniel. He also wrote a Penitential, which was discovered by Binterim, A.D. 1822 and a poem of the virtues and vices and a grammar, the titles of which have lately come to light. It is a display question whether he was the author of the Life Livinus, Bishop of Ghent; but he could not have urn the Life of S. Lebuin, which has sometimes scribed to him, because that saint survived Charlemagne also ordered that, besides cathedral and convent schools, primary schools should be generally established by the parish priests. It has often been thought that these were parochial schools intended for the education of the whole population. There is, however, every reason to suppose that they were intended to recruit the ranks of clergy, and for the education of boys employed in the choir and in the service of the altar. The canon of the English council of Cloveshoe, of the year 747, which has been alleged to prove the existence of such schools, plainly refers to monastic schools, as appears from the title. Again, an attentive reading of Charlemagne s famous capitulary of 787 shows that its object was to establish schools for the younger clerics and choristers. The same is still more evidently true of the canons of the council of Vaison, the original of many subsequent enactments. It expressly provides for the education of the unmarried lectors. It is true that such often-repeated enactments as that of the Capitulary of Theodulfus, Bishop of Orleans in 797, prove that the education of any who are willing to learn, was a part of the duty of parish priests even in the country. But this is a very different thing from the universal attendance of children in a village school. In fact, the house of the parish priest was looked upon as a seminary for clerks, and the home of those who wished to learn but there was no such thing at that time as a network of parish schools throughout the empire. The idea of teaching reading and writing to all indiscriminately, whether ploughmen or woodsmen of the wild forest, never entered the thoughts of this most practical generation. And even had it flitted across their imagination, the scarcity of books and costliness of writing materials would have quickly dispelled so fantastic a dream.

The fact that it should have been found necessary to repeat, not merely once as a mere form, but over and over again during more than a century, minute directions on points which now seem matters of course, proves how difficult was the task of Christianizing and educating the wild men who, caught in the toils Divine love, were now pressing by hundreds thousands into the churches and abbeys.

When one passes from the education of the clergy and monks to that of the great masses of laity, there appear an appreciation of the value of each soul and a paternal solicitude for the instruction of children and she poor and most ignorant classes, which are very striking The great object was, that each individual should be taught the Creed, the Lord s Prayer, and Christian morals, not merely as a parrot-like recital, but with such explanations and cross-questionings as would secure his knowing all that was necessary for his salvation; and accordingly, for the attainment of this end through oral instruction, minute and pressing directions were five. It is touching to behold Charlemagne, the hero of chivalry, pause in his career of victory and conquest, to tell the poor barbarian poor that he must not fancy that he may dare to pray "to God only in three languages; for God may be prayed to in any language and every man will be heard if he asks what is right." And again, to hear him command "all his subjects to learn the Creed and the Lord's Prayer," and "to send their children to the monastery or parish priest to learn them, so that on their return home they may teach them to others. And all who could not do more were at least to learn them in their mother tongue." Again and again he presses on bishops the duty of preaching, and of seeing that the priests explained the Lord's Prayer clearly to the people, so that every one should know what he was asking God for; and that the Gloria Patri was sung reverently by all, and that the priest himself joined with the holy angels and God s people in singing the Sanctus. And as if all that he had said or done through others was but little, he himself addresses his "most beloved brothers" from his imperial throne, and teaches them in the fullest detail what they should believe and what they should do, affectionately pressing on them, that as "life is short and the hour of death uncertain, we should always be ready that God may have mercy on us, and grant us that happy life to come with His saints in eternity."

Confession, too, was ordered to be made at least once a year in Lent for which the form, almost word for word the same as is now used, was given, with full directions about instructing the penitent and securing contrition and resolutions of amendment before he was absolved. With tender sympathy for sinners, the priest was told to say to his hesitating and trembling penitent, "My brother, blush not to confess thy sins, for I too am a sinner, and perhaps have done worse than thou Let us confess, then, freely what we have done freely. But perhaps, my beloved, thou dost not at once remember all thy acts. I will then question thee. Hast thou committed homicide by accident, or intentionally, to avenge thy parents, or in obedience to thy master" and so forth. The priest was, more over, recommended 1 to fast for a week or two with his penitent, "since one cannot raise a fallen man without stooping to him." And he was told to impose upon slaves only half the fasts and penances that he required from the rich.

But it may be objected that all this legislation was thrown away, since the same synods which issued these decrees, proclaimed also the vices of the clergy who were to carry them out into practice. The existence of scandalous vices among the Frank clergy, consequent on nearly a century of anarchy, is undoubted. But it ought to be noticed, that these vices do not come to our knowledge through the ordinary historical channels, but through the earnest protests of the most influential persons in the Church and State, who fought boldly and perseveringly to exterminate them. This fact shows, that however numerous the delinquents may have been, they were still only a minority, and no doubt a diminishing minority of the clergy, for vice cannot long hold out against the out-spoken and resolute opposition of the heads of society.

Moreover, a corrupt clergy cannot possibly exert a powerful influence either on literature or as missionaries. The literary labors of the period, the incessant study of Holy Scripture, and the almost exclusively religious tone of all that was taught, studied, or prized, prove how large was the number of clergy and monks who were free from these vices. Their missionary success is a further proof of the same. For no sooner was a church or monastery founded, even in the wildest district, than there sprung up around it a village, the inhabitants of which submitted themselves to Christian discipline, exchanged their barbarian life of wandering and rapine for the peaceable and settled habits of dawning civilization, and imbibed from their teachers a spirit of deep piety, which, after the vicissitudes of a thousand years and centuries of heresy, still continues to be a national characteristic of the German.

But the most remarkable monument of the influence of the clergy on the mass of the people is the German language. The district in which German is now the popular tongue was the principal field of S. Boniface's labors. When he entered on his work, each of the countless tribes, among whom this region was divided, had its own peculiar dialect, which was identified with its national history, religion, and independence. But through the patient, loving industry of the clergy and monks, this Pagan Babel of tongues gradually gave place to the Christian German language, which now asserts its supremacy not only within its own district, but as the sole literary vehicle wherever German is spoken. No conquest can compare with that of a nation s language. Foreign arms may subdue a state social revolutions may overthrow its reigning dynasty and its political constitution but it is only a thorough change in the heart and mind of a nation, which can transform its spoken and written tongue. This transformation the Christian clergy wrought, thus proving their great influence on their flock, and vindicating their own moral character from reproach.

The process by which this linguistic revolution was effected, may be traced in the glossaries and glossed, or interlineated MSS., of this period. It is evident that the difficulties of S. Boniface and his fellow laborers must have been greatly increased by the multiplicity of dialects, and that it was essential to create a common medium for expressing thought. This might be done either by obliging all the converts to learn Latin, as being the language of the Church, or by translating Christianity into the vernacular. The latter is the course which the Church has always followed, translating the original Greek and Hebrew Scriptures, and the Offices of Divine worship into Latin in the parts of the Roman Empire where Latin was in common use, and retaining Greek and the Oriental languages in the East. The same principle was carried out in Germany, where gradually a common vernacular idiom was created, as the popular vehicle of Christian thought; while Latin was used only in the sacred Offices, where it was necessary for the preservation of Catholic unity.

In the glossed MSS the daily difficulties of the foreign missionary are seen, the check on his eloquence from ignorance of a word to express his thought, the puzzling search for it, the writing it down as a treasure for future use, with corrections and re-corrections by successive generations of philologists. In many cases the Latin is interlined with a running Latin explanation, with German words interwoven. In others the Latin and German are intermixed. Some glosses are inter linear, and others are on the margin of the pages. They are not always by one hand, for successive students often added to them, or corrected them. And often, too, they were in a secret cypher, to prevent their being used by pupils as a crib. In fact a well-glossed MS.

was a treasure beyond price, gratefully borrowed and generously lent, and carried by a master from school to school.

Many Christian ideas, as for instance, the Holy Ghost, humility, bishop, found no expression in the old Pagan language. And a far greater number of words, such as God, faith, confession, penance, had a totally different meaning in the Pagan and in the Christian sense. In the countries in which Latin had once been the common language, this difficulty had been met by the use of Latin or Latinized Greek words; but in Germany the word in the provincial dialects, which most nearly approached the Christian idea, was adopted or if, in a few cases, a Latin word was introduced, it was completely Germanized. Some times two or more such words seem to have been taken up and used by way of experiment, till the popular voice, or the decision of learned men, or some principle of natural selection now unknown, gave the preference to one of them, which henceforth was applied to the Christian idea alone, till at length its heathen sense was forgotten. So completely was this process carried on through the medium of the provincial dialects, that though the first missionaries were English, yet very few English roots found entrance into German, and even these few were completely transformed in tin course of their adoption.

The details of this subject would carry us too far, but a few examples may be quoted as illustrations. For instance, humility being a purely Christian idea, there was no word for it in the Pagan language, and the new words, demuth and niedrigkeit were coined. The name Christ was necessarily borrowed ; but in all its compounds, Christen, Cliristenlieit, Cliristliclie, it was Germanized. Also, our Lady s name, die Jungfrau Maria, was Germanized by the German prefix. Again, the novel idea conveyed by the word Pagan, which was taken in Latin from pagus, i. e. the country district where the old religion longest held possession, was translated into German by heiden, taken from heide,

heath or forest wilderness, the abode of the unconverted, wandering tribes, as distinguished from the villages in which the Christian converts settled down near the church or abbey. Kreuz was derived from the Latin, crux, but its compounds, Kreuzigung, Kreutzen, Kreutschen, were Germanized. It may in general be noticed that words connected with the outer organization of the Church, such as bischof, priester, alt, moncli, were adopted from the Latinized Greek but German words were used for what concerned its inner life and was essentially popular; such as the names of the Trinity, the Persons of the Godhead, the attributes of God, and of the virtues and vices. The great feasts of the Church, too, had German names, as Weihnacht, or Christstag, Christmas, Osterfest, Easter, Himmelfahrtstag, Ascension, and so forth. As for the words which in Pagan times had conveyed a different idea, they gradually came to be used exclusively in the Christian sense. Thus Gott has totally lost its polytheistic meaning, and is associated only with the Unity of the Godhead. Beicht and btisse, formerly used in a general sense, are now confined to the Sacrament of Penance and so on with many others.

The earliest German glossary is one made by S. Gall himself, which has already been mentioned. Another glossary was made by Kero, a monk of S. Gull, who also translated the Benedictine rule into the Alleman dialect, about A.D. 750, when his brethren adopted this rule. But the great impulse to glossing dates from the beginning of the next century, when it was given from Fulda by Rabanus Maurus, and his pupil, Walafridus Strabo, afterwards Abbot of Eeichenau.

From the old German MSS. interesting glimpses may be obtained into the interior of those old abbeys, and the daily life of those barbarian converts and their teachers, whose very existence is other wise enshrouded in such mystery. In these MSS. have already been discovered their reverent devotion to Holy Scripture, their careful study of the laws of the Church and the duties of their state, their appreciation of the best patristic writings, their passion for poetry, and their aspirations after the highest purity. If it be asked what was the daily occupation of these holy men, the answer is found in the numerous translations of the Creed, of the Lord s Prayer with and without explanation, and of many other prayers, forms of confession, abjuration of the heathen gods, and profession of love to the Blessed Trinity, simple exhortations, and other similar works, which proclaim their love of souls and their activity as missionaries and parish priests. Moreover, a collection of medical prescriptions in Latin, glossed with German words and Runic letters, shows that they were physicians of the body as well as the soul while the glossed grammars of Alcuin, Donatus, Priscian, and others, a treatise on the proper choice of words, and exercises in dictation to give facility in writing quickly, prove their patient industry as schoolmasters. Nay, even the secrets of their hearts and their favorite subjects of meditation and popular instruction, are revealed by the fact, that the earliest German works treat of our Lord s life on earth, as for instance, the translations of the Gospel of S. Matthew, of S. Isidore s Treatise on our Lord s Nativity, Passion, and Resurrection, in the eighth century, and of Ainmonius's Harmony of the Gospels, and Otfried's rhymed "Liber Evangeliorum Domini," both of the ninth century, besides other MSS. from the Gospels written in the eighth and ninth centuries. One of those from the Abbey of S. Gall, contains a picture of our Lord's Stigmata, with the note, "pictura in corpore, ut Scotti pingunt." S. Paul s Epistles, too, were early prized, a glossed MS. of them by Winitharius, a monk of S. Gall, being dated A.D. 761.

Great as has been the development of the German language in modern times, especially since the sixteenth century, it ought never to be forgotten that the far harder task of making it Christian was begun by S. Boniface and his disciples, and carried on to its completion by successive generations of unknown monks. The motives which prompted this earlier work enhance its value. No hope of wealth, no thirst for fame, no selfish gratification of taste or genius, stirred the industry of these men, whose very names and personal identity were merged in their community. Their sole spring of action was the love of God and of souls and inflamed by this Divine fire, they wearied not at the tedium of their monotonous task, they fretted not at their own obscurity, but they labored on humbly, patiently, with heroic self-denial, hour after hour, and year after year, looking only to the day when He whom they loved should appear, and they should rise to meet Him surrounded by the souls, who, through their labors, should have been won to His greater honor and glory.

CHAPTER XXVI. THE CONCLUSION

Within a few years from Charlemagne's death his empire broke up through the natural tendency of matter to disunite, and the obstinate revulsion of its discordant elements against that intolerable material unity in which his strong arm had forcibly bound them. But Europe did not fall back into anarchy and Paganism, as it had done on the fall of Rome and the decay of the Merovingian race. For the spiritual unity which S. Boniface had breathed into it, still survived, and though the body politic had been dissolved, the life-giving soul continued to animate and sustain society.

In the modern, as in the ancient world, Rome was the centre of unity and civilization. The barbarians of old had fallen prostrate before the fierce Roman eagle or perished in its pitiless claws and now they bowed reverently before Rome's new sovereignty, which came to them in a loving and paternal character with the Lamb, the Dove, and the Cross as its banner. In the ancient world all was material there was no faith, and hence no efficacious ideas. But in the modern world, society rests, not on material facts, but on ideas and the author, inspirer, and maintainer of these ideas is Christianity, which alone can give faith in them, and make them forcible in the eyes of reason. The great idea which distinguishes Christian society from the Pagan world, is the awakening of conscience, the notion of moral right, and the force of duty springing out of a supernatural faith something which cannot be seen or touched, against which violence is powerless, but which is, therefore, all the more irresistible and Divine.

This was the weapon which S. Peter's successors opposed to the physical force which surrounded and threatened them, and with it they conquered the barbarians, who for seven centuries had been fluctuating between Paganism and Christianity. It was no new weapon forged for the occasion, for it was co-existent with Christianity, and with it all the Church's victories had been won. But through the perfect ecclesiastical organization and discipline which S. Boniface had established and Charlemagne fostered, it was brought more fully into action. Its power was now felt throughout Europe by the frequent recurrence of ecclesiastical synods, the multiplication of bishoprics, parish churches, and abbeys, and the constant presence of the clergy and monastic bodies, all exercising their respective functions in subjection to that unseen power, of which each individual in that vast Christian army, were he bishop, abbot, priest, or poor cleric or monk, was equally and at once the servant and the representative. In every corner of Christian Europe, side by side with the royal or baronial castle bristling with armed men and warlike engines, rose the cathedral, or abbey, or parish church, in which the prince or baron beheld the seat of a rival power, which eluded the grasp of his mailed hand, which his sword and lance could not reach, and yet which irresistibly checked and controlled him in his proudest moments, while to the victims of his passions it was ever a sure refuge and defense.

During century after century of struggle between physical and spiritual force, between barbarism and Christianity, amid the invasions of fresh hordes of barbarians and the ceaseless strife arising out of the feudal system, in spite of the frequent revolt of princes and barons against any restraint on their lawless passions, nay even in spite of the pretensions of the Emperors to control Christ s Vicar, still the Church fought steadily on, and in the end always conquered.

Marvelous, indeed, was that supernatural power which could bring these fierce, proud, self-reliant barbarians to fall contrite at the feet of a fellow-man and humble themselves in confession and after once seizing them under the impulse of compunction, could hold them firm, in penance and fasting, solitary, barefoot, clad in sackcloth, stripped of their arms and social rank, for weeks,, months, or years nay, even, for their whole lifetime.

Under the influence of this spiritual force the warlike Franks submitted the question of their change of dynasty to S. Peter's unarmed successor, and exercised their proud privilege of free national election in obedience to the decision of a feeble old man, whose very existence seemed to be dependent on their fidelity and prowess.

Impressed by the same Divine idea, the Emperor Louis II, the boasted successor of the Caesars, confessed that he and his family held their title in virtue of the Papal unction. And when the Emperor on the day of his coronation would present himself to his subjects in solemn state, the crown on his head, the sceptre and globe in his hands, the Cross, the spear, and the sword borne before him, and his nobles all standing around him, the people would greet him, not with acclamations of joy or personal honor, but with the cry, "Christus vincit, Christus regnat, Christus imperat." Thus teaching him, that he, too, equally with the lowest serf in his realm, was subject to a higher law than his own will, that his sword could not annul the least of God's commandments, and that for every act of violence, treachery, or oppression, an inevitable retribution awaited him.

But never did this spiritual power appear stronger than when it had been most violently resisted; for instance, when Louis VII of France strove to atone for the revolt of his youthful years, by a life of devotion to the Holy See and by the protection of S. Thomas of Canterbury. Again Henry Plantagenet, exhausted by fasting and a weary pilgrimage, bled under the scourge at the martyr's tomb. Still more strikingly the excommunicated Henry IV of Germany, hard and impenitent, but terrified by his subjects faith and the doom that hung over him, hurried over Alpine precipices amid frost and snow at the risk of his life, and stood day after day, shivering, fasting, and an outcast, at the gate of Canossa, begging forgiveness of the old man whom his sword afterwards drove out of Rome but of whom, dying in exile and possessing not even a stone on which to lay his head, it has been aptly said, "He had nothing, yet he had every thing hunted down on all sides, but triumphant."

Nor was faith the Church s only spiritual weapon. She wielded another yet more powerful, which was supernatural personal love.

Love is the very source and essence of Christianity, and thus it was the master of the new Christian world. It had inspired the martyrs, and triumphed on the rack and in the arena; and now it shone forth no less resplendently in the missionary. It was the light of the schools creating new languages, English, German, Italian, popularizing music, painting, poetry, and learn ing for the service of the poor and of souls. It gave birth to that generous enthusiasm which heaped up all God's best gifts on the Church's altars, and lavishly devoted to His service the noblest powers of great intellects, the warmest affections of loving hearts, rank, wealth, strength, and every moment of life from youth to old age.

Quickly did the sparks from this Divine fire kindle the souls of the barbarians. They, too, penetrated forests, and waded through swamps in pursuit of lost sinners. They, too, tore themselves from all that made life dear, pressed into the abbeys and schools, became priests and monks, and were content to live, nameless and unknown, in toil, poverty, obedience, and penance, for the love of Him who had loved them and died for them, and of that heavenly kingdom in which they hoped to live with Him for ever. So rapidly did the flame of love spread that before many years had passed the missionaries, clergy, monks, and scholars in most of the newly converted Teutonic nations, were almost all of native birth.

Even those who aspired not to such heights of perfection, were softened and purified by the genial glow from this vivifying fire. When the barbarians beheld the fearless intrepidity with which the unarmed monk, Cross in hand, bore the Gospel to bloodthirsty Pagans, or reproved lawless tyrants, they imbibed a noble courage, which put their own drunken war fury to shame; and they, too, in course of time assumed the cross, devoted their swords to the chivalrous defense of the feeble and oppressed, and performed deeds of supernatural heroism. The celibacy of the clergy purified their ideal of chastity, and set before them higher objects of love than they had hitherto dreamt of. The community life of the monks, their industry, obedience, self-denial, and charity, gave a new dignity to labor, and gradually broke down the barbarian habits of selfish isolation, independence, rapacity, indolence, and sensuality. The personal inviolability of the clergy taught the value of human life. The ecclesiastical courts substituted new principles of justice and mercy for the old duties of revenge and pitiless cruelty, and inspired that horror of blood which is a characteristic of modern times. While in the schools the Christian faith, learning, and the arts, were diffused freely among all, rich and poor alike, who were willing to acquire them; and in the churches painting, music, poetry, and eloquence, softened the hearts and enlightened the minds of the wild men, and drew them gently and lovingly to God's house, in which they found both beauty and truth. As the barbarians were thus fitted for and trained to the arts of peace, war ceased to be the sole avocation of whole nations, arms were no longer borne by every free man, and law and order took the place of barbaric violence and confusion.

Thus was the Church the mould of the new society. In her crucible of pure charity she fused the disjointed and discordant barbarian units into a harmonious spiritual unity; through the framework of her marvelous organization she placed their entire being, moral, intellectual, and social, on a Christian basis and with her supernatural weapons of faith and love she wrought them, heart and mind, into Christians while they still retained their barbaric form. In the lapse of centuries the slough of barbarism wore off, and then, when she had Christianized, educated, and civilized them, she led them on to the grand awakening of European intellect in the fifteenth and sixteenth centuries, and enabled them to take their place in the foremost ranks of modern Christian progress.

Eleven centuries have run their course since the days of S. Boniface and Charlemagne, and the whole aspect of Europe, its empires and kingdoms, its political and social relations, its manners and customs, and all its outer being are totally changed. But its highest, inner life is still the same. The same ideal of Christ's sovereignty on earth through His Church, is reflected in every part of it. The same spiritual unity breathes through it. The same perfect organization and the same supernatural weapons of faith and love, still exist in active operation binding Christian society fast to S. Peter's Rock, and ever renewing its youth like the eagle s. Great and marvelous as have been the deeds of the Church in past ages, they were but the same as she is working today, more or less visibly and consciously, in countless millions of hearts, so that only through her influence, even on those who reject her authority, is the modern Christian world held together.

But the labors and combats of the Church on earth never come to a close. For as thunder-clouds gather round the sun in the zenith of its meridian splendor, so at the very time when the Church was most prolific in great saints, and civilized Europe was entering on the full enjoyment of the fruit of her long labors, there burst forth in Germany that fatal revolt, which has torn the greater part of the Teutonic race from the Church, has infected the whole civilized world with a spirit of infidelity, and has not yet fully run out its malevolent course.

Beginning with the revolt of the will against the Church s authority and pure code of morality, it has led, as a necessary consequence, to the revolt of the intellect against her dogmatic teaching, to the negation of all revealed or certain truth, to cold skepticism, bold atheism, and scoffing blasphemy. And as if to prove how closely the cause of the Church is bound up with that of society, this rebellion against her has marched side by side with outbreaks against civil authority and violations of natural law and order. Princes and their ministers have frequently been the victims of conspirators and assassins. Kings have been arraigned before mock tribunals, have shed their blood on the scaffold, and have in such countless numbers been placed on their thrones, or hurled from them, by rebellious subjects or the fortunes of war, that imperial and royal crowns have fallen into contempt, as the playthings of popular caprice or the ephemeral trophies of military success. Europe from end to end, and especially the old Teutonic soil of Germany and Belgium, has again and again been ravaged and deluged with blood in order to satiate the pride of rival monarchs or the ambition of aspiring adventurers. While the people, reft of the succour and protection which the Church was wont to afford them, have too often been the victims of the most cruel oppression, sometimes on religious pretences, at others for the sake of class privileges, or from sheer selfishness and disregard of Christian justice and charity, till at length it has come to pass, that in the places where wealth and luxury have most abounded, the poor have been most crushed down, living in hopeless want and misery, and dying of starvation.

But now a great crisis is impending. A new paganism and its attendant barbarism are springing into life. Countless forms of heresy and infidelity, at variance in all else, are banded together with apostate Catholics against the Church. Christ's Vicar is a prisoner, despoiled, insulted, and begirt by the lawless successors of the Lombards, while all the rulers of Europe look on approvingly or silently acquiesce. Whole nations are arming as in barbarous ages. The invention and multiplication of the most deadly weapons is the great object to which national wealth and science are devoted. Unheard-of principles of atheism, murder, incendiarism, and rapine are openly disseminated. A world-wide war of extermination against religion, morality, property, and civilized society, is boldly proclaimed with the avowed object of overthrowing the entire existing fabric of moral and social order, and erecting on the ruins of Christian civilization a new world, godless, lawless, selfish, bloodthirsty, acknowledging no authority except brute force, and wallowing in the foulest depths of sensual corruption.

In this tremendous crisis, though the thunder growls ominously and the gloom of the horizon is unbroken, though no imperial hero now exists to rush to the world s rescue and no sign of approaching aid can be seen, yet the history of the past sheds its light on the dark future, and reveals the course and issue of the coming war.

In past times the foes of the Church have been disunited or comparatively few, their attacks have been indirect or partial, and their warfare has been desultory, intermittent, limited in area, or even hidden under the mask of friendship. But now the whole civilized world is arrayed on either side. The Church's foes are united, at least in enmity to her; they are marshaled in overwhelming numbers and disciplined bands, and are supported by the civil powers. Her extermination is their avowed object; and the combat is a outrance.

The citadel of Christianity and central point of attack is the Chair of S. Peter. There sits one whom no threats can intimidate, no danger can cow; who his beheld two successive pontiffs imprisoned, insulted, and cruelly tormented, yet unflinching and triumphant while their oppressor pined away his life, a prisoner on an ocean rock and who, once a fugitive and exile, has himself experienced God s love and power in his own unexpected return to Rome. From his prison in the Vatican he now looks with hope and confidence to his children scattered over the wide world, who are the true heirs of S. Boniface and Charlemagne, who have inherited their spirit of faith and love, and who cling with them in close spiritual unity to the Chair of S. Peter.

The length of the struggle and the trophies of victory will depend on the fidelity and fervor with which each individual Catholic in his own sphere, wields his weapons of supernatural faith and love. The combat may be long and fierce, nay, even bloody, but the final triumph of the Church, now as in all past ages, is infallibly certain. For against that Church which our Lord has built on the Rock of Peter, the gates of hell shall not prevail; no weapon that is formed against her shall prosper; whosoever shall fall on this stone, shall be broken; but on whomsoever this stone shall fall, it shall grind him to powder. He who hath made these promises, is He not essential and immutable truth, yesterday, and today; and the same forever.

84163453R00109

Made in the USA
San Bernardino, CA
04 August 2018